The Upper Room
Disciplines
2003

The Upper Room

Disciplines
2003

UPPER
ROOM BOOKS®
NASHVILLE

Contents

Foreword

Welcome to a new year of exciting, passionate reading of and reflection on the Bible through the helpful "lenses" of *The Upper Room Disciplines*. State-of-the-art computers, E-books, and Internet services that can open up thousands of worlds and books for us in a blink of an eye surround us; but here we are, still holding a precious book in our hands.

As a New Testament professor, I emphasize to my students the importance of reading the biblical text with all our "baggage": our joys, fears, beliefs, doubts. It is crucial to keep an honest perspective on who we are and what we bring to the text in order to understand why we read the way we do. But to approach the Word of God with all our passion, willingly offering our vulnerable selves in openness for transformation and growth is also vital.

Even before I could read, I was passionate about books. I still recall the day I fearfully went into the library at home searching for the big book of stories that my mother used to read to my siblings and me. I had loved that book until I found the illustration of a little devil on one of its pages. I hadn't even been able to get near the room for fear of the devil in that book. But I decided to overcome my fear. I took the threatening book and, in one quick move, tore out the offending page. I had solved the biggest problem of my life.

I no longer tear pages from books. My interaction with books has changed. Now I use colored pencils to scribble marks and comments that express my fears, doubts, joys, and disagreements. Sometimes those marks seem like blood shed on a battlefield; at other times they resemble decorations at a joyful party.

When I open a book, I try to approach it with a willingness to grow and change in the process of reading it. I always hope that by the time I finish reading it, I have become a better person, even if I don't remember all I read. I can always go back and browse through my notes and remember the lessons I learned.

This year, before you prepare to read and reflect on your Bible and the meditations from the *Disciplines*, I invite you to prepare a self-inventory. Write about the ways in which your family history, religious formation, cultural and ethnic background, political perspectives and other crucial experiences of your life have become your lens for interpreting the biblical message. Bring yourself and your understanding of who you are to your reading. Then enter the world of the Bible to dialogue with God, with biblical writers, and with the authors of *Disciplines*. Be ready to question their ideas, to doubt their opinions, to embrace their truths, to engage in a lively conversation. Don't tear out pages in fear, anger, or doubt. Rather, bring all those feelings to God and be ready to wrestle with the Living Word.

Perhaps you have found your own creative ways to mark those special moments in your reading when a feeling is changed, an attitude improved, a lesson learned. As you read the Bible and the *Disciplines* this year, may you mark many such transformations in the act of reading and reflecting passionately on the Word of God. May God grant us courage to read the book of life with new eyes every day.

—*Leticia A. Guardiola-Sáenz*
Assistant Professor of New Testament
Andover Newton Theological School

The Creating God Redeems

January 1–5, 2003 • Don E. Saliers[‡]

WEDNESDAY, JANUARY 1 • Read Jeremiah 31:7–14

Have you noticed that any significant event in scripture seemingly encourages someone or something to break into song? A prophet like Jeremiah cannot contain his vision in flat prose. The picture of God's promised redemption and reunion practically "sings" off the Bible's pages.

God's call to praise permeates the whole of scripture. "Sing to the LORD a new song" echoes in every generation—through bad times and good, in ever-changing circumstances of history. So in today's passage we hear again the invitation to praise God in Zion, to "sing aloud on the height of Zion" (31:12).

Why should God need all this praising? C. S. Lewis once wrestled with this question. He at first thought it strange that God asks for our praise. But it finally dawned on him. Lovers praise their beloved; patriots praise their country; beauty is praised by the poets. Could it be that the praise completes the love and serves as the delight of the relationship itself?

Yes, that's it! God provides a way for our relationship with our Creator and Redeemer to overflow into its completion. The act of praising God is an act of love, discovery, and exploration of God's very nature. In this way God is "enthroned on the praises of Israel" (Ps. 22:3) and adored by naming all of creation in light of God's Word made known to us. The One who declares a word to Jacob is the God whose providential care in nature and in history is also for us and for the flourishing of all humanity.

PRAYER: Your Word, O blessed God, runs swiftly to all the earth. Deepen and broaden my praise day by day in Christ. Amen.

[‡]William R. Cannon Distinguished Professor of Theology and Worship, Candler School of Theology, Emory University, Atlanta, Georgia.

For what in your life do you offer praise and thanksgiving to God? Most of us naturally begin by naming family, loved ones and friends, good health, home, or some recent good fortune. All of these things are certainly worthy of thanks. But we do much more when we express praise to God.

Our psalm of the day recites what God has done and is doing, moving back and forth between compassion for human beings and divine providence in human history and nature. Consider how praise of God may already be opening up your life. In the act of praise in what ways do you see, hear, and perceive the world more clearly? When you take a moment for praise, how does it comingle with thanksgiving? How does praise somehow train a grateful heart to receive and name life as a gift? How do you evidence praise growing in you over time, enabling you to refer all things to God?

Amidst human blessings God also speaks a word of command to the earth's snow and frost, the wind and hail and waters. These verses remind us that the natural world is not entirely under human control. Yet that same divine word comes to Jacob, to the human community called out to acknowledge God before all the nations of earth. How deep, how broad, and how high are the power and providence of God! The God who numbers the stars, gathers the outcasts, heals the brokenhearted, and lifts up the downtrodden takes pleasure in those who see the world as the arena of God's glory.

We do well to take time to name all the things in life that we deem worthy of praise. To obey the command to praise God and to "sing to the LORD with thanksgiving" is a joyful coming-to-life. As the whole Book of Psalms concludes with the doxologies of 145–50, may we so complete our lives—beginning and ending each day with such praise.

PRAYER: God of awesome wonder and tender care for your children, teach us to name you in all things and to listen for your word in all things earthly and heavenly. Amen.

The praise of God we hear in Hebrew Scriptures now flows over into the church, like a melody that you can't get out of your head. At the table a few weeks ago, my wife, Jane, asked, "Do you ever have a hymn tune running through your mind, but you can't quite recall the words?" She had been humming a melody to herself all day long. "I wonder," she said, "if it has to do with a troublesome situation at work?" She sang a few notes. It hit us both at the same time: "Hope of the World, Thou Christ of Great Compassion." Oh, the shock of recognition! Jane realized that this melody had come to her as she struggled to bring more understanding to a difficulty in her work setting.

Ephesians is like a melody that keeps running through my mind and heart—and the song is about Jesus Christ. The first chapter is itself a true canticle of thanksgiving for the blessing and wisdom God has given us in this unforgettable One from Nazareth. I must confess that more than once I have gone back to these words when I have been struggling with uncertainty and with hard issues of faith. I hear again the opening words: "Blessed be the God and Father of our Lord Jesus Christ, who has blessed us...." Even when I feel far from God or full of self-preoccupation or simply dull to the gospel, this song bears me up as on eagles' wings. We need this testimony, this ringing truth of how the "riches of his grace" have been lavished upon us, even when we cannot fully claim them.

Suddenly (or gradually) we come to realize that by grace we are being gathered up with all things in Christ, destined for God's promises and good pleasure. So this very day, when a melody haunts you, think on this hymn that underlies all our life: God has "freely bestowed on us in the Beloved" forgiveness, love, and redemption.

PRAYER: Source of life and all holiness, gather me up into your beloved community in Christ that I may praise you with my lips and my daily life. Amen.

Several years ago a friend told me this story. The family matriarch, a grandmother to twelve and a great-grandmother to twenty, died at the age of ninety. She had lived a simple life, having been widowed for some time. The family knew she had little money left. So it surprised those gathered to find a handwritten will in her nightstand drawer. The will took the form of a letter to all the grandchildren. She mentioned a locked wooden "hope chest" in the attic. After a lengthy search for the key, several of family members gathered to open the hope chest. In it they found twelve beautiful hand-stitched quilts with notes carefully pinned for each of the grandchildren. The notes read, "I have little money to give you, dear ones. But each of you must take one of these quilts. They were made by my grandmother— your great-great-grandmama Mary Elizabeth. Cherish them, use them, then give them to your children in time. My inheritance is yours. When you do these things remember me and all the children before you who were protected and comforted by the quilts. Remember all who have taken delight in the designs and the colors."

This is the message that the author of Ephesians passes on and names for us today: We have received an incredible inheritance. In hearing the word of truth, we have been given a testimony—a will. In receiving this word gladly and by opening the gospel in our life through the grace of baptism, we are marked with the seal of the Holy Spirit. Each of us receives a note with his or her name on it: You are my children, the inheritors of what has been given in Christ. And we, by word and deed, are to pass on the gift. To set our hope on Christ compels us to love God and neighbor and to "live for the praise of [Christ's] glory." The glory of the Word becomes human, that we might be numbered among the saints. There can be no greater inheritance than this!

PRAYER: God of all mercies, you have called me to the riches of a glorious inheritance. May I live each day in the light of your creating and redeeming glory. Amen.

At the abbey church of the Benedictine monastery of St. John's in Minnesota is a remarkable wrought-iron figure of John the Baptist by the artist Doris Caesar. During my first winter visit there I walked to the church in a blowing snowstorm. In such conditions a person can become snow-blind for a while. I entered the front door and walked into what seemed like complete darkness.

Moving in the darkness cautiously, I backed up and felt a strong finger poke my back. Startled, I whirled around to see a thin, seven-foot-tall figure. "Who, who are you?" I nearly shouted. Silence. Finally in the dim light, I could make out the bronze-black figure of John the Baptist with his bony finger pointing to the baptistry, his other arm rising toward the ceiling.

When we read the Gospel of John's powerful prologue, we all bump into John the testifying prophet whose word is always the same: He points toward the water and the light, toward the Word become flesh. John remains the startling witness to an astonishing gospel. That the God who flung the farthest stars into incomprehensible space, the God who fashioned this beautifully fragile earth, the God who called Abraham and Sarah and who made covenant with ancient Israel to witness and to be a light to other nations, that this God should come fully into our human life as one of us—we "scarce can take it in." The One who created all things is now the God who redeems all things. This reality is what John the Baptist points to and what John the Evangelist unfolds.

Today, this very moment, behold as if for the first time this truth: The Word, the breath, the very life of God has become flesh, living among us. And we have seen the glory, "full of grace and truth." Consider how astonishing this news is. Jesus, the beloved of God, now shines incarnate and arisen on this earth as the beginning and ending Word of God.

PRAYER: O Morning Star, how brightly you shine in our midst. Be a lamp to my feet and a word of freedom and mercy. As you have been sent from God, so send me forth. Amen.

Enfolded by Grace

January 6–12, 2003 • *Marjorie Hewitt Suchocki*[‡]

MONDAY, JANUARY 6 • **Read Genesis 1:1-5**

We begin a week of meditation on baptism: the baptism of our Lord and our own baptism. The Genesis text that begins our reflections is magnificent: It speaks of God's creating by moving over the waters and speaking a word. In our baptism too the Spirit is said to move over the waters. We understand there to be a new birth, a new creation. And in our baptism, God speaks a word—the word of the gospel.

Is it too fanciful, then, to imagine in this Genesis text that God's very act of Creation is like a baptism of the world? We see the parallels: the waters, the Spirit, the word, the pronouncement of good. What might these parallels mean? Even as we understand Christian baptism to be a work of grace, we must also understand Creation itself to be a work of grace. The world is not simply given, like a stage on which we play out the dramas of our lives. This world in which we live exists in and through grace and forms an integral part of how we live our lives. Our baptism is an extension of the same grace that encompassed the original Creation of the world.

Look around you! See the loveliness of this world—its mountains and plains and rivers and seas, its sky in all its subtle varieties of color! All of it, all of it, is the work of God's grace! To see creation in light of baptism is to see how surrounded we are by grace, how imbedded we are in grace. Thanks be to God.

PRAYER: O God of grace, whose very being is gracious, give us eyes to see how wondrous is this world you have made. And seeing, let us so love this creation that we shall live responsibly within it, contributing to its good in ways that are in keeping with grace. Amen.

[‡]Ingraham Professor of Theology at Claremont School of Theology, Claremont, California; United Methodist laywoman.

The psalm begins with a blessing to God and concludes with God's blessing to God's people; the psalm, then, is like a promise or covenant of blessing. In between, we have dynamic storm imagery from nature. If, as in yesterday's meditation, we connect God's creation of the world with the same grace we experience in baptism, then we read the storm imagery from within the confidence of grace. "The voice of the LORD is over the waters" inaugurates the storm imagery—and those words remind us, before we read what follows, of those baptismal waters, both from Creation and from recreation in Christ. But then! Lightning and thunder crash; great trees are uprooted; leaves are blown from limbs, and the very earth shakes.

The text describes a storm of frightening proportions, like some great hurricane that combines lightning, thunder, and wind and that occurs simultaneously with an earthquake! Yet this storm occurs between those covenantal passages of blessing! What are we to make of this? Imagine the difference between the sensation of being caught without protection in the middle of a fearful storm and of watching the same storm from the safety of a warm home that is secure against those winds and that rain. The covenantal blessings and the baptismal reminder provide a safe home in the midst of life's storms. Surrounded and embraced by covenant, we can face our storms with confidence and courage.

PRAYER: O God, my safety, my shelter in a time of storm, replace my anxieties with courage. For you are my hope and in you I trust. Amen.

In yesterday's reading the blessings that surrounded and framed the psalm's storm imagery encouraged us. We took heart from the reminder of our baptism even as the text took us into the eye of the storm. God is our shelter in a time of storm.

But look once more at the psalm, and ponder once more its imagery. Yes, the storm imagery is fearsome: thunder, rain and flood, broken cedars, shaken lands, lightning, earthquake, forests turned bare and baby animals born before their time. The storm seems like nature out of control, the natural order of things totally overturned. These aspects of the storm cry out with emotive effect, and we remember our baptism and are thankful for its shelter!

But the text teases us to see more than this. It is the Lord's voice in the thunder, over the waters, breaking the cedars. It is the Lord hewing out those "flames of fire," the Lord who strips the forests bare. Who is the Lord but the God of covenant and blessing? Yet the text tells us that this very God is in the storm, actively evoking it! Do we tremble at such a text? Does it tempt us to withdraw our trust? To the contrary. Those storms from which we shrink are not so alien as we have feared. God is in the storm. Psalm 139 reminds us that nowhere we can go is beyond the presence of our God—even in the storm, God is there. Even more, God is creatively there.

If God is in the storm, we can dare to move outside the safety of our homes. We can deal headlong with life's problems, for the God of blessing and baptismal covenant is also there in those storms. And since God is there, we need not fear them quite so much. "And in [God's] temple all say, 'Glory!'"

PRAYER: God, give us the grace of confidence no matter what the storm. Let us see you in it and therefore dare to face it in courage and hope, knowing that ultimately you surround us with blessing even in the midst of storms. Amen.

Finally we come to the baptism of our Lord. Have you noticed that there are two baptisms for Christ: the baptism through John that begins his ministry and the baptism through the cross that ends his ministry? We are so familiar with the first. John the baptizer comes preaching a baptism of repentance for the forgiveness of sins. He announces the coming of One who is "more powerful than I." And Jesus is this one, who nonetheless submits to baptism. We protest, If this baptism is for the forgiveness of sins, why should *he* be baptized? He is no sinner!

The second baptism gives us the reason for the first. Do you recall that Jesus referred to his coming Passion through the imagery of baptism? In Mark 10:38 he asked the disciples, "Are you able to drink the cup that I drink, or be baptized with the baptism that I am baptized with?" In Luke 12:50 the words are, "I have a baptism with which to be baptized, and what stress I am under until it is completed!" And he was speaking of the baptism of his death.

Jesus' ministry, then, begins and ends with baptism: first the baptism of John and then the baptism of the cross. The baptism of the cross is for us; he identifies with us and our sin in death. Even so in the initial baptism: He inaugurates his ministry in solidarity with us, identifying with us and our sin in repentance. What do we make of this? If Jesus identifies with us, then we are invited to identify with him. And if he, in union with us, undergoes our death, then we, in union with him, undergo his resurrection. The double baptisms bespeak the mission of Jesus, which is our salvation.

PRAYER: O Lord, you have been gracious to us beyond all our deserving. You are not a distant God, far from us, but in and through the baptisms of Christ you show yourself so near. You bind yourself to us and us to you. For this we give you thanks and praise. Amen.

In yesterday's text we contemplated the double baptism of Jesus: the first to inaugurate his ministry, the second to complete his ministry. We rejoiced at the strange union that God brings about through faith: Jesus Christ is one with us; and by grace through faith, we are one with him. So we too are baptized to symbolize and enact this grace.

It is right that we "remember our baptism, and be thankful." The church's rite of remembrance is a beautiful and important sign to us of God's grace. But we must never relegate our baptism to a past event that is merely to be remembered. If Christ's baptism is double, like bookends of his entire ministry, then we can view that ministry as entirely within the scope of that double baptism. Christ's baptism is not a once-and-then-over event; it is an event that spans his ministry. Even so with our baptism. Our initial baptism that brought us within the covenant of God will be met by the final baptism that brings us into eternal life. Our whole life is a living between these baptisms. Baptism, an event that lasts our whole life long, is past and future and therefore sustains our present. We live in and from and toward our baptism, first in the community of God's people and everlastingly into the life of God's own self.

When you remember your baptism, be thankful: not simply for that which is past but for that which continues to sustain you day by day until that final day of days in the life of God.

PRAYER: O God, you have baptized us into the body of Christ, your people. You have graced us with the life of this community and with your own life. You are the God of our salvation; we remember our baptism and are thankful. Amen.

What does it mean to be baptized with the Holy Spirit? And why did John contrast Jesus' baptism with his own in such a way? For all we know, Jesus never took water and baptized the disciples; he was not a baptizer in the sense that John was at all. So what should we make of this text?

Notice that John's baptism for repentance emphasized a person's past. People came to him confessing their sins. Matthew's account tells us that John even called those who came to him a "brood of vipers" (Matt. 3:7), and Mark tells us that John baptized them for the forgiveness of sins. Thus John's baptism seems to have dealt primarily with persons' lives prior to baptism—although surely, they were to "bear fruit worthy of repentance" (Matt. 3:8) following their baptism.

Baptism with the Holy Spirit does not simply refer to past events and behaviors; rather, it entails empowerment for how we will live now and in the future. Baptism with the Holy Spirit doesn't just cleanse; it opens us to the grace of God that guides us into a life in which holy loving is possible.

Baptism was not the focal point of Jesus' ministry perhaps because his own baptism was not yet complete—it awaited that second baptism of the cross. And because he himself is the one into whom we are baptized when we are baptized with the Holy Spirit, we are baptized into his body. Therefore we are empowered by his Spirit, the Holy Spirit of God.

PRAYER: O Lord our God, how excellent is your name in all the earth. You have baptized us with yourself and into yourself to the end that we may live in holiness all our days. Keep us mindful of this joy; conform us to your image. May we ourselves be witnesses to your grace in all the earth. Amen.

Baptism of the Lord

Notice the communal nature of this story in Acts. Apollos had visited this group of disciples in Ephesus, preaching Christ and baptizing, as did John, for the forgiveness of sins. Paul meets with this new band of twelve, these new disciples, and queries them about the Holy Spirit, which puzzles the men. So Paul instructs them about baptism in the name of the Lord, then baptizes them. Immediately they experience unusual phenomena that bear witness to the Spirit's presence.

Most of us do not *speak in tongues*, if by this term we mean ecstatic utterances. Yet perhaps in a deep way we do. The speaking in tongues gives vocal expression to an experience that defies any words the disciples in Ephesus know to express. They speak in this way together, interspersing this form of speech with the regular form of prophesying, which in those days would have meant something like preaching to one another, witnessing to one another about the presence of the Spirit.

Does not ordinary Christian worship with its ritual and its preaching constitute something like the experience of those believers in Ephesus? Our rituals—whether of an order of service or Communion or other sacraments—give expression to that which seems somehow deeper than our language knows how to say. Our hymns and sermons are a mode of prophesying, telling one another the good news of the gospel.

The band of twelve in Ephesus were inaugurated into a new way of being together through their baptism into Christ and their reception of the Holy Spirit. We are their spiritual heirs.

Prayer: Lord, when worship seems "ordinary" to us, remind us of its extraordinary power. May we be worthy successors to those early believers of so long ago. May our worship, as was theirs, be edifying to all in the faith community. May we, as were they, be a blessing to those who come after us. Amen.

God Searches for Us

January 13–19, 2003 • *Toby Gould*[‡]

MONDAY, JANUARY 13 • Read Psalm 139:1-6

The psalmist relates how intimately God knows us. God knows our movements, our thoughts, our sleeping, and our speaking. And then the psalmist says, "Such knowledge is too wonderful for me; it is so high that I cannot attain it."

Do these six verses make you uncomfortable? The psalmist says that here we stand, exposed before God, all that we are and all that we have been. From our malicious thoughts to our studied indifference to our ego-centeredness, God knows it all. Our hurts and grievances that we cling to so we can feel even sorrier for ourselves, God knows. Our desire for revenge, God knows. Our reliance on the other gods of our lives, God knows.

Yet the psalmist rejoices at his nakedness before the Lord. Clearly a song of loving praise, these six verses can wash over us as God-given reassurance—if we let them.

What do we need to do to hear these verses positively? First we remember that God is God, and we are who we are. The fear of standing before God is part of the human condition. Only if we have pride without measure might we stand before God and feel the least bit self-righteous.

So let's get over it. God sees us as we are whether we allow it or not. God knows who we are and how we are. Yet God still loves us. That is reassurance.

PRAYER: O God, you search my heart and know me. Quiet my fears and help me know that in Christ you love me. Amen.

[‡]United Methodist pastor; Project Manager for Mission Studies, General Board of Global Ministries, New York, New York.

"Can anything good come out of Nazareth?" What on earth did Nathanael mean? Certainly, from our perspective, someone very good came out of Nazareth.

But the Gospel writer has a different perspective and probably a different purpose for quoting such a question. Nazareth, a town in Galilee, was a place of religious and political turmoil during Jesus' time. The Roman governors always kept a wary eye focused on Galilee, for they were never sure when trouble might break out there.

Nathanael's question fits the public perception of a town in Galilee. "Can anything good come out of Nazareth?" The accepted answer would be, "Of course not!" It's a dumb question; everyone knows that Nazareth is nothing but trouble.

Yet out of Nazareth and onto the stage of human history walks Jesus, the son of Joseph the carpenter. He calls Nathanael, and Nathanael's life is forever changed.

Nathanael should have known. God often chooses the strangest people from the strangest places. Moses, a tongue-tied fellow, was tending his father-in-law's flock when he was chosen. Ruth was a young widow in a strange land. Saul walked toward Damascus with righteous violence in his heart.

All of these events should tell us to expect God's chosen to come from strange places. Can anything good come out of Afghanistan? Can anything good come from the other side of the tracks where we wouldn't be caught dead? Can anything good come from the wild-eyed, young woman who always questions our moral choices? Can anything good come from the immigrant who speaks with an accent we often choose to find too difficult to understand?

"Can anything good come out of Nazareth?" Once the very best of humanity came out of Nazareth, and not many people noticed.

PRAYER: O God, come into our world where you choose and help us to see your way for us. Amen.

"Samuel! Samuel!" Old men often need help in the middle of the night. Sometimes sleepy young helpers stumble out of bed and go to do the bidding of the old one. This night young Samuel responds to old Eli three times, but Eli denies calling his young helper. Samuel thinks, *What's going on? Is the old man losing it? I heard my name, even in my sleep. Now he says that he didn't call.*

But Eli knows. Another voice is calling Samuel. Back in the past of his mind, Eli vaguely remembers that voice—a voice that needs to be identified as we respond to it.

But Samuel has not heard this voice before. So the old and tired Eli, with the wisdom of his years, tells Samuel, "Go, lie down; and if he calls you, you shall say, 'Speak, LORD, for your servant is listening.'" Eli discerns the nature of that divine voice, then tells Samuel who it is and how he must answer.

The Lord searches us out, and we need not be on a solitary mountaintop. We do not need to be alone. In fact, other people sometimes point out God's call when we do not hear or will not understand.

Too often our romantic religious feelings obscure God's call. "O Lord, you must call me in the dramatic fashion of my choosing. A burning bush would be nice, but I'd settle for a thunderous voice in the middle of the desert."

God can call us through the words of a friend or colleague, through the events that happen in front of us, anywhere, anytime, any way. May our response be, "Speak, LORD, for your servant is listening."

PRAYER: O God, open my ears that I may hear my name when you call. Amen.

Here's the situation. Many people in Corinth are arguing with Paul that fidelity in marriage isn't important. In essence they maintain that the body is a minor annoyance; it is our souls that count. What we do with our bodies isn't important to God in the long run.

Paul never lets go. Though the Corinthians never seem to learn, he remains steadfast in his teaching. Paul forcefully and impatiently tells the Corinthians that all that they are is God's creation. God didn't just create their souls with their bodies following along in random fashion. All that they and we are, body and soul, comes from God. Consideration of physical actions requires careful decision making, as do thought and prayer.

The lawyer Paul needs to drive his point home. Our bodies are of ultimate importance because we are part of the body of Christ. Paul doesn't say we are part of the mind of Christ or the soul of Christ, but as Christians we become part of Christ's body. Later Paul describes those parts of the body to the Corinthians assuring them that each of them has a place, a distinctive place, in the body of Christ.

Each day presents us with situations that call us to affirm that we are part of the body of Christ. Our issues may differ from those facing the Corinthians, but our response to Christ's call to be part of his body is as important today as it was then. "Do you not know that your bodies are members of Christ?"

PRAYER: Open my senses, O Lord, that I may know that my body is part of the body of Christ. Amen.

It seems that neither Eli nor the Lord is too thrilled with secret spiritual knowledge. After the Lord speaks to Samuel, the old man Eli asks the obvious question, What did God say?

Samuel hesitates. The Lord's words to Samuel are angry and vengeful: Because of the blasphemy of Eli's sons, the house of Eli will be punished by God. When Samuel hears these terrifying words, he does not go running to Eli to share the news. Samuel hides in his bed. But Eli persists, "What was it that he told you? Do not hide it from me."

Then young Samuel tells the old man what God has in store for his family. What is Eli's response to the news that his family will be wiped out? He says simply, "It is the LORD; let him do what seems good to him."

One verse drives home the point that when we are called by God to speak, we speak when and as God directs: "As Samuel grew up, the LORD was with him and let none of his words fall to the ground." If words fall to the ground, they are not heard. God has ensured that the words of God's chosen prophet will not fall.

As Jesus' followers, we are called to share God's words. On many pulpits are the words *We would see Jesus*. Whether we are in a pulpit or not, whenever we speak, we speak as Christians and need to remember who has called us to speak. Let us speak bravely and clearly, knowing who we follow. Our words will not fall to the ground.

PRAYER: God, give me the courage to share my faith openly and honestly with all who seek your word. Amen.

Too often what we see first determines how we act. We Americans are impulse buyers. We buy cars because of the way they look when we first see them. We order meals based on the aroma coming from the restaurant kitchens. We go to the movies based on movie posters.

We all would be wise to follow Nathanael. We shouldn't believe the first argument we hear. The opposite side might make more sense. We certainly shouldn't use those seven last words of the church, "We've never done it that way before." Try a new way and learn something.

Nathanael has heard about Jesus from his friend Philip. Though skeptical at first, Nathanael goes with his friend to meet this rabbi. He takes a second look. As Nathanael approaches him, Jesus calls to Nathanael, "Here is truly an Israelite in whom there is no deceit."

Jesus and Nathanael engage in a conversation. Jesus appreciates Nathanael's questions about Jesus' knowledge of him. As the conversation continues, Jesus' words convince Nathanael that Jesus is that unique person to whom he will declare his allegiance. He states, "Rabbi, you are the Son of God! You are the King of Israel!"

Children want instant gratification, and parents often lovingly and quickly give them what they want. But as we grow, we need to put away our childish impulses. Mature faith raises questions about easy answers and comes to different conclusions: Don't assume teenagers are up to no good. Allow a former enemy to become a friend. Take a personal risk for the sake of justice. Don't follow the crowd when you suspect that the members are wrong.

Be ready to have your mind changed. Wait for God to show you the way.

PRAYER: Lord, give me the patience to question my motives and await your response. Amen.

How do we respond to God's call? The psalmist says that first we respond with a hymn of praise. Before all else, God be praised!

It is God who has called us—the first miracle here. God cares for each of us so much that God has woven us together. "You knit me together in my mother's womb."

The psalmist does not praise a distant creator who set the stars in motion and then left creation alone. The weaver of the stars in the sky knitted us together as well. Then the psalmist says, Not only did you begin my existence, O God, but when life ends, I am still with you. The sense of wonder in the psalmist's heart comes through in these words. It's as if the psalmist asks, "How can God care for me?" And in the same breath, the psalmist answers, "Because God is God."

Despite physical pain or troubled thoughts, despite injustice done to us, despite disappointments too bitter to swallow, it is God who knitted us together. So praise God.

This psalm offers no lesson plan for praising God. It does not tell us to play the lyre, raise our hands in worship, or dance a particular dance. Our life itself praises God.

In an increasingly noisy world, it is not easy to focus our lives on praising God. Start a daily discipline that carves out some space for remembering who created you. Develop your own spiritual exercise in praise of God. After some days of practice, your spiritual muscles will remember and will call you to praise God.

PRAYER: O God, I praise you for creating me. May my life reflect your creative hands. Amen.

Sounds Like a Plan!

January 20–26, 2003 • *M. Garlinda Burton*[‡]

MONDAY, JANUARY 20 • **Read Jonah 3:1-5, 10**

And the people of Nineveh believed God; they proclaimed a fast, and everyone, great and small, put on sackcloth.

—Jonah 3:5

My pal, Jeneane, is not one to make up her mind in a hurry. Whether it's what movie to see or how to ask her boss for a raise, she has to be absolutely convinced that her choice is the right one before she'll proceed. Unlike me, she's not given to snap decisions.

I can always tell though when I've hit upon the perfect, most persuasive argument to convince her to see things my way. Whenever I say the right words, she suddenly perks up and says, "Sounds like a plan! Let's do it!"

The people of Nineveh had chosen previously to ignore the call to repentance and reconciliation with God. So God had decided to do away with them and had sent Jonah to read the death sentence. However, when faced with the choice to change or die, the Ninevites repent—quickly but sincerely. And their impassioned and genuine change of heart persuades God to change as well and say, in essence, "You wanna work together with me for good? Sounds like a plan!"

God's open hand reminds us that it is worth making room in our lives for the love that never gives up on us. Will you take God's hand right now? Sounds like a plan!

PRAYER: God, who like a patient parent forgives and embraces your wayward children over and over again, thanks for giving me another chance to make my way to you. Amen.

[‡]Anti-racism trainer; editor of *Interpreter* magazine; member of Hobson United Methodist Church, Nashville, Tennessee.

God is a refuge for us.
—Psalm 62:8

Three o'clock on a spring afternoon the sky turned black and eerie yellow. The tornado was coming.

Most children in the neighborhood were home alone because their parents could not afford after school care. There were frantic calls from mothers and fathers trying to reassure their children and work out a safety plan. Then came that first clap of thunder, and most phones went dead.

Suddenly the children filled the streets and ran toward the big church on the corner. Formerly a dying, older congregation, the members in recent years had opened a free after-school program as a service to the community and as a way to bring new life to their church. It worked. Children came after school and for Sunday school too. They knew it to be a loving, welcoming place. They knew they'd be safe there. When the storm threatened, their first instinct was to run to the church.

Adults welcomed the children and herded them into the fellowship hall. They sang songs and talked as the thunder cracked and trees fell. Not one child sustained an injury. After the storm, church members kept the children busy by involving them in emergency assistance to others in the community. The children even made a news video chronicling the church's ministry in the storm's aftermath.

Today the children still remember that day, not with fear but as the day they found refuge when they needed it most. God's people are also called to be a refuge. Does your life's plan include being a listening ear, a shoulder to cry on, a helping hand?

SUGGESTION FOR MEDITATION: Name in your heart people who have reached out to you in your time of trouble. Give God thanks for them.

Once God has spoken; twice have I heard this: that power belongs to God, and steadfast love belongs to you, O Lord.
—Psalm 62:11

Some people say I'm a good public speaker, but often I don't feel competent. The speakers and preachers I most admire seldom seem to use written notes or texts. They simply step to the pulpit and the words come, powerfully, effortlessly, and true. Even though several preacher-friends have explained that they practice and practice to achieve that "effortless" presentation, I still view them as being imbued with some extra power, unattainable for an amateur speaker like myself.

But sometimes when I'm asked to preach on a topic or a biblical text that has special meaning for me, I feel something like hot water start at my toes when I take the pulpit. It happens whenever I preach from my favorite text—the story of the paralyzed man and his four friends in Mark 2. Something about Christ's compassion and power and the witness of those friends makes me want to shout every time I even think about that story.

So whenever I read the text aloud, the hot water roars up my spine, and my voice gets stronger. Suddenly my speaking is no longer just words over which I have labored and planned; it is balm for the world, and God gives me the honor of pouring it out. And, doggone it, I'm preaching!

God reminds us daily that our strength, talents, and spiritual gifts are handmade and sent special delivery to us from God's realm. We all have a calling; we are all part of God's plan. And the tools we need to do our part are there for the taking, if we will lean on God for strength.

PRAYER: God, thank you for the loving strength and holy power poured out for me every day. Help me harness that power for good in your world. In Jesus' name. Amen.

*From now on, let...those who buy [be] as though they had
no possessions, and those who deal with the world as though
they had no dealings with it. For the present form of this
world is passing away.*

—1 Corinthians 7:29, 30-31

Many people point to First Corinthians as an example of Paul's
misogynist predilections, for he seems to favor the celibate,
unmarried life for Christians over marriage and family. He seems
to urge true believers—particularly men—to avoid the distractions of marriage in order to be better followers of Christ.

Paul, preaching to people in his own time, believed the end
of the world was imminent: "The appointed time has grown
short." Therefore, he urged disciples to spend what he believed
to be their last days focused on Christ only, because the institutions of the world would not last.

Today most of us admit that we don't know when the world
will end. But what might our lives be like if we knew? Perhaps
we would find ourselves less attached to outward "things," be
they relationships or possessions. If these days were our last, we
might choose more carefully, attempting to find wholeness and
healing for ourselves.

Also, if we believed, as did Paul, these were our last days, we
would probably put Christ first in more aspects of our lives. What
might result from single-minded devotion to God? Repentance,
forgiveness, and a more fervent prayer life would likely be front-
burner issues, instead of being something we'll get around to
later in life.

How would you express your faith differently—in your
home, at work, in your prayer life, or in your church—if you
believed these days to be your last?

SUGGESTION FOR MEDITATION: **Make a list of the things you
would do differently if this were your last week on earth. In
what ways can you clear the clutter and begin living as if every
moment matters?**

The kingdom of God has come near; repent, and believe in the good news.

—Mark 1:15

An elderly friend of mine has had a running feud with a member of her church for nearly forty years. My friend can't even remember when or why she and the other woman first crossed paths, but she's really clear about who is the more pigheaded. She ends every diatribe with words about her sister church member: "Peggy's so stubborn; they'll have to knock her up 'side the head on judgment day!"

Most of us reading this devotional have heard God's good news. Many of us have joined churches, and we say we love Christ, who has redeemed us. We express our gratitude to him in many different ways, and we're planning to take up residence in heaven when our time comes.

But while we're waiting for that celestial condo, are we living lives of humility, gratitude, forgiveness, prayer, and love? Or do we put those qualities away with our Sunday clothes and live the rest of our time with so much stubbornness, combativeness, and even silliness that someone will have to "knock us up 'side the head on judgment day" to get our attention?

The kingdom of God hovers near at all times. It has come in Jesus, the Word made flesh. It comes in the unexpected smiles of children, in the quiet strength of a recovering drug addict, in the withered hand of an old woman who has forgotten more about survival than I'll ever know, and in the witness of those who have learned when to be hardheaded for Christ's sake and when to lay anger aside.

Hear the good news! Christ died for us while we were yet sinners. That proves Christ's love for us. Conflicts will come, but the kingdom of God is at hand.

PRAYER: Forgive me, Lord, when I am stubborn or willful in ways that run counter to your desires for me. Help me embrace your plan to seek allies on the journey. Amen.

And Jesus said to them, "Follow me and I will make you fish for people." And immediately they left their nets and followed him.

—Mark 1:17-18

Talk about a big promotion! Picture Simon and Andrew, simple fishermen dragging their lines—another day, another dollar. Suddenly Jesus calls, and they go from being net jockeys to having the most important jobs in human history—helping bring people to Christ.

But, as many of us know all too well, no promotion comes without a price. By leaving the comfort of a low-profile job and following Jesus, Simon and Andrew faced ridicule and scorn from the old-guard religious authorities. The two men worked long hours in often hostile environs, sometimes not knowing where they would sleep and what they would eat. Their CEO was a guy given to telling strange stories they didn't understand and healing without official religious authorization. To top it off, they signed on with what would be a rag-tag crew—yes, the disciples—who had no action plans, flowcharts, or support staff and little if any start-up funding.

Thank God that the two brothers yielded to the temptation of pursuing a more excellent, if unknown, way. To paraphrase Robert Frost, Simon and Andrew took the road less traveled and helped establish the foundation for our faith.

By clinging to the safe and mundane in our lives and ministries, we sometimes miss opportunities to take on a challenge that would fulfill and stretch us. True, a promotion often means more work and more responsibility, but it also means that we have more chances to bless and be blessed.

SUGGESTION FOR MEDITATION: Listen. Look. Pray. Isn't it time for you to drop your net and go?

As he went a little farther, he saw James son of Zebedee and his brother John, who were in their boat mending their nets. Immediately he called them; and they left their father.
—Mark 1:19-20

We settled in Nashville with the idea that when my mother-in-law got too feeble to live on her own, she could move in with us. Although we had first planned to move to another city and we both dreamed of pursuing that one great job before turning our minds toward retirement, the reality that my mother-in-law might need us kept us anchored here.

We'd been no more than two years in our new—and what we had planned as our final—home, when my mother-in-law got sick and died suddenly. She died the way we all want to go: still caring for herself, still driving herself to any mall or church meeting or vacation she liked, enjoying her retirement and her family with her usual relish and zest for life.

With her death, my husband and I realized that all our plans for the next twenty years had changed in an instant. And though we don't regret our choices, we were also reminded that had we pursued our own dreams my mother-in-law's life would have come to the same conclusion. Could it be that we used her as an excuse not to take a leap of faith by leaving the familiar behind to pursue some frightening but exhilarating risks?

James and John could have used their father and the family business as excuses for declining Jesus' offer to become followers and fishers of people. Instead they left their father in God's care and hit the road with the Messiah—a life-altering choice.

I'm glad we were here for my mother-in-law, but I'm also grateful for the lesson I've learned: If you feel in your heart that you're following God's plan, God will supply what is needed. Trust in God's plan is essential for living in fullness of life.

PRAYER: Loving Creator, help me find the balance between my dreams, the needs of my family and community, and your will for my life. Guide my feet in the name of Jesus. Amen.

To Know As God Knows

January 27–February 2, 2003 • *Jay Voorhees[‡]*
Kay Hereford Voorhees[‡‡]

MONDAY, JANUARY 27 • **Read Psalm 111**

My seven-year-old's favorite TV show of the week is called "Fear Factor," which pits the beautiful and successful of the world against one another, challenging them to overcome their fears in the pursuit of fame and fortune. The program features much macho posturing as these celebrities attempt to appear invulnerable, powerful, and fearless.

Our world is uncomfortable with fear. Our literature does not generally lift up fear as a virtue; rather, we value the strong and courageous. For us fear is about losing control or finding ourselves at the mercy of powers greater than ourselves.

The psalmist's suggestion, that fear is connected to wisdom, startles us. "Doesn't love cast out fear?" we ask. Aren't we irrational when we are afraid? How can fear lead to wisdom?

Somehow the psalmist knows that fear isn't necessarily a bad thing. Psychologists tell us that healthy fear is necessary in helping us identify challenges to our safety and security. Fear helps us prepare for the journey ahead.

The fear of God likewise serves to tell us something. The fear of the Lord reminds us of who we are. To bow before God is to be reminded that we aren't in control, that we serve a higher power, that we are vulnerable. Wisdom is found in remembering our place in the world, which leads us to set aside our illusions of power and instead live out our lives as children of God.

PRAYER: Creating God, help us to remember our place in the world. Amen.

[‡]Associate pastor, Bellevue United Methodist Church, Bellevue, Tennessee.

[‡‡]Associate pastor, West End United Methodist Church, Nashville, Tennessee.

Have you noticed that prophets seem to be everywhere these days? The supermarket tabloids hail the latest prediction by the seers and sages of the day. All sorts of pundits on TV attempt to predict what will happen and to interpret complex concepts into palatable sound bites. Religious bookstores are filled with books that proclaim the latest and greatest revelation of God, translating the sometimes troubling words of God into "relevant" lessons that are easy to grasp. "You figure out what's going on," we tell these folks. "It's too hard to deal with these things ourselves."

God's people have fallen prey to this tendency throughout the ages. The Hebrews, poised at the foot of Mount Horeb, ease Moses out ahead of them rather than experience God directly. "You go, Moses," the people say. "You tell us what God says because it's simply too scary to hear God ourselves."

So, because we are too afraid to connect with God ourselves, God gave us prophets to do the work for us. But there's a catch. "If you're going to have prophets," God tells us, "you have to be willing to listen to them." If we don't, then God says *we* will be held accountable.

That is the problem, isn't it? We want prophets to do the dirty work, the hard work of facing God. But we also want the option of ignoring what they say when their message doesn't fit into our lives. Prophets are popular as long as they tell us what we want to hear. But when they veer too close to home, challenging those things that we hold dear, then we want to head back to Egypt and live in our familiar slavery.

The options are simple. We either listen to those whom God has called and faithfully follow their guidance, or we do what God wanted the people to do in the first place. We head up the mountain ourselves, braving the fire and the terrifying voice to experience God's message directly. The choice is up to us.

PRAYER: Dear God, cast out our fear so that we may experience your Word fully. Amen.

To my ears, this story reads like a scene from a B-grade horror flick. The synagogue is filled; the rabbi is seated at the front, teaching. Murmurs of approval and astonishment arise from the crowd at his powerful lesson, but overall the mood is peaceful. Suddenly, from among the crowd, a voice cries out: "What do you want with us, Jesus of Nazareth?"(NIV) Heads turn, and a crazed-looking man stands center stage, ranting at the teacher. Rabbi Jesus, dressed in shining white robes, interrupts, "Hush! Come out of him!" and with one great convulsion the ghostly demon leaves the man's body and flies away across the screen. I giggle nervously, proud that my Jesus is such a hero but a bit embarrassed to admit that such a story could belong to me.

As long as the man in the story is demon-possessed, of course, I don't have to identify too closely with him. Or if I think of him (using modern terminology) as mentally ill or schizophrenic, I might still manage to disassociate myself. What could I possibly gain by removing myself from the story? Or, to ask the same question from another perspective, What have I got to lose by finding myself *in* it?

Yet the evil spirit that possessed this man actually gives voice to the deep fears that reside in me. When I find myself in Jesus' presence and I hear his authoritative teaching, my divided heart wants to cry out, "What do you want with us, Jesus? Have you come to destroy us?" Parts of myself and my life that I hold most dear are precisely the parts that Jesus comes to exorcise: my self-interest, my wealth-interest, my self-inflicted ignorance of God. If I let Jesus have his way with me, all my props will crumble.

Which is more powerful: my demon fear or the authoritative grace of Jesus Christ? I pray that I will be like the man in the synagogue, speaking my heart's truth to Jesus and being blessed beyond measure by a power far greater than my own.

PRAYER: O Holy One of God, I know myself too well; you know me fully. Dispel my demons, I humbly pray. Amen.

Like the church at Corinth, today's Christian community is riddled with conflict. Liberals versus conservatives, hand-lifters versus pew-sitters, guitarists versus organists, each group certain that its way is best. At the core of the rampant conflict is the assumption that what we *know* is more important than *how we act* toward one another.

In Corinth, some who "knew" the grace of Christ were causing confusion for those who were new to the gospel. Those in the know reasoned that since there was only one God, food that had been sacrificed to idols couldn't really be connected to other gods. Through freedom found in Christ Jesus, they felt free to buy meat at the market without regard to its origin. So what if it had come from Artemis's temple? Eating it would not make them followers of Artemis. She wasn't a divine being anyway.

Other people though—those looking into the Way from the outside and those who were new to faith in Christ—had yet to grasp the theological intricacies of Christian practice. To them it appeared that Christians might be joining themselves to other gods by eating meat that may have been sacrificed to those gods.

Sin, Paul explains to the church at Corinth, is more than a matter of breaking rules that once were chiseled into stone. Sin is breaking relationships among ourselves, others, and God. When we value our own personal knowledge above the faith life of another, we betray Jesus Christ who gave his life for that person. What we think we know and even what we deeply believe to be true are no more than hot air. But our gentleness toward those who believe differently than we shows that we both know and love God, who knows and loves us and our neighbors more fully than we will ever know.

PRAYER: Lord Jesus Christ, have mercy on me, a sinner. Forgive my habit of looking down on those whose knowledge differs from mine. From this moment on, may I know only your love in all my relationships. Amen.

The notion of a great judge in the sky who waits for me to mess up so that I can be struck down by lightning does not attract me. On the other hand, the image of God as a kindly old Santa Claus figure on the throne among soft white clouds is not accurate or helpful either. Somewhere along the way, as the church tried to teach the children of the 1960s about God's love and grace, we lost touch with the glory and majesty, mighty acts and fierce jealousy, the absolute power of God.

"The fear of the LORD is the beginning of wisdom," writes the psalmist. What he means by "fear" is knowledge of the wholeness of who God is and what God has done. In other words, to fear God is to have a grasp on the immeasurable greatness of the One who has absolute hold on everything. How can we stand before the One who formed every detail of countless universes without our knees trembling at least a bit? How can we address the One more powerful than death itself in much more than a terrified whisper? How can we know ourselves to be fully known by such a One and still live to tell?

I accompanied a group of inner-city kids on a backpacking trip. They moaned and complained about the loads on their backs and the strain on their feet. Then we got to the waterfall—an idyllic scene with columns of water splashing down into a perfect swimming hole, surrounded by lush green forest. One of the most cynical young men of the group threw his backpack on a boulder, sat down beside it, and said, "Wow. God must be pretty big to have made this." I'd never heard him refer to God before, except when cursing. While the other kids explored and swam that afternoon, this young man spent most of his time sitting on that boulder gazing at the sight of the waterfall and, as I later learned, pondering the bigness of God and the smallness of himself. May we all be so wise.

PRAYER: Holy God, though I love you as the dearest of friends, may I feel how small I am compared to you. Give me the courage to fear you well. In Jesus' name. Amen.

The members of my family are addicted game players. I remember many nights sitting around a table placing wooden squares on the Scrabble board or rolling dice as I tried to get five of a kind in Yahtzee. I was never good at math, so number games eluded me. I did OK with word games, but I often failed to see the patterns of letters that made up words. My specialty was trivial knowledge: the capital of Austria or the author of *War and Peace*. I enjoyed playing Jeopardy or Trivial Pursuit—any game that let me demonstrate my intellectual prowess.

My love of knowledge continued into adulthood. I understood education to be a source of success. Growth came through gaining knowledge. The pursuit of degrees and credentials gave a person authority. I bought into the notion that titles and knowledge could provide security and significance.

For many years I didn't recognize the value of Paul's words in First Corinthians. As I move into my forties, I've learned that the older I get, the less I know. Facts and certainties have become less certain. Knowledge doesn't seem nearly as powerful as it once was. Degrees and credentials mean less to me as I file them away.

Instead I have learned that love is the only certainty in our world. It is the most significant power, the center of life with God, the source of strength and hope. As Paul tells us, the experience of love is life-building and life-changing; it provides knowledge that goes beyond accumulation of facts. Love, as Paul says later in chapter 13, is eternal and the greatest of all virtues.

Our goal might be to know love in its fullest, for when we know love, we are known by God. When we are known by God, then all the knowledge of the world begins to make sense, and we experience the reality of God's kingdom here on earth.

PRAYER: Loving God, help us to see that love is stronger than knowledge. Help us to love others as you have loved us. Amen.

Authorities on all sorts of subjects fill our world. Psychiatrists are authorities on the workings of the human mind. Sociologists are authorities on how society operates. Economists are authorities on how money and markets affect our world.

To be an authority today requires special knowledge about a particular topic. Authorities are people who have studied a subject and learned as much as they can about it.

However, the most authoritative among us today are those who have firsthand knowledge about a topic. Persons might study for years about lions, reading all there is to know about the physiology of lions. They might have seen videos and photographs depicting all the types of lions in the world. Yet they will never have the same authority as a person who regularly interacts with lions, who lives with them, who plays with them, and who sees them in their natural home.

Jesus amazes the people of Galilee because he has firsthand knowledge of God and God's ways. The theologians of the day—the preachers and teachers of Judaism—are considered authorities on the law because of their years of intense study. But Jesus comes among them, living the law, embodying it, making it real. The scribes can talk about how the law restores one's relationship with God. Jesus lives that understanding into existence by casting out demons and healing the sick. The teachers have knowledge; Jesus has authority.

We can easily confuse knowledge with authority. The great sages and teachers of our day may not have a great deal of "book learning." Rather, they are people who know God intimately, who experience God's grace daily, who have the faith to cast out demons in Christ's name—true marks of authority.

PRAYER: All-knowing God, grant us the grace that we may know you fully, that we may feel you completely, and that your love will be manifest in the world through our lives. Amen.

Not One Is Missing

February 3–9, 2003 • James E. Sargent[‡]

MONDAY, FEBRUARY 3 • Read Isaiah 40:21-31

The theme of this week's readings takes its cue from the prophet Isaiah. He speaks to the exiles of a hope that "not one is missing." What memories might this phrase have stirred in those who heard it? All the exiles are survivors or children of survivors. They have heard the awful stories of the collapse of Jerusalem, the round-ups, the forced march, the terrible separations and losses. Every family has a heartrending story of loss. This week's scriptures express concern for individuals.

My mother used to tell a story of a day at the beach when, as a toddler, I'd gotten away from the gathering. Mom asked, "Where's Jim?" Immediately sandwiches and drinks, picnic baskets and beach balls were dropped. Everyone looked. I'm told that great relief swept through that group when I was found.

For people who have suffered loss, the announcement of a day when no one will be missing comes as an inexpressibly wonderful promise. One of the most poignant memorials in Yad Vashem, the memorial to the Holocaust in Jerusalem, is that in which the children are remembered. In a dark room with flickering candles someone reads aloud the names of hundreds of thousands of children who were lost. A day will come when no one is missing.

In England every chapel, church, and cathedral has a plaque that lists the names of soldiers from that parish who were lost in the Great War. The day will come when no one will be missing. Across the United States one can see flags that commemorate the lives of those missing in action in Vietnam. The day will come when no one will be missing.

SUGGESTION FOR PRAYER: Pray for families suffering loss. Pray for the promise of the prophet, that no one will be missing.

[‡]Retired clergy, The United Methodist Church, living in Cincinnati, Ohio.

I recall our three sons' earliest steps. They balanced themselves carefully and then tentatively took a few steps. After they'd developed walking skills, they learned to run. Later each of them became a varsity athlete. Today two of them watch their own children learn to walk. Crawl, walk, run, and soar. We see this rhythm in human development. The prophet concludes his chapter with exactly the opposite rhythm, a peculiar reversal? Isaiah begins with flying as with eagles' wings, then running with the speed of an athlete, and concludes with ordinary walking.

The prophet has paid attention to life. He has seen lots of people caught up in the enthusiasm of a new movement and witnessed the enthusiasm of new converts. The initial impulse is to soar as with eagles. However, the prophet has also seen what inevitably follows the flush of enthusiasm that accompanies great beginnings. The first generation of exiles anxiously anticipated returning to their beloved homeland. Their children are not as enthusiastic; grandchildren are even less enthusiastic.

Many people feel as if they have been left behind in the spiritual realm by others who seem able to soar with eagles or run as effortlessly as conditioned athletes. Some feel disqualified from faith because they have not had a moment of high enthusiasm. Others suspect that they don't have as much faith as people who give vivid witness practically every day.

To people who fear that their faith is somehow not enough or second-rate, Isaiah speaks a most welcome word of encouragement. The measure of faith is not how high one can fly or how quickly one can race. The measure comes in our placing one foot in front of the other and continuing with the mundane tasks of faithful living.

SUGGESTION FOR PRAYER: **Recall a moment in your life when your faith strengthened you to continue your efforts for another hour, another day. Now bring to mind someone you know who is discouraged; pray that the prophet's promise will be fulfilled in that person's life.**

Some years ago, on a midsummer night near Jackson Lake in the Grand Tetons, I gazed into the heavens. I'd never seen anything like that night sky. It appeared that God had dust mopped the entire universe to gather every possible particle of starlight, then scattered the stars as one might scatter dust. The sky was littered with more stars than I thought possible.

We have names for stars and constellations: North Star, Dog Star. All of us have stared into the heavens and identified the Big Dipper or Orion. The psalmist says that God names every one of the stars. Staring at the stars, I called to mind a biblical character. God promised Abraham that his children would outnumber the stars in the heavens. Imagine Abraham's seeing a sky similar to the one I witnessed, a sky littered with stars. He may have wondered how God's promise could come true.

Imagine all the people over the course of thousands of years who have believed in God's purposes, who have trusted in God's grace, who have been blessed by the stories of Abraham, Sarah, Jesus, and Paul. How many people have stared at the stars, recalled the promises made to Abraham, and wondered how God can keep track of stars and individuals? Yet we are assured that God cares for and tends to both the minute and the vast.

In one of his volumes on the Army of the Potomac, Bruce Catton includes a scene in which two recently freed slaves stand near a road as the victorious Union army marches past. Endlessly long ranks of blue-clad soldiers pass. At one point one of the slaves speaks, "There are so many of them, they can't all have names." We know that each of those soldiers had a name. Each individual has a name, and in God's knowing each star has a name.

SUGGESTION FOR PRAYER: **Bring to mind a friend and imagine that person in a large stadium surrounded by thousands of other people. Now imagine that stadium in the midst of a large city. God sees each individual just as you have been able to picture one friend.**

We have all waited in lines at the post office, doctor's office, grocery store, or hotel lobby. Picture this home in which Jesus ministers to people. Word has spread that Jesus of Nazareth is in town. People have lined up to see him—some reluctantly, others with unbridled enthusiasm and anticipation. Long lines of people, each person with a special concern, wait to see him. We join the line as one of many people seeking his healing touch and comforting word.

When on pastoral exchange in England I had the opportunity to serve Communion at church. Members knelt at the rail with hands extended and cupped to receive the bread. I noticed their hands: gnarled, old hands; young, slender fingers; arthritic, bent fingers; work-worn palms and callused knuckles.

Whenever I read stories of Jesus' healings, I imagine the details of people's appearance. Jesus would have noticed hands. In one of my imaginative moments I picture a man who has accidentally smashed his thumb with a hammer. As he extends his hands to Jesus, our Lord notes the blackened thumbnail. With a knowing look in his eye, Jesus shows the man his own blackened index finger. Jesus knows and understands people.

I can easily imagine Jesus leaning forward to catch every word whispered by a young man too self-conscious to speak loudly. I imagine Jesus reaching out to touch the young man on the shoulder and speaking softly. The young man's eyes brighten as he whispers, "I hope so."

These scenes continue for hours. That long line of people is not just another mass of humanity. Each person has a name and a face, eyes and hands. Jesus notices and cares for each of them.

SUGGESTION FOR PRAYER: **Notice someone's hands and eyes. Look deeply into his or her eyes; if you can, hold hands. Then picture Jesus looking and holding the hands of an endless line of people. Imagine Jesus speaking to each of them, "God bless you." Listen as each person responds, "Thank you, Jesus."**

To the psalmist the expression God's "delight is not in the strength of the horse, nor his pleasure in the speed of a runner" means that a person's measure does not reside in advancements claimed or amassed, nor is it in personal achievements. The significant criterion by which anyone is measured is faithfulness to God's purposes.

I know a man who has worked with chronically mentally ill people for many years. The burnout rate in his profession averages three years, yet he has been doing this work for over sixteen years. When I asked him how he managed to stay at it for so long a time, he said his primary concern has always been to fulfill his calling. Therefore, he has chosen to work with a part of the population that has too often been marginalized, neglected, or ignored.

Occasionally I ask my friend about his work. He tells me about people that the newspaper would categorize as mentally ill. To him, however, every person he works with has a name, a life story, loves, and fears; each is a distinct human being.

As I write this meditation news reports speak of deployment of military forces; news articles analyze defensive weapons systems; and economic news always mentions wealth that exceeds that of kings and queens. Headlines seem always to focus on the maneuverings of the powerful or the privileges of the rich and famous. Against that backdrop my friend continues his work with men and women for whom God seems to have a particular concern and care. Hebrew Scriptures always characterize God as having a special concern in this area because unless God cares for the poor, downtrodden, and marginalized, seemingly no one will care. My friend is among those whom the psalmist mentions as "those who fear [the Lord]." My friend cares for individuals so that none will be lost.

SUGGESTION FOR PRAYER: Pray for people who work in obscurity with otherwise forgotten people.

Something must have happened deep within the apostle Paul's soul. Perhaps he had been thinking about the conflicts that raged in his beloved Corinthian congregation. He'd poured his soul into that group, from its inception to the final day when he had to depart for other mission fields. At length word reached him that the congregation had split into factions. After days of anguish a different, imaginative thought occurred to him.

The kinds of things the congregation argued about or fought over seemed to him to be largely irrelevant. He remembered his own inclinations in earlier years. He'd been adamant in his demands, inflexible in his expectations. He'd insisted that people behave in a certain way or believe as he believed. Along the way he had learned that if he were to speak to people about Christ, he would first have to understand life, issues, dreams, and aspirations from their perspective. He must have wondered, *Why can't people bend a little? Why can't they see that what really matters is how people got along with one another?* Somehow he knew that at the root of it all, the stuff of Christian discipleship has to do with relationships. Paul was willing to forego his own inclinations regarding correct doctrine and proper creed so that other people might come to know the freedom, the life, and the joy that are central in the life of faith.

The old Beatles song includes the line, "Try to see it my way." The apostle Paul sees life from another person's perspective so that no one will be lost to the saving knowledge of Christ.

SUGGESTION FOR PRAYER: Recall one person from whom you have felt distant. Loosen up your imagination, and try to see the situation from that person's perspective. Pray that the spirit of Christ may change you so that the other person may come to know the presence of Christ.

The evangelist notes that crowds of people come to see Jesus toward sundown. Again, without doing violence to the scripture, we can cast loose our imaginations. People have been working all day. Only "after hours" can they seek out Jesus. Imagine a line of people. Here a man with leprous hands stands, his arms revealing the dreadful disease. There a woman long haunted by demons talks to herself. There a man holds his fever-wracked son. In turn each person enters the house where Jesus has been working all day.

One man anxiously cranes his neck to see how many people are ahead of him. He has heard about Jesus and wants desperately to see the man from Nazareth. But the sun is setting. The day draws too quickly to a close. A memory of an Old Testament story comes to mind. He recalls the story of Joshua and how the sun stood still. He prays that the sun might stand still now, lest Jesus conclude his healing for the day.

In your imagination, recall someone you know for whom you wish a healing, an encouraging word, or gentle touch by Jesus. Now stand with that individual in line. Notice the people around you. Listen to them, to the low murmur of their voices. Watch their eyes as they glance to see how much longer they will be waiting. They too wonder whether Jesus has time for them before the sun sets.

Watch Jesus as he leans forward to hear the whispered requests, sensitively receiving each person. Note how the individuals react to what Jesus says, what he does, how he touches them and speaks to them. Listen to him ask, "What do you want me to do?" Watch as they hesitantly make their request. See Jesus hold their hands. Listen to hear his prayer. Then watch their eyes brighten as God's grace overwhelms them.

SUGGESTION FOR PRAYER: In your imagination, stand beside the friend you have brought to Jesus. Listen as Jesus asks, "What can I do for you?" Listen. Pray in the faith that Jesus' touch and voice will heal.

Healing for God's Purposes

February 10–16, 2003 • Larry Ousley[‡]

MONDAY, FEBRUARY 10 • Read 2 Kings 5:1-14

The number 911 signals a call for help. In 2001 the crisis call that occurred on the ninth month and the eleventh day changed the shape of the world for all time, transforming the lives and economies of the entire globe.

One of the many losses in the aftermath of 9/11 is the world's willingness to slip back toward greater fear and hatred of persons and things that seem foreign. Yet one of the main tenets of our Hebrew heritage is providing assistance to the alien in our midst.

Naaman's time, like our own, involved wars and rumors of wars. Israel felt oppressed by its more powerful neighbors. And at such a time Naaman, an Arabic military figure, comes to ask for help. As commander of the army of Aram (modern Syria), he represents perhaps the most feared enemy of the Hebrew people. Recently he and his army have conquered the nation of Israel.

Naaman's household maid is a young "foreign" girl captured in a raid on the Hebrews. Her role in pointing toward a spiritual solution to Naaman's skin disease makes her the hero of the first part of the story. Naaman follows her advice to visit the prophet Elisha in Samaria. Elisha sends Naaman to wash in the Jordan, and his flesh is restored. He returns to Elisha's abode and declares his faith in God: "Now I know that there is no God in all the earth except in Israel." What a different story would be recorded had Naaman viewed the maiden as subversive or had he himself been seen as an enemy and therefore been denied help.

SUGGESTION FOR MEDITATION: How do we view those who are not like us? Pray for peace in the Middle East, as well as in our own country.

[‡]United Methodist clergy; spiritual/life coach; director of the Intentional Growth Center, Lake Junaluska, North Carolina.

The Bible contains so much subtle humor. In the Naaman story, we witness the humiliation of the most powerful foreign military figure in the world of the Hebrews. Oh, how the oppressed Hebrews must have laughed as they told and retold this wonderful account of the proud being humbled and coming to faith.

Of course, faith is the point of this passage. Wealth, power, and status cannot protect the mighty Naaman from a debilitating skin disease. He is diminished with every turn of the story line: his foreign slave girl utters his prescription; the prophet Elisha won't even come out to greet him, much less administer a sophisticated healing ritual. A servant helps him see the merits of the simple procedure, and Naaman has to wash in foreign waters instead of the beautiful, familiar home streams of his native land. Nevertheless, his vulnerability and desire for a cure finally make him open to faith in God.

This story reminds us that our salvation does not reside in material goods, military might, or status; our salvation comes from the Lord who has made both the waters of Israel and the rivers of Damascus.

We exhibit the beginnings of wisdom when we can shift into God's perspective without having to be hit up 'side the head with the proverbial two-by-four. G. K. Chesterton wrote, "The reason angels can fly is that they take themselves so lightly." Humility helps open us to divine insight and cooperation with God. Anthony de Mello offers this prescription: "For peace of heart, resign from being the general manager of the universe."

SUGGESTION FOR MEDITATION: Assuming a receptive posture, pray for the humility to be open to God's guidance and for the willingness, courage, and faith to follow God's leading.

In the dark of winter, in an age of malaise, we are called by Psalm 30 to find meaning in a life of joyful praise of God. A new perspective enables us to move from "mourning to dancing," from fear to praise.

A cursory reading of the psalm might discern a message of prayer and praise, followed by God's making everything right. A deeper look enables the understanding that our hope rests not in God's taking away threat and suffering but in God's being with us, giving us confidence—"I shall never be moved."

How do we get to that place of strength? How do we find our empowering sense of direction in life? More and more I believe we discover that place of strength by responding to the Creator's call to fulfill the purposes in our creation. Knowing and living out our purposes have a powerful, transforming effect upon our lives. One way to express this concept is in hearing and singing a song that is peculiarly our own. Our song is born of a unique calling and embodies a distinctive shape of that calling for us. We are born to express our song as part of God's universal chorus.

Praise is indeed the mode of being at one with God's purposes for us. When we "sing praises," we "vibrate" in response to and in harmony with God's movement toward love, compassion, justice, and opportunity for all people. When our whole being resonates with God's purposes, then all our life is praise.

SUGGESTION FOR MEDITATION: Spend some time reflecting and journaling about your understanding of God's purposes for your life. What action steps will you take to fulfill this calling? Then spend some time in praise of God. Singing is good and appropriate!

I love the name of our organization—the Intentional Growth Center. Our founder, Dr. Mark Rouch, chose the name wisely and well. Our purpose is to assist persons in their personal and professional growth. The part I like best is the word *intentional*. Undirected growth, like cancer, grows without purpose or benefit. God's growth direction for us is intentional!

One problem with the word *intentional* in our name is that one slip of the finger leads to mail addressed to the Untentional Growth Center. As yet, we haven't received anything addressed to the Unintentional Growth Center. However, John Miller, one of our feisty, retired pastors at Lake Junaluska, hit me where it hurts. Standing next to my predecessor, Dr. Jim Warren, and me, John pointed to our rotund midsections and said, "Now here is an example of unintentional growth!"

Paul urges us as followers of Christ to disciplined living. We avoid "aimless" running around by living purposefully. Our purpose is not to look good or to win a prize but to harness our total life energy toward serving God. I am working on intentional balance in my own life with a coach who has helped me see the spiritual and servant perspective of healthy living, including stewardship of my body. What a difference it makes to envision the purpose toward which one is moving—servanthood —and then maintain intentionality.

SUGGESTION FOR MEDITATION: **What direction of growth is God calling you to in your life? How will you be intentional in moving toward God's call? Write down your plans. Share them with a partner on the journey and decide on a way of being accountable for your intentional growth.**

In this passage, Paul prods us with the metaphor of running a race. Not only do we have a finish line toward which we move intentionally, but we have disciplines that transform and enable us to run the race effectively. Staying with these disciplines of training and living is the challenge.

When we think of athletes in training, we naturally think of coaches who assist them. One of the exciting new opportunities for me in the last few years has come in assisting persons in their growth through spiritual/life coaching. This new way of working with persons parallels mentoring, pastoral counseling, consulting, and spiritual direction. Yet there are distinctive differences among them. Coaching is an ongoing partnership that helps persons clarify their vision and values for their life and move into action toward specific goals.

One of the main benefits of spiritual/life coaching comes in developing a plan and a practice of accountability. A coach can help persons stay focused and responsible to their plan for living out the call of God for their lives.

Think about Jesus as a spiritual coach. He certainly guided the disciples over time in a "run" of growth in values and behaviors moving toward the realm of God. Jesus regularly asked powerful questions that caused persons to assess their commitments and actions. As Paul reminds us, seeing a coach implement this approach in his or her own life becomes a source of integrity and trust "so that after proclaiming to others I myself should not be disqualified."

As persons stay with Christian disciplines over time, they experience increasing fulfillment of God's purposes in their lives. It is beautiful to behold their expanding wholeness and deepening faithfulness as energized servants of God.

SUGGESTION FOR PRAYER: Pray to discover and follow practices that enable you to run God's race in all areas of your life.

We who follow Jesus attempt to grow intentionally in the pattern of life he depicted and calls us to live. This passage in Mark illustrates Jesus' responsive nature to a request of one who suffers. Jesus takes immediate action in answer to the man with leprosy, despite Jesus' desire to remain out of full-blown public attention until the time is right.

What a contrast there is between Jesus' response to need and Elisha's in the Second Kings passage of the week. Although Elisha did allow Naaman to have new experiences by not catering to his every desire or by working on his timetable, Elisha did not respond quickly. Nor did Elisha respond in the way Naaman desired, a marked contrast to Jesus' reaction to the leper's request.

One of the marks of the Christian is compassion ("pity" in this passage). However, Christian concern moves beyond realization of need to actual response. We express our compassion in concrete human acts of love and care. Our means of healing normally will not result in immediate and direct cures, but our acts of caring can be a healing balm to those in need.

In a culture of achievement and reward for accomplishment, acts of giving often take last place in popular thinking. Yet Jesus continually celebrates the behind-the-scenes actions of compassion by ordinary people. What can those of us who have one talent do for God's realm? We can use our gift to care for those who suffer.

SUGGESTION FOR MEDITATION: Ask for sensitivity to the persons and the needs to which God wants you to respond. Commit yourself to being God's agent of healing through acts of caring.

What is our level of faithfulness in following the way of Jesus? The leper in our passage received a tremendous gift. So have we! The leper received some clear instructions on how to use the gift. So have we! The leper violated clear directions and requests from Jesus. So have we!

What are we to do? Certainly the gospel tells us of forgiveness for the repentant. We have the opportunity to turn again to faithfulness. However, our journey seems to involve turning and turning to the point that we are on the verge of being mistaken for whirling dervishes.

Progress in the Christian life involves growing in integrity and faithfulness in all our thoughts and actions. Wesleyan Christians live in a tradition of Christian nurture that sees formation groups as being integral to maturation in the faith. Relational, covenantal accountability with other Christians enhances our patterns of growth.

The genius of early Methodism came through nurture of the faithful in small groups guided by a Class Leader. In recent years, we in The United Methodist Church have witnessed strong attempts to recover the benefits of these early patterns of support through accountable discipleship, covenant discipleship, Disciple Bible Study, *Companions in Christ*, and spiritual/life coaching. Whatever the form of our faithfulness, we need accountable and relational interactions to best foster our growth.

Regardless of the specific means, we as Christians are called to live in disciplined ways that enable us with God's help to align ourselves more fully with God's purposes in the world. We know God's choice for our lives; let us affirm that choice and live in wholeness and faith.

SUGGESTION FOR MEDITATION: **Discover a means of accountable discipleship that fits for you. Make a commitment and plan to use that particular means of grace to stay in alignment with God.**

Perceiving God's Provision

February 17–23, 2003 • *Juanita Campbell Rasmus*[‡]

MONDAY, FEBRUARY 17 • **Read Isaiah 43:18-21**

Seeing God provide

Imagine all that God has provided for you over your lifetime. God in essence says to the people: "What I've provided for you in the past is nothing compared to what I will provide for you. I'm already doing it." Sense the energy in verses 18-19 as God states that God is going to take provision up a few notches as in "you ain't seen nothin' yet!" Then God asks the pivotal question in this passage: Do you not perceive it?

How often has God made a provision in our lives that we did not see? We are often blinded to God's provision by convenience, technology, material possessions, power, and ego. They can obstruct our ability to "perceive it" and ultimately to see God. When have you lost a valued item that you later discovered amidst the ordinary "stuff" of life? It was there all the time, yet not perceived by you. Remember your joy when you shifted something and the valued item came into view: "There it is; I see it now!"

God goes on to proclaim the types of provision the Israelites can anticipate: a way in the wilderness and rivers in the desert. God asks us to perceive God's provision, to seek it out and be able to identify it as the handiwork of a loving God! Verse 21 implies that God expects our praise and enthusiasm as we perceive God's provision at work, revealed in our lives.

PRAYER: God, my provider, I give you thanks and praise. May I clearly see your provision in my life. Amen.

[‡]Copastor of St. John's United Methodist Church-Downtown, Houston, Texas; coparent to Morgan Elena and Ryan Victoria.

Seeing God's patience

The Israelites and God seem forever to be involved in a soap opera of sorts. God speaks of awesome plans and then wonders where God's loved ones are. We too dance with God, promising faithfulness when life brings challenge, but once the pressure's off we don't "perceive" God anymore. We grow weary of God and the relationship.

God lists those practices the people have relinquished when their relationship with God is not a top priority. God waits patiently. But as any loving parent knows, there comes a time to address the broken rules and to list the offenses. God states, "You have burdened me with your sins; you have wearied me with your iniquities."

God, like any parent, realizes that a "clearing of the air" about sin may bring restoration to the relationship. After making the offense perfectly clear, this great parent says, Now that you understand, I will not discuss this issue again. I'll forget this ever happened.

We in our own parenting understand this need to confront problems in a relationship. At times enough is enough when dealing with our children's errant ways. And while *we* may have difficulty forgetting the offense, God declares that our transgressions and sins will not be remembered. Despite all our offenses, misplaced loyalties, and failed commitments, God patiently seeks to restore relationship.

SUGGESTION FOR MEDITATION: Since love is patient and God is love, meditate on being filled with the patience of God. How might being filled with God's loving patience express itself in your life? Three times today stop and visualize yourself as an empty pitcher being filled with God's patience.

PRAYER: Father, allow your patient kind of love to flow through me today. Amen.

Seeing God's trustworthiness

Writing to the church in Corinth, Paul builds a case for God's trustworthiness. The case begins with verse one. Paul's plans to go to Corinth have changed, and he attempts to comfort the Corinthians' disappointment. Paul speaks of God's not being wishy-washy and compares his personal faithfulness and trustworthiness to falling in line with God's plan. Tying his integrity and character first to God's faithfulness and now to Christ's, he says in effect: I stand on what I have said to you, and you can stand on it too! It's not a shaky word but rather a firm foundation established by God, laid by Christ; and now we build on it.

In your own life can you point to such a direct connection between your character and integrity that follows the pattern of God? Are we not made in God's image? Are we not to pattern our lives after God's desires for us and after the life Christ made visible for us?

Paul reminds the Corinthians that everything God has promised is a "go," a "yes," and in him "Amen" (so be it). Paul then extends this "shield" of protection both to the Corinthians and to us. God has established us, putting God's seal on us. We have received the Spirit as the down payment to the full promise. God's stamp of approval connects us all. We can trust God!

So often we say we trust God, but do we really? Do we trust God when the plan changes? Do we trust God with our lives? Do we trust God with the lives of those who impact our own: spouse, children, boss, enemy? God is trustworthy even in the midst of change!

PRAYER: Father, I know you live in me. Teach me trustworthiness so that my yes will be yes and my no will be no. Bind my mind to the mind of Christ in all that I think and do and say. Amen.

Seeing God gather

There is something absolutely incredible about the presence of God that draws people. Jesus has once again come to Capernaum, and the word is out that he is in town. Jesus allows the God-power within him to gather all kinds of people to hear the preached word in a life-giving way. Jesus' energy evidenced in his life and words makes people drop what they are doing to go and hear the word of life—a word not confined to parchment and quill. Jesus paints word pictures while speaking with love, peace, and clarity.

Have you ever seen a three-dimensional children's book in which the pages pop up for added depth? Jesus' words "pop" and the dead words of the religious come alive. So the people of Capernaum gather together because Jesus is in the house.

Four men allow the power of God to move them not just to gather in assembly with the others but to be gatherers also. Gathering is one aspect of the work of the Holy Spirit in the life of the believer. It is not enough that we should gather with Jesus, but we become driven to gather others as well. So the four men come, bringing a paralytic to him. The paralytic's impairment has created a state of helplessness; he is unable to act and to gather with Jesus without the help of others.

Jesus told Peter, "Follow me and I will make you fish for people" (Mark 1:17). It is not enough that we routinely gather with Jesus and receive from him words of hope and encouragement. We must be willing to bring others needier than ourselves to him as well. God draws us, yes, gathers us. We, in turn, gather others whose paralysis of mind, body, or spirit needs Jesus' healing touch.

SUGGESTION FOR PRAYER: **Reread slowly verses 1-3; then pause and ask this question: "Lord what do you want me to learn from this passage today?"**

Seeing God's compassion

The psalms are rich with human emotion and experience. Psalm 41, called the psalm of the compassionate, acknowledges personal crisis and reminds us of God's compassion toward us. It also reminds us to *be* compassionate.

Just what does it take to be compassionate? One definition of compassion is "suffering with another." How willing are you to walk alongside someone who is suffering? You need not resolve the conflict or even ease physical, mental, or emotional pain. You listen intently and perhaps laugh with him or her at the weird humor that can emerge from suffering. Perhaps you cry with the sufferer, exchanging no words at all.

Ironically this psalm starts with a blessing for the compassionate and then speaks the blessings. But midway the psalmist speaks of the lack of compassion he is experiencing: apparently his best friend has failed to be compassionate toward him. Could it be that the psalmist realizes that he has not lived compassionately himself?

Perhaps after this realization, the psalmist pleads with God to give him a second chance: "Be gracious to me, and raise me up, that I may repay them" (in a way that will reflect compassion, we would hope). Then he says words to this effect: If you do this for me, Lord, I'll know I have become a person of integrity, and you will set me in your presence.

Compassion is not an insurance policy against bad times, grief, disappointment, or loss. Compassion is a way of life in the midst of our day-to-day experiences that can offer an umbrella during the storms of life.

SUGGESTION FOR MEDITATION: **What would motivate people to visit me and pray for me during a crisis?**

PRAYER: **Father, allow me to see how I treat others. Remove any defects of character, and let love lead the way. Amen.**

Seeing God's compassion

The psalmist says promise number one is that God will deliver persons in time of trouble. The heading for this psalm attributes its writing to David. David certainly knew about God the troubleshooter—God, who showed up to support him against a lion, a bear, a giant, and an outrageously jealous King Saul. David also knew that God would sustain people. Some things in life we just wade through, trusting God's word that though we pass through the waters we will not drown. So the sustaining grace of God, the divine ability to keep us in the midst of a stormy period, is a promise.

Sometimes you and I need God's sustenance during a trying time, but more intense are the times when the power and presence of God are *all* that sustain our lives. "The LORD...keeps them alive." And we will experience happiness. In Jeremiah 29:11, God speaks of plans for us: "For surely I know the plans I have for you, says the LORD, plans for your welfare and not for harm, to give you a future with hope." God's ability to protect us, to keep us alive, and to bless us all exemplify God's compassion toward us. God willingly suffers with us.

David reminds us that God will sustain us on our sickbed. What greater vulnerability do we face than our alert awareness of the body's weakness and frailty? The mind, body, and spirit connection causes a synergy that can keep us in bed or see us restored to health. Our compassionate God wills wholeness and health in mind, body, and spirit. In our times of trial and distress, may we hold fast to God's promise of deliverance, buoyed up by the compassion of God.

SUGGESTION FOR MEDITATION: **Reflect on how God has shown compassion in the three most challenging or pivotal areas of your life.**

PRAYER: **Father, help me to see your compassion toward me. Teach me to respond to others with compassion. Amen.**

Seeing as God sees

We saw how God's loving presence and the power of Jesus' word gathered people in Capernaum and filled a house. Four men, driven by the presence of Jesus, bring a paralyzed friend to him. Unwilling to allow the large gathering to hinder their companion from being brought to Jesus, these four men begin to see a new possibility. Before long they have made their way to the roof and begin to tear it off! What on earth? What's going on here? What kind of people would do such a thing? Certainly these questions must have come to the minds of those gathered around Jesus—or perhaps at least to the mind of the homeowner. But the scripture only records, "When Jesus saw their faith, he said to the paralytic, 'Son, your sins are forgiven.'"

Jesus surely saw the pieces of roof tumbling down around him. No doubt he saw the four men struggling, maneuvering, and eventually lowering a mat with a man on it to the floor at his feet. But while viewing all this activity, he looked beyond the distractions and the destroyed roof and "saw their faith." Seeing more than just the faith of four men and their friend, Jesus also sees straight through to the hearts of scribes who are present, and he asks them why they raise such questions in their hearts. Why do they not see what Jesus sees in this situation? Jesus sees the scribes' unbelief and decides that some people only believe what they see. So Jesus tells the paralytic, "I say to you, stand up, take your mat and go to your home."

God sees faith—mustard-seed sized faith, roof-wrecking faith! Will you choose to see as God sees?

SUGGESTION FOR MEDITATION: What role do you play in this passage? Why?

PRAYER: Father, help me to see what you see in every area of my life. Amen.

Rooted in Love

February 24–March 2, 2003 • *Kristen Johnson Ingram*[‡]

MONDAY, FEBRUARY 24 • Read 2 Kings 2:1

Although Gilgal is the name of the town that Elijah and Elisha have just left, the word also means a tumbleweed. The Hebrew word *gilgal* literally means "rolling." If you've visited the American Southwest, you're familiar with the round bushes that are green for a few days, then quickly turn dry and thorny: As soon as a good desert wind comes along, they detach from the soil and blow over the ground and often onto highways, creating driving hazards. In this country we call them tumbleweeds. Like thistles, tumbleweeds roll in the wind; they have no say in where they go or against what fence or hill they end up. They're passive and make no decisions.

When Elijah heads out of Gilgal and toward Bethel, he is no tumbleweed. Without hesitation, he sets his face toward the place where his life will end. He heads into death the way I might charge into a store for a big sale. Because he's lived a pure, holy life devoted to God, he has no fear of the next world. But most of us resist death to the end.

Entering into the movement of death doesn't mean denying God or grace or resurrection; it means looking death in the eye and saying, "I'm coming." Elijah knows he is going not toward an end but toward a beginning. He displays his willingness to go anywhere God calls him, even the end of his mortal life.

God doesn't want a world full of tumbleweeds but men and women firmly rooted in God's will. A tumbleweed mentality makes us helpless, but commitment to God's will is voluntary and requires no strong winds to move us.

PRAYER: Root me in your love, O God; help me firm my faith in you, and give me the strength to face the future without fear. Amen.

[‡]Spiritual director, licensed lay preacher, writing teacher, book doctor, and grandmother living and working in Springfield, Oregon.

When I was a child I collected some monarch caterpillars and raised them in a dry aquarium. Every day I fed them damp leaves, but one day they quit eating and their orange stripes turned brownish. They hung off the twigs I'd furnished and began to look dry, dark green and brown like dead leaves. My father told me this was the chrysalis stage, so we set the aquarium outside, with the top open. One morning about a week later I rose from bed, leaned out of my bedroom window and saw bright monarch butterflies rising out of their glass home. They exercised their new wings for a while, and soon they hovered over the flower beds and our blossoming Arizona palo verde trees, then soared into the morning sky. We believe such miracles occur in nature, but we rarely stop long enough to witness the process.

Elisha, the prophet-in-training of Israel, also believed: He knew his mentor, the prophet Elijah, would be transformed that day at the Jordan, but he'd not expected to see the process. So when he asks to inherit a "double share" of the prophet's spirit, he is probably shocked to hear Elijah say, "If you see me as I am being taken from you, it will be granted you." Elisha doesn't know he'll soon see blazing horses and a chariot of fire or watch a desert whirlwind lift the old man and take him away.

The thumbprint of transformation is all around us: caterpillars become butterflies; eggs crack open to reveal fluffy chicks; redwood seedlings turn into the world's tallest trees; and tiny babies grow up to be adult men and women. Everywhere on earth we see evidence that God's promises of new life are true. So keep your eyes raised, and who knows? Keep your eyes raised; one day you just might see chariots and fiery horses swooping down from heaven.

PRAYER: Dear God, help me not only to love and care for your creation but to see in it your promise of transformation. Amen.

I heard sirens wailing into the summer afternoon and knew a tornado had set down nearby. The siren was insistent and so was the fierce wind battering the store windows. I locked up the shop where I worked and headed for the shelter in the mall basement. The sun was gone, maybe forever. Clouds had turned the world a dark green, summoning wind that threatened every house and wheat field.

About a hundred of us huddled among parked cars on the lowest basement level, where we could barely see one another's faces in the dim light. Suddenly we heard a crashing sound and found ourselves in total darkness. We sat in suffocating heat, disoriented and frightened, not knowing what we'd find when we returned to the surface. Occasionally someone spoke, but most of us were silent. Finally we heard the three siren toots that signaled the storm's passing. Someone outside opened the heavy door that led to the street. The splinter of light that burst into the room made us gasp: Outside, the sun had already returned, and the world was still there.

We crept outside to find broken tree branches and broken glass. The fallen elm had cut off our electrical power; the wind had blown newspapers and other debris into the streets, but most of the city was relatively unhurt. That first shaft of sun that broke into our basement darkness was a messenger of good news, and the washed sidewalks gleaming in the light were more beautiful than we had ever seen them.

Even oppressive, sorrowful darkness is never without the promise of light. Whether you're mourning or depressed or ill or in desperate financial circumstances, light is waiting and God shines forth.

PRAYER: We give you thanks, Lord, for the shining light of your love and for the safety we find in it. Amen.

When we first read the words, "faithful ones, who made a covenant with me by sacrifice," we might assume that humans made the sacrifice. Thousands of bulls and goats and lambs were offered on the altars of Israel, but did that make the people faithful? It seems that every few sentences in the Old Testament we find the Israelites doing what was wrong in the sight of the Lord.

A covenant is God's invention; more than agreement or a contract, a covenant is a promise not to be broken. When Noah and his family stepped off the ark, God made the rainbow the sign of a covenant. Later God told Abraham, "As for me, this is my covenant with you: You shall be the ancestor of a multitude of nations" (Gen. 17:4). Indeed, the children of Abraham's sons, Isaac and Ishmael, became the people of the Middle East: Arabs, Israelis, Palestinians, and Yemenites are just some of Abraham's descendants. The Ten Commandments were part of the great covenant God made with the Hebrew people. An animal sacrifice accompanied each of those covenants. And though the people deserted their side of the contract over and over, God was faithful and continued to restore the nation.

"This is the covenant that I will make with the house of Israel," God told Jeremiah. "I will put my law within them, and I will write it on their hearts; and I will be their God, and they shall be my people" (Jer. 31:33). God affirmed the covenant when Jesus passed the cup of blessing at a Passover dinner, saying, "This is the new covenant in my blood." The people "who made a covenant with me by sacrifice" never kept the covenant; God kept it. And ultimately God made the sacrifice in the person of Jesus Christ.

PRAYER: Lord Jesus, you established the new covenant for all of us, and you have been faithful. Help us to be worthy of your love for us. Amen.

Women living under Taliban rule were forced to wear the head-to-toe burqa with its grid that allowed little air and even less vision. The very conservative Taliban rule turned highly educated, active Afghan women into cowering creatures who could expect violence. If they laughed or sang, they were beaten; if caught walking with a male relative other than their husband, they were flogged in Kabul's empty soccer stadium. Women were invisible and disposable.

On the day Kabul was freed, a television camera caught the picture of a man and woman in the street watching the Northern Alliance march into town. Suddenly the woman pulled back her burqa enough to show her face and grinned at her husband. He grinned back, gazing into her face as if he had never seen her before. Music, until that day forbidden, rose from the nearby houses, and the husband and wife joined hands in public, perhaps for the first time ever.

As with the Taliban's harsh rule, the face of God has been hidden from humanity, often covered with the veils of power and control. But on a remarkable night in Bethlehem, a child was born. When he grew up, his words revealed God's nature and character; and as he was led to the cross, he became the image of the God who is willing to die for God's people. Jesus is God's picture; someday we will throw off the veil and see God face to face while the music swells throughout heaven.

PRAYER: We ask only one thing of life beyond this one, O God: that we may come into your presence and behold you. Amen.

I took Maria, my friend's five-year-old daughter, to the ballet to see her mother dance for the first time. We sat in box seats. Maria pictured Mommy at the practice barre in their house. She'd even visited rehearsals a time or two, but she was hardly prepared to see her mother dance the lead in "Swan Lake." When her mother came onstage in a cloud of white tulle, dancing on the toes of her silken shoes while the blue spotlight played over her, little Maria gasped with shock. She stood up, holding to the edge of the balcony, and finally breathed, "Will she still be my mother?"

The people around us chuckled; a few in the orchestra seats below looked up, smiling. But Maria wasn't laughing; she was awed and close to terror at the sight of her transformed mother. She had to learn to accept that Mommy was more than the gentle, warm lady who fed her, read stories, and sat beside her on airplane trips. Her mother had metamorphosed into a woman of strange powers and transforming presence.

When Jesus—the humble man who shared the disciples' bread and water, the gentle teacher who patiently guided them, their traveling companion on the dusty roads—is transfigured, he suddenly turns into someone else. Even his clothes change, looking whiter than any bleach can make them. To further terrify Peter, James, and John, Jesus is talking to Moses and Elijah, the greatest men of ancient Israel. The disciples must wonder, *Will he still be our Master?*

Who changed? In Maria's case it was her mother who had donned a tutu and exotic makeup. But perhaps on the mountain, the three disciples are the ones transfigured, so they can see Jesus glorified, see him without his humanity—the way God saw him. And since we're all immortal beings, perhaps we can try to see one another in that same transfigured way.

PRAYER: Extend our understanding, Lord, and give us grace so that we may know you better. Amen.

Peter's proposal to erect three dwellings on the Mount of Transfiguration serves as his desperate attempt to get back the Jesus he's known. The season is probably Succoth, when Jews build outdoor shelters of boughs and rushes and dwell in them for a week to remember their time of sojourning in the wilderness. Now Peter, having glimpsed the glorified Christ, wants to democratize the young rabbi. If he can only build Jesus a house of branches, perhaps they can be ordinary men together again. He wants Jesus to stay with him, to be human, a man who will keep the law as best he can, fishing all day and spending the evenings talking with him and the other men. Deep down, though, Peter must know it is too late: The die has been cast; and sure enough, on the way downhill Jesus speaks the mystery of resurrection.

We still want to keep Jesus human. In fact, we sometimes like him best as a helpless baby in the manger rather than as God. Jesus the baby or the boy in the Temple or the traveling preacher threatens us less than the resurrected Christ. The splendor of his light blinds and frightens us. But if we take our hands from our eyes and look at him glorified, we see the Savior whose love is poured out on all humanity.

Up there on the mountain, Peter gets a glimpse of who his master really is. Reluctant to look, he tries to deny the reality of Jesus—just as he will deny him later on the night Jesus is betrayed. But after the Resurrection, it is Peter who recognizes his risen Lord and sloshes ashore, willing to see the God-man who died for him and stood before him transformed into an eternal being.

We may love Jesus, the Son of Man, and we should; but our salvation depends on the Christ whom God glorifies forever.

PRAYER: O God, who made the miraculous human mind, grant us the ability to comprehend your divinity as we have understood your humanity. Amen.

Gracious Water, Gracious God

March 3–9, 2003 • *Terrell M. McDaniel*[‡]

MONDAY, MARCH 3 • **Read Genesis 9:8-17**

God seems to love using water as a symbol in covenants with earth creatures. Water, one of the strongest elements known, cannot be destroyed by normal means. It can only change form—from liquid to solid to gas. Yet it can, on occasion, cause great destruction: by flood, as it did in Noah's day, or one drop at a time until a canyon is formed.

On the other hand, water seems to be quite gentle and obedient to God's will. It meanders downhill finding its own way, respecting obstacles in its path until it finds a way around or through them. Water portrays the perfect balance of power and passive acceptance—the ingredients of serenity. Perhaps that is why we often feel so comforted in its presence.

Don't forget that water is also the mystical, essential "stuff" of life itself. It heals, cleans, and nourishes. It covers most of the earth and is the main component of our own bodies! Water protects us in the womb and replenishes us as we live each day.

It is no accident that God chooses water and light—two elements of life-giving power—as the central symbols for the new covenant with us: the light of the world, reflected through something common—earthly but powerful—to reveal the possibilities of a world reconciled with God.

SUGGESTION FOR MEDITATION: If you don't see a rainbow today, sip a tall glass of water. Enjoy the blessing of having your thirst quenched and your body refreshed. Express your praise and gratitude for the blessings of the earth, those of the spirit, and the life-giving, mystical connection between the two.

[‡]Clinical and corporate psychologist; attends Belmont United Methodist Church, Nashville and New Community Church, Hendersonville, Tennessee.

God reveals to us the divine desire for reconciliation with God's children. And although we often read this passage as symbolic of God's covenant with us humans, we are reminded that it is a covenant made with all the earth. Every time God mentions humanity, all the other living creatures and the earth itself also are mentioned. This is no small matter: If you read the passage aloud, you cannot help but notice this emphasis on inclusion in God's promise. We are a part of something bigger, and we must view ourselves in the context of a living world in which God is in loving control.

This point has not been lost on the sparrow (Matt. 10:29), a happy creature whose bird-sized brain rests assured that God is looking out for him or her. But we humans, with our impressive neo-cortex, are a more complicated matter. We have the potential to be God's helpers in extending grace and righteousness to the world, but we become alienated. We seem to have more difficulty than the rest of nature in accepting God's grace to us and thus feeling the joy of true reconciliation—reconciliation not just with God but with nature, one another, and the rest of God's family.

Jesus taught us that we must be like the sparrow. If so, perhaps we could find happiness. Today's passage reminds us of a God who desires to be in relationship and to celebrate an everlasting covenant where no one—and no thing on earth—is left out. To live in such communion is our heart's desire. So why can't we let go and let our heads believe?

PRAYER: God, I suffer when I am disconnected from you and the rest of our family. Thank you for your love for me and for your commitment to help me be whole through reconciliation. Amen.

ASH WEDNESDAY

On this special day we celebrate our connection to the earth; but we also experience, in concrete terms, the humility of our earthly limitations.

While most of nature rests securely in God's loving arms, humans seem restless. Realizing our potential, we long to do more than live out our lives on earth. We yearn to actualize our spirits, to realize the promise of our ability to think and feel, and to find immortality. Ironically, we end up feeling alienated, acting primarily in disobedience to God's way.

To say, "I come from ashes, and to ashes I will return" in the Ash Wednesday ceremony is not to degrade the earth, for the earth is God's blessing to us. The earth is our partner in God's creation and covenant. Instead of indicting us, being "grounded" by our earthly nature is a good place to start our journey toward reconciliation with God. Being made of ashes, we must reach outside of our physical world for the power to be more.

Today's passage reveals that, once reconciled, we can become "the righteousness of God" on earth, no less! Imagine! To become a living instrument of God's grace! However, as Jesus demonstrated to us, this kind of greatness is born only of humility. We begin our journey from the lowly place of dirt, ashes, and water.

SUGGESTION FOR MEDITATION: **Tonight accept and appreciate the sense of water's gentle touch as you wash off the cross of ashes. Pledge to respond in good conscience in the coming days to God's movement of reconciliation in your life.**

"Show me your ways, O LORD" (NIV). David is certainly responding in good conscience as he implores God to show him God's ways and to teach him God's paths.

What is the way of the Lord? I'm not sure that anyone can really define it in its entirety. It's big…really big…like God is. It's profound, elegant, simple, and right in front of our noses. We see it in scripture, the structure of DNA, a child's laugh, a sunset, broccoli. (Yes, broccoli!)

For instance, we would do well to follow the example of water (described on Monday) for following the path that God has set out for us. We can learn from water if we are humble enough. Consider the carving of a canyon one drop at a time, signifying both power and passive acceptance.

But living humbly is the problem, isn't it? At least it is for me. I may have some profound moments when I feel close to God, humble, expectant, open, thankful. But a lot of my life is spent being full of myself. I get wrapped up in and react to events. And while I am fretting, I miss the green in the broccoli, the beauty in the sunset, or the moment (ah, that moment!) of hearing my own child's laughter.

Embarrassing as it is to admit, God shows me the way; and I ignore it. And when I try to live by the way, I inevitably blow it. I think that the psalmist knows this about himself too, because he asks for mercy, love, and forgiveness. Thankfully we need not rely on our own perfection but on God's love for us in order to live in God's covenant.

PRAYER: **I was born of earth and water, but on my own I cannot even be as obedient as they. Have mercy on me, and according to your love remember me. My hope is in you, O Lord. Amen.**

"All the ways of the LORD are loving and faithful for those who keep the demands of his covenant" (NIV). Uh-oh. I'm in trouble.

"According to your love, remember me, for you are good, O LORD." Whew. Thank goodness for God's grace.

I believe that grace is a big part of the way, and it seems the psalmist shares my perception. Grace is a goodness, a connectedness, an acceptance drenched in love and inseparable from God. It is powerful and reflected in everything God has made. Most important, grace is so abundant that it flows over us like water, quenching our thirst and making us clean, fresh, and whole.

And, oh boy, do we ever need it. We need it extended to us. We need it to heal us. Ultimately we need to reflect it through us toward everyone and everything else with which we have contact. We just can't quite make grace happen on our own, though. So we become alienated. We struggle. We allow ourselves to be put to shame, as was the psalmist.

Here is where Jesus Christ comes in. He literally embodies grace and extends it gladly. He teaches us to live with, by, and for grace. He reconciles us with God and loves us because of, and in spite of, our humanness. Jesus "went the distance" for us because he knew we needed hope and salvation. He does these things not because he *knows* the way but because he *is* the way.

From ashes I have come and to ashes I will return, but to you, O Lord, I lift up my soul.

SUGGESTION FOR MEDITATION: **Breathe normally in meditation, but as you inhale, humbly pray, "Teach me your ways, O Lord." As you exhale, allow yourself to feel God's grace flow over you.**

For those of us baptized as youths or adults, our excitement about acknowledging God's grace is mixed with some concern about the future. What changes will our newfound profession of faith require of us? Exactly how are we to handle things differently now that we have submitted to God's will (or at least committed to learn how to do so)? How do we learn to rely on grace?

It is reassuring to know that Jesus must have experienced some of the same concern as he looked to his future. In his traditional role as part of the Godhead, dealing with this old world might have been a snap. But in human skin, it is likely that Jesus felt some of the same anxiety—and maybe even some of the resistance—that you or I might feel about facing our futures.

Yet despite any anxiety or resistance Jesus might have felt, he submitted to the Father's plan, communing with our world through baptism with earth's water. As soon as he emerged, Jesus, the human, got to feel the exhilaration of the Father's approval! Not long after, he also got a heavy dose of temptation. Later he began to translate his commitment into action.

Once again water is central to the covenant, a soothing balm for our worries. It serves as an earthy reminder of God's gentle, indestructible, and powerful gift of grace, and of God's promise to be with us as we fulfill the missions of our lives.

Today remember your baptism. How might you rely on grace to get you through today's trials?

PRAYER: O God, how I want you to be pleased with me! But I fear what is in store for me if I truly submit to your will. Please help me to rely on you, your promises, and your grace. Amen.

I just realized what I like about this passage. Although we are in the first week of the Lenten season, this passage gives away the ending.

You and I are the beneficiaries of a most gracious deal. The problem is that on our own we can't live up to our end of the bargain. Miraculously our benefactor paid our debt by sending the Son, who taught us how to live. What's more, the Son defeated death for us so that we may be permanently reconciled with God, living forever in communion. The water of our baptism symbolizes the extraordinary grace that is synonymous with God's way. Praise be to God, the author of this miraculous love!

It has been an honor to have you with me each day of this special week. The presence of your spirit and the awareness of your journey were a blessing to me as I wrote. Whether this is your first Lenten season or your one hundredth, I would like, in the words of Paul (2 Cor. 5:20), to "entreat" you on behalf of Christ, be reconciled to God. God waits patiently and lovingly for your commitment. Drink in the blessings of grace that fall on you like rain each day, and seek to be humble, mindful, and obedient to your Lord. And I look forward to hearing the miraculous stories of how God used you, an humble servant, as an instrument of God's perfect righteousness and outrageous grace.

PRAYER: God, Father, Mother of all the earth, I accept your incredible gift of grace and, most important, the sacrifice of Christ Jesus when he defeated death so that I may have eternal life. I pray that I might understand more each day how to be mindful, thankful, and obedient to your will. Amen.

Encountering God

March 10–16, 2003 • *L. Cecile Adams*[‡]

Monday, March 10 • Read Genesis 17:1-7

Abram stands in the shade of a tree and looks at the land spread before him as far as he can see. Abram thinks about the vision he has seen in which God had given him this land and promised that his descendants would number as many as the stars. Time has passed. Abram is now ninety-nine. Ishmael is his only child—by Hagar, not Sarai. Abram sighs wearily and wonders.

Abram does not see or hear the visitor until a voice says, "I am God Almighty; walk before me, and be blameless. And I will make my covenant between me and you, and will make you exceedingly numerous." Abram falls on his face in respect and praise for the One who has brought him to this land.

Then Abram hears God saying that Abram's name will become Abraham, which means "ancestor of a multitude." Furthermore, God insists that Abraham's descendants will constitute nations, will become kings, and will be God's people forever.

Abraham: the name sounds strange. He has lived with the other name for so long. Yet he likes the idea of countless descendants and God's covenant extended to them. He still cannot fathom how that will come to be.

Suggestion for reflection: What does God keep repeating that you have difficulty hearing? During this Lenten season, how are you walking before God? How are you moving toward being blameless? What is your sign of the covenant with God? How are you relating to other descendants of Abraham, particularly Jews and Muslims?

Suggestion for prayer: Quietly listen to God's response to the question that is the most difficult for you to answer.

[‡]Personal and corporate coach, writer, and advocate for children; Executive Director of Treutlen House, Savannah, Georgia.

Suddenly Abraham realizes that God is still speaking to him. Has he dozed off or has he just been lost in the euphoric image of his multitudinous descendants? He remembers God's instructions about circumcision as the sign of the covenant. Perhaps his attention has drifted momentarily. Is his name being changed again? No, God is telling him about Sarai's name change. She will be called Sarah and will be blessed by God.

Abraham can hardly believe what he is hearing. Once again, as in the much earlier vision, God promises that a son will be born to him and Sarah. They will share equally in the rise of nations and the numbering of kings among their descendants.

Abraham falls on his face again. This time he responds not in awe-filled, respectful obeisance. This time he responds with laughter: a head-thrown-back, knee-slapping, spontaneous belly laugh. Yet he dares not risk exposing his incredulity to God. So he falls on his face in an effort to hide the intensity of his laughter from God.

Having almost reached the century mark, and with Sarah at age 90, Abraham cannot imagine that he and Sarah will have a son. Yet here God speaks to him, instructing him to name his son Isaac, which means "laughter." Perhaps Abraham wonders what Sarah will say when she hears the news and considers it best to wait a bit before telling her about this visit from God.

SUGGESTION FOR REFLECTION: **What promise of God do you find most laughable? When do you find yourself doubting what God will do? What blessing are you promised about your role in God's future?**

SUGGESTION FOR PRAYER: **Confess God's promise that you find the most difficult to accept. Ask God to provide what you need to live as if that promise is already being fulfilled in your life. Listen for God's response, and close the prayer as you choose.**

How long ago Abraham and Sarah walked this earth. How long they waited for the birth of their promised son. Yet their laughter and incredulity live on in us when we wonder how God's promises will be fulfilled.

In the depths of their hearts, Abraham and Sarah hoped against hope that a miracle would happen to bring about the promised multitudes of God's people. It did not happen through Sarah's giving Hagar to Abraham or at the usual age of birthing and parenting. The miracle happened in God's time and in God's way and because of Abraham's and Sarah's faithfulness.

God asked only that Abraham walk before God and be faithful and trusting, following God's lead. From leaving his home in Haran and journeying to Canaan to waiting for the birth of his son and beyond, Abraham walked in trust before God. That is all God asks of us today as we keep the covenant.

This portion of Romans reminds us that Abraham's faith is what is remembered and valued. Our faith, like Abraham's, moves us beyond legalism and motivates us to participate with God in creating a future. That future is what God intends. We cannot know fully the results of our faithful actions, yet we can hope and trust that what God intends will come to be in spite of our intermittent doubt. Paul reminds us that this is Abraham's legacy of righteousness, one in which we can participate and, by God's grace, pass on to others. Paul also reminds us that what we have, which Abraham did not, is the witness of and our belief in the redeeming work of the Christ. How much more powerful then is not only our legacy but also our witness.

SUGGESTION FOR REFLECTION: How are you moving beyond legalism? What legacy of righteousness are you passing on to others?

SUGGESTION FOR PRAYER: Ask God what faithful witness is needed from you today. Listen for God's response, and close the prayer with gratitude.

Subject: What's Ahead
Date: Late Winter, approximately 33 C.E., God's Time
From: Jesus
To: Simon Peter, James and John (Sons of Zebedee), Andrew, Philip, Bartholomew, Matthew, Thomas, James (son of Alphaeus), Thaddeus, Simon the Cananaean, and Judas Iscariot

Just wanted you to know we have tough times ahead. We are going to be observed very closely. More people will ask questions about what I'm doing. People will call my words blasphemy. The healings and numbers of people following us will make the elders, chief priests, and scribes nervous and jealous. They will want to silence me. I will be killed. The glorious news is that I will rise again after three days. Please remember this: I will rise. Death will not keep me down. Thanks, guys, for keeping quiet about my being the Messiah. Thanks too for trying to understand what I'm doing. I hope that's becoming clearer.

Subject: What?!
Date: Midafternoon, approximately 33 C.E., My Time
From: Peter
To: Jesus

What's going on? I know you're the Messiah. And, no, I haven't told anybody else. How can you talk about difficulties when so many people are following us? Everybody is talking about you and what you are doing. We just fed a crowd of thousands. Word is spreading about your miracles. Next thing you know, mothers will want you to bless their children. This idea about your death is ridiculous. Those people aren't that angry. Who would listen to them anyway? Will you just stop this talk?

SUGGESTION FOR REFLECTION: **What in your agenda gets in the way of God's agenda? What is God saying to you about that?**

SUGGESTION FOR PRAYER: **Breathe and listen for God's direction about your time and your actions today.**

Peter: Guys, I really messed up yesterday. I jumped on Jesus for talking about suffering and death. He let me know quietly and emphatically that I wasn't following him.

James: I guess that was why he called us and the other followers together late yesterday afternoon.

Thomas: I don't like all this talk about taking up my cross and following Jesus. Haven't you seen a man carrying the cross on which he is to be hanged? That is not a welcome sight.

Peter (shuddering): I'm not sure I want to lose my life for him and for the sake of what he's teaching and preaching. And I certainly don't want him to die!

Judas: I just want Jesus to bring in this new kingdom he's heading up and end the waiting.

John: Well..., I think Jesus is asking us—and others—to choose. Our decision is to keep things the way they are; that is, maintain the status quo or to live and love radically like he is doing.

James: Oh, I can decide that. I choose the latter; and I'm willing to do whatever it takes, including the suffering. It can't be any worse than the argument with the Syrophoenician woman or the word traps set by the Pharisees.

Peter: I'm not sure about that. His words about denying myself and taking up my cross make me a little cautious, even though I know he's the Messiah.

John: I don't have a need to gain the whole world and forfeit my life. I just want to live and love as radically as he is doing.

SUGGESTION FOR REFLECTION: **What have you left behind in order to follow Jesus? What cross(es) have you chosen to carry in following Jesus? What suffering have you experienced in following Jesus? When has embarrassment or fear kept you from following Jesus?**

SUGGESTION FOR PRAYER: **Pray for courage in living and loving as radically as Jesus did.**

The Jerusalem Bible subtitles this psalm "The sufferings and hope of the virtuous [person]." The New Revised Standard Version uses the subtitle "Plea for Deliverance from Suffering and Hostility." The psalm begins with the words Jesus spoke from the cross, "My God, my God, why have you forsaken me?" The words that follow recount the horrendous difficulties the writer is enduring, the likes of which we will probably not experience. Beginning with verse 23, though, a distinct difference emerges: The psalmist begins praising God.

Take a few moments to count the number of times the word *praise* or similar words and phrases appear in verses 23-31. All of those words and phrases express adoration and thanks for who God is and what God has done and is doing. This latter part of Psalm 22 is the radical culmination of a litany of difficulties and an ultimate affirmation of hope in the midst of suffering. God's deliverance is evident. The comfort of God is palpable. Unreserved faithfulness is rewarded. Hope lives! Praise is a natural response in life and in death, now and in the future, by one and all regardless of circumstances.

Take some time now to look at each clause in verses 23 through 26. After each one, write your words of praise to God.

SUGGESTION FOR REFLECTION: **Which phrase was the most difficult for you to paraphrase? How does that difficulty relate to your current experience of suffering? What words and actions do you use to praise God in the midst of that suffering? How do you encourage others to praise God? How might a more intentional focus on praising God influence your relationship with God?**

SUGGESTION FOR PRAYER: **Offer the words of your paraphrase as a prayer of praise to God.**

Why do good people suffer? And what do good people do with their suffering? My son-in-law has a phrase that he often uses (with a degree of humor) when experiencing or reflecting on difficulties: "It builds character!" We are apt to think that we have enough character already and do not need more experiences to fine-tune character. One of life's realities is that suffering simply exists. We will experience difficulties, and we decide our response to those.

One of the stories told after the Hutu/Tutsi conflict in Burundi in the early 1990s involved a Christian woman who was a Tutsi. She took some Hutu people who were being hunted by the Tutsis into her house and gave them shelter. The Tutsi combatants, after being informed of the situation, came to her house and killed everyone.

What the good woman did lives on and provides a witness to her faithfulness. She willingly pursued humane action, even though it cost her life. She praised God up to and beyond her death.

What would we do in such a situation? What do we do in situations that are less life-threatening? In what ways do our choices abbreviate our praise of God and dull the witness of our lives? How willing are we to give thanks in all things?

Continue with yesterday's practice of writing your own words of praise after each clause in verses 27-31.

SUGGESTION FOR REFLECTION: **Which phrase was the most difficult for you to write about? What thoughts about community—your congregation, your town, your denomination, interfaith exchanges—did you have as you worked with this section? How are you living so that "future generations will be told about the LORD?" If you were writing a litany based on these verses, which phrase would you choose as the refrain?**

SUGGESTION FOR PRAYER: **Stop every hour today and praise God for whatever you choose.**

The Divine Initiative

March 17–23, 2003 • *W. Paul Jones*[‡]

MONDAY, MARCH 17 • Read Exodus 20:1–3

The theological heart of the Reformation can be stated in three words: *the Divine initiative.* Yet this insight is the one that Protestants keep losing, needing additional reformations. Part of the reason for loss of insight is the church's tendency to emphasize giving and doing, rather than instructing people in how to receive. This is why *grace* is such an indispensable word for Christianity, meaning God's graciousness. God lavishes us with so much, not because we deserve it by what we do or are but because of who God is and promises to be.

How we read the Ten Commandments offers an excellent example of how we misread the good news—as something we are required to do rather than the declaration of what God is doing for us. When I was a boy, my minister always preached "Do this!" or "Do that!" Often I wanted to shout back, "Why?" He may have communicated the "what," but he failed to give me the "because."

The Ten Commandments do not begin with "Thou shalt," which is the beginning of the "whats." We must begin with verse two, which is the "why." "I am the Lord your God, who brought you out of the land of Egypt, out of the house of slavery." Only those of us who have been freed by Christ can understand why the "whats" should even be done. But when we fall in love with God who first loved us, the "thou shalts" are transformed into "thou mayest."

PRAYER: God, I do better with the "what" if you keep reminding me of the "why." Amen.

[‡]Trappist monk, hermit, priest, and writer who combines spirituality and social justice as he alternates between life in the monastery and his hermitage among the poor; living in Pittsburg, Missouri.

Yesterday we acknowledged that the commandments are not a way of earning God's favor and reward. Obedience for the Christian is always a response to the Divine Initiative, a response of loving because God first loved us. But immediately two problems arise.

1. Israel and many of her leaders violated each of the commandments. In fact, even while Moses was on Mount Sinai receiving the commandments, Israel was at the foot of the mountain already disobeying the first two by worshiping a golden calf: "You shall have no other gods before me," and "You shall not make for yourself an idol." So the scriptures are often less concerned with the "what" as with what to do because we don't obey. A rebellious streak in all of us urges us to do things our way. This powerful urge is so strong that Luther insisted that the purpose of the commandments was to convince us of our inabilities. Being a Christian does not center in a moral code. It begins with confession, followed by forgiveness and healing.

2. God breaks most of the commandments, such as six (killing) and eight (stealing). God commands the Israelites to "borrow" silver and gold from the Egyptians on their way to receive the commandment that prohibits stealing (12:36). Likewise God directs the Israelites to invade lands not theirs, killing all the inhabitants, and becomes angry when the destruction is not total.

Some interpreters believe these discrepancies relate to Israel's developing understanding of God. Yet what I discern is that only God is absolute, willing whatever God wants. All else, even the commandments, are guidelines, never absolutes. Jesus Christ discloses the nature of God as essentially that of love. Therefore, the context in which the concrete will of God is known in each unique situation is this: We must act out of love (as means) for love (as end). Using this context, Jesus broke idolatrous laws, those done for their own sake rather than as a vehicle of love.

PRAYER: God, may I hold nothing absolute except you. Amen.

The value of committing scripture to memory lays the foundation for lifelong assurance. This psalm has been my favorite for a long time, ever since I received a gold star at age seven for memorizing it in Vacation Bible School. Religious educators today tend to discourage memorization. Likewise different Bible translations make it difficult even to memorize the same Lord's Prayer and Psalm 23 for corporate worship. Yet I am impressed that illiterate monks of the Middle Ages memorized all 150 psalms in Latin, so they could praise God by chanting them as they worked.

I remember visiting with my parents a man who was dying. In his delirium he quoted scripture from memory. I am told he died saying Psalm 19 as a gift to the God he was going out to meet.

This particular psalm also elicits my concern that much spirituality taught today is most natural for an introvert. For example, Elijah experienced God not in fire or earthquake but primarily as a still small voice. The stress is on contemplation—losing one's self in God.

But equally valid is a spirituality more natural to extroverts—rendering the world as God's temple. "Thy Kingdom come on earth...." Indeed every night "the heavens declare the glory of God" (NIV), so that every sense needs to be attuned to God's "handiwork." While the Divine paints portraits, God also paints with a very large brush—"day after day" and "night after night" (NIV). Here God is known ecstatically through everything that lives and moves and has its being in God.

PRAYER: Lord, may I never take the splendor of your earth for granted, for you give it to me afresh each morning as a gift. Amen.

It is not easy to know what Jesus requires of us. Sometimes he declares invitingly that his yoke is easy and his burden light. But almost as soon as the attractive side of being a Christian settles in, we hear Jesus speaking of the narrow gate and the few who can pass through. After he uses the analogy of the camel and the eye of a needle to present the odds of rich persons entering the kingdom of God, his disciples raise their voices in protest, "Then who can be saved?" Jesus has waited for this response in order to make his point. "With God," he claims, "all things are possible." Our hope never resides in our efforts but in the unimaginably foolish love of God. And foolish it is when seen from the perspective of this world.

The beginnings of Jesus' ministry required after his baptism that he immediately enter the desert, where he was tempted. The basic temptations were the three *P*s—power, prestige, and possessions. He wrestled with these for forty days, until Satan left him, promising to return at the most opportune moment.

Here we reach the depth of the gospel's foolishness. In our society, these three *P*s are not temptations at all. Instead they are the basic promises advertised all around us as the rewards for living society's values. There is no escaping the seriousness of Christianity. Either it is a stumbling block to the people in our society, or the values of modern society are foolishness to the serious Christian. It cannot be both ways.

PRAYER: Lord, I ask not only the courage to resist our society's game of winners and losers, but help me lose my taste for all such games. Amen.

Five years ago a friend gave me a finely finished walnut cross. I appreciated it as a token of our friendship. Yet it remained in my sock drawer in the original box. When packing for a retreat in my hermitage, I took the cross with me, determined to come to terms with it or give it away. Once there I put it on my desk, waiting to see if either of us would initiate a friendship. For two weeks we simply exchanged side glances. Then came the evening that I had given myself to decide.

I went outside. I don't remember making any decisions, even though it appeared that I knew what I was doing. I picked up some bent twigs and an acorn with cap intact. Fifteen minutes later, with the help of glue, my cross had become a crucifix. I knew then that in the morning I would hang it as the center-piece in my chapel.

Somehow I had learned with Saint Paul that the cross of Christ is not a polished surface appealing to those who know the wisdom (and the art) of this world. Rather it is a cross that is rugged, unattractive, unfinished, and so unappealing that it is capable of radiating God's foolishness. The empty cross says too little or too much.

In this world of suffering, terrorism, and bloodshed, that for which we cry out is not the empty cross but the one on which God hangs, sharing suffering and death with us. Jesus is called Emmanuel, God with us. Thus nothing we are called upon to face is outside the experience of Christ, suffering with us. To the dying I give a crucifix to hold—with the words, "Behold your God." We are in it together, always, in every way.

PRAYER: God, I do not know why good people suffer, but this I do know—that no matter what, you are our companion through it all. Amen.

Repressed anger is destructive. Stored up, it tends to erupt inappropriately with a confused focus. Yet the church is not helpful here, often denouncing anger as un-Christian. An early saint said, "A person who is angry, even if he [or she] were to raise the dead, is not acceptable to God." Angry words may not break bones, but they certainly can break hearts.

In amazing contrast to what we have been taught is the frequency of Jesus' anger. His names for his foes are choice: "brood of vipers," "hypocrites," "blind fools." Even remarks to his friends would strain any friendship: "O faithless and perverse generation, how long am I to be with you and bear with you?"

Then is there an appropriate anger for the Christian? Yes, and with Jesus as model, it needs to be directed to a cause not a symptom, focused on the present rather than the past, free of personal advantage and having love as its motive and end.

What about anger directed toward God? The psalmists freely express their displeasure at God's doings and failures. "You have made us like sheep for the slaughter" (Ps. 44:11). Anger is the test of authentic friendship. Prayer means asking. So Jesus pleads three separate times with God to remove the cup. And on the cross he screams at God for abandoning him. Only then does he acquiesce. "Into your hands I commend my spirit" (Luke 23:46).

God's anger toward us is often tough love, holding a mirror of self-disclosure to persons and nations. But it is love, for to accept the judgment is the beginning of redemption. Then we discover that the Jesus with the whip is also the Jesus who carries lost lambs in his bosom.

PRAYER: Christ, cleanse me not of my anger but of its smallness and its misdirection. Amen.

The portrait of Jesus overthrowing the tables of buying and selling in the Temple is one of the most controversial for many Christians. Up to this point Jesus has appeared to be nonviolent, serving as a model for Gandhi. Yet here Jesus commits not only property violence, but he drives sellers from the Temple with a whip. This portrait could make local churches defensive, for they are always selling something. Yet the issues go deeper.

1. Jesus knew that the authorities wanted him killed. To upend their lucrative commercial arrangements was an act guaranteeing his fate.

2. Everything changed for Jesus when John was beheaded. After much prayer Jesus set his face steadfastly toward Jerusalem, intent on dying. On the Mount of Olives he surrendered even though he could easily have escaped over the hill. This willingness to die for what he believed renders Jesus our model and possibly our call. More Christians have been martyred during the last century than in the church's whole history.

3. If something is not fit for the Temple, is not this a criterion for what is fit anywhere?

4. Since Jesus' zeal is for "God's house" as a place of special presence, is the sanctuary more than a gathering place for Christians—perhaps as a place of prayer, day and night, with special symbols of God's presence?

5. Paul uses the temple analogy for the Holy Spirit as the permanent resident in the Christian's soul. What needs to be driven out of your temple?

6. The merchants were no doubt selling in the Temple bright and early that Sabbath morning after Christ's death. To be an advocate of social justice requires a deep life of prayer, for, viewed from the human perspective, it entails unending defeat. It is faith, not success, that is in our hands.

PRAYER: God, dwell in me so that I am willing to die for you— then I shall be free to live for others. Amen.

Lessons Learned in the Wilderness

March 24–30, 2003 • *Cheryl B. Anderson*[‡]

MONDAY, MARCH 24 • Read Numbers 21:4-6

The people of God have left slavery behind and are on their way to the Promised Land! However, they have not yet entered the Promised Land; they remain in the wilderness. Their stay in the wilderness is a time of transition—they no longer have their old lives in Egypt, but they do not have their new lives in Canaan either. During this time in the wilderness, the Israelites learn lessons that will enable them to remain faithful to their new covenantal relationship with Yahweh. These lessons learned in the wilderness are significant because the New Testament readings for this week develop the same lessons. As a result such lessons are instructive for us as Christians as we seek to remain in relationship with God during our own times of transition.

In today's reading the people of God no longer appreciate the miraculous events of their deliverance from Egypt. In fact, they complain that Moses even brought them out of Egypt. While the Promised Land lies ahead of them, they are impatient that the goal has not yet been reached. They complain about the lack of food and water. Though God has provided for them during this time in the wilderness, they describe this food as "miserable." Does any of this sound familiar? How do we react when we set a goal for ourselves but achieving it takes a long time? How do we deal with times of transition in our lives? The Israelites' experience reminds us to remember with gratitude God's acts on our behalf and to appreciate the blessings that we have received while still on our own journey.

PRAYER: Most gracious God, may I never take for granted the miracles that you have performed in my life. Today help me to appreciate all that I have in my life right now. Amen.

[‡]Assistant professor of Old Testament Interpretation, Garrett-Evangelical Theological Seminary, Evanston, Illinois; ordained elder in The United Methodist Church.

For their insolence and ingratitude the Israelites are punished. Poisonous snakes show up in their midst, and those who are bitten die. The people, admitting that they have sinned, ask Moses to intercede on their behalf. As a result God tells Moses to set up a bronze serpent, and those who have been bitten will live if they look at it.

The people do not get exactly what they desire. They want God to take away the snakes, but the snakes are left among them, serving as reminders that all our actions have consequences. God does not take away the consequences of our actions. In God's mercy, though, a means of reducing the negative consequences of our actions exists. God provides a means of healing that restores us to wholeness.

During times of transition in our own lives, we can become impatient, disagreeable, and ungrateful. We can even try to return to the old familiar ways rather than risk an unknown future. Although such attitudes and actions will have consequences, the journey does not have to end just because we have faltered. God provides a way of restoring us so that the journey may continue.

We are accustomed to hearing the words "limited time offer." We expect that anything offered will only be offered for a limited time. Notice that no time limit is placed on the efficacy of the bronze serpent. Presumably it is available as long as the people need it. God's healing methods are always available.

PRAYER: Eternal God, help me to understand that my mistakes cannot stop me from completing the journey you have set before me. Enable me to see the means of healing that you have set in my midst. Amen.

The setting for this psalm is not the wilderness. It is a worship service of the people of God. However, this psalm of thanksgiving liturgically enacts the lessons learned in the wilderness, among them God's healing of the sick and dying. God is good and has a steadfast love that endures forever!

In the wilderness the Israelites learned that God offers help in times of need. This psalm mentions four different contexts to demonstrate the variety of ways in which God works—a caravan lost in the desert is rescued; prisoners are set free; those who are sick are healed; and sailors who were caught in a storm are brought back home safely. These four situations fall into a pattern. Those who need help are desperate; they cry out to God; and God comes to their aid. One of the wilderness lessons is that God can help, but today's psalm emphasizes that we have to ask for that help. Asking for help can be the most difficult step to take, but it is the most necessary one. How quickly we seem to forget that fact!

After God has acted on our behalf, today's reading reminds us that there are two more requirements of us. First, we must thank God for the steadfast love and wonderful works we have experienced. Second, we must tell others what God has done for us. It is simply a matter of giving credit where credit is due.

PRAYER: Creator God, in the midst of my own wilderness experience, may I have the strength to reach out to you. Keep me ever mindful of your steadfast love and your ability to rescue, deliver, set free, and heal. May pride never keep me from the sense of wholeness only you can give. Amen.

THURSDAY, MARCH 27 • Read Ephesians 2:1-3

With today's reading we move from the Old Testament wilderness setting to that of a New Testament epistle. Yet the description of human nature remains the same. In the wilderness the people were impatient and complained, just as we tend to act even now when we are in a time of transition! In Numbers 21:4-9, the people learned that such an attitude results in death. Although the death described in the Numbers passage is a physical one, this passage from Ephesians suggests a spiritual death that results from similar negative behaviors and attitudes.

We read that such spiritual death results from following the wrong powers of this world and from living according to our own needs, wants, and desires. Similarly the Israelites in the wilderness wanted their own timetable followed and their own desires met. The wilderness experience reinforces the belief that our actions have consequences. God cannot protect us from the judgment and punishment warranted by our attitudes and behaviors.

The lesson from the wilderness is repeated in today's scripture when those who are spiritually dead are referred to as "children of wrath." We are children of God who should experience God's wrath because of our disobedience, but we will not experience its harshness because of God's mercy and love. When we struggle with our failings, we need not worry that we are alone.

Straying from the paths that God has set before us may occur during the unsettled times in our lives. Yet knowing of God's love will enable us to forgive ourselves and resume our journey.

PRAYER: Gentle and loving Spirit, sometimes we can be so hard on ourselves because of what we do, think, or feel. Help us to acknowledge our failings and to accept your gracious help so that you can nudge us forward. Amen.

Our negative tendencies result in our being spiritually dead, but this is not the end of the story. While we find ourselves trapped in old destructive ways, God moves toward us and makes us alive with Christ. Our movement from death to life occurs solely because of God's grace. We cannot initiate God's saving acts. We can only avail ourselves of the divine help that is in our midst.

In earlier readings this week, we learned that God loves us and offers wholeness when we are in distress. In today's reading the extent of God's love is made clearer. God is "rich in mercy" and loves us even when we are still spiritually dead. Divine love, then, does not exist just when we are on our best behavior or looking our best. It exists even when we are at our worst!

Because of God's love, we who were the living dead are made alive with Christ and are seated with him "in the heavenly places" so that we might experience the "immeasurable riches of his grace." Having been made alive in Christ, we find that new possibilities open up for us. We can move not just from death to life—but to abundant life (John 10:10). Plus, in Christ we can do the good works that God would have us do without letting negative influences hinder us.

At those times in our lives when we feel insignificant, insecure, and unlovable, we must remember that God is at work. How reassuring it is to know God's profound love for each of us and the power of that love to enliven us and give us a new life.

PRAYER: Eternal God, a love that is unconditional and eternal is a difficult concept for us to understand. Be patient with us as we mature in the faith. Help us be more receptive to your loving guidance toward new ways of being and doing. Amen.

Responding to questions raised by Nicodemus, a Pharisee, Jesus provides answers that instruct us all. Jesus indicates who he is and what will happen to him, basing his explanation on a story that Nicodemus knows and that we know—the bronze serpent. Just as the bronze serpent was lifted up, Jesus promises he will be lifted up, anticipating his own crucifixion and resurrection. In the context of this week's readings, we learn the significance of his crucifixion and resurrection for each of us. Our passage from Ephesians told us that through God's grace, we who are still spiritually dead have been made alive with Christ (Eph. 2:5). In today's passage from John, we learn how God in Jesus Christ brings about our renewal. When Jesus Christ was lifted up, we too were lifted up.

We are saved by God's grace, a grace fully expressed in the death and resurrection of Jesus Christ. What good news! As a result of God's gracious act in Jesus Christ, believers may experience eternal life. Though we were spiritually dead because of our separation from God, now, through Christ, we are no longer dead. Instead we are alive together with Christ and can remain forever in union with God. God's gift of the bronze serpent allowed the people to live and not die. God's gift of Jesus Christ enables us to stop being the living dead and allows us to have eternal life.

PRAYER: Gracious God, thank you for the gift of Jesus Christ and for the gift of faith that allows us to believe. Thank you for your abiding presence and care. Thank you for making new beginnings available to us. Amen.

This passage summarizes a basic tenet of our faith—that God's love for us was expressed in the gift of Jesus Christ. Jesus was sent for our salvation. Earlier, John's Gospel describes Christ as "the life [that] was the light of all people" (John 1:4). Here Christ is again equated with the light, and those who believe in him will have eternal life. We are told that some people do not come to the light because of their past deeds (John 3:20). Yet today's passage reminds us that Jesus was not sent to condemn us. Regardless of our past histories, the gift of salvation in Jesus Christ is available to all. However, we must choose. If we desire eternal life, we must choose the light rather than the darkness. If we remain in the darkness, we cannot then blame God for our condition. We have not been condemned by God to the darkness, but by our own failure to choose the light. The choice is ours.

Today's passage reminds us of our responsibility as persons of faith. We can remain mired in the past, or we can take steps toward a new future. Even though we may make only gradual moves from the darkness to the light, we can rest assured that Christ's presence will be with us through it all. "The light shines in the darkness, and the darkness did not overcome it" (John 1:5).

For those experiencing their own time in the wilderness, this week's message offers profound comfort and assurance. God loves you; and God's salvation, that divine wholeness, is offered through Jesus Christ. You just have to choose the light.

PRAYER: Eternal God, help me to experience your love more deeply. Strengthen me to choose the light over darkness. Enable me to appreciate the blessing that you have offered—an eternal life in Christ. Amen.

Going Deeper, Lifting Higher

March 31–April 6, 2003 • *Sidney D. Fowler*[‡]

MONDAY, MARCH 31 • Read Psalm 51:1-9

On Ash Wednesday we began the Lenten journey by reading Psalm 51. We read it again today as it signals a call to a more fervent spiritual examination than when first prayed. Go deeper.

Tradition identifies David as the writer of Psalm 51. Confronted by the prophet Nathan, David reflects on his deceit and desire for the beautiful woman Bathsheba (2 Samuel 11–12). Along with David, we are unavoidably challenged to reflect on ways we break our relationships with God and others. The psalm moves us to face the full truth of our lives and to confess.

Mornings and evenings, we recall our comings and goings.
The daily blunders and broken ways prick our hearts.
"Have mercy on us, O God."

Remembering usually lasts a moment.
Breakfast or sleep comes fast.
We get on with living.
Transgressions linger, however, in our bodies,
in despair, in hopeless expectations.
"Have mercy on us, O God."

For more than a moment, take us to the shadow places.
There may we imagine our days—those injured relationships,
selfish habits, addictions, violence, withholdings, deep
disappointments.

Have us hold them long enough to hand them to you.
Crush and cleanse our sin. Forgive us.
"Have mercy on us, O God."

PRAYER: Revealing and forgiving God, help us trust you so we can be honest about our lives. Forgive our sins. Amen.

[‡]Minister for Worship, Liturgy, and Spiritual Formation with Local Church Ministries: A Covenanted Ministry of the United Church of Christ, Cleveland, Ohio.

Lent's penitential Psalm 51 moves in these verses from confession to restoration. The psalmist calls on God to create something new in us, foreshadowing Saint Paul's declaration, "So if anyone is in Christ, there is a new creation: everything old has passed away; see, everything has become new!" (2 Cor. 5:17).

Take time today to pray, reflect, breathe, and sing "Create in me a clean heart, O God, and put a new and right spirit within me." This prayer, born out of the truth of our lives, focuses both on the discipline and the redeeming hope of the season of Lent. What do we do once washed and forgiven? Who are we now as forgiven people?

We close our eyes and breathe deeply.
We exhale ways that choked us from life in God's spirit.
We inhale the new, the fresh, God's spirit.
"Create in me a clean heart, O God,
and put a new and right spirit within me."

We open our eyes and breathe deeply.
Before us is the new day.
Give us the joy of life renewed in you, O God.
Keep us vigilant. Teaching, defending, living your way.
"Create in me a clean heart, O God,
and put a new and right spirit within me."

We breathe deeply.
From broken spirit to new spirit, we give you our lives.
The gift of one's self, you offered.
Now we offer the sacrifice that you treasure—our whole lives.
"Create in me a clean heart, O God,
and put a new and right spirit within me."

PRAYER: Renewing Spirit, give us the courage to live as a new people—willing to live more fully for you in hope, joy, and obedience. Amen.

What do you think about God on the other side of heartbreak? What is your request of God once death, exile, isolation, or injury has occurred? After heartbreak what do you imagine the living God desires to speak to you?

The prophet Jeremiah speaks to a people, the houses of Israel and Judah, scattered and broken during the Babylonian exile. On the other side of that heartbreak, that desolation, Jeremiah declares there will be a new word: "The days are surely coming."

Despite Jeremiah's declaration that a new thing is happening, the words proclaimed are ancient covenant words: "I will be their God, and they shall be my people." Those same words led God's people through the Red Sea and to Sinai. On this side of the heartbreak, the words seem old, so what is new?

"I will be their God, and they shall be my people." Over and over those covenant words seem to work for a moment and then things fall apart. The people break the covenant; they fail. The covenant has not gone to heart.

"Jesus loves me, this I know, for the Bible tells me so."
I sang it as a child. For as long as I live, I figured,
the melody line will be there in my head.

"Jesus loves me, this I know, for the Bible tells me so."
The world crumbles around us. We despair. I sin. We sin.
I miss the mark with my life. We miss the mark with our common life.
Where are the verses and melody that
protected and delighted my childhood?

"Jesus loves me."
"I will be their God, and they shall be my people."
O God, sing your covenant to us again.
Make melody again. Go to our hearts.
This time, get to us—really get to us.

PRAYER: O God, this day in spite of any heartbreak, help us to live as yours. Amen.

The prophet Jeremiah declares that God will write a holy covenant upon the hearts of God's people. The heart in the Old Testament is the source of the will. It is from the heart that God's people remain faithful. For the covenant to go to the heart means the words "I will be their God, and they shall be my people" will be known in the deepest of ways. There will be no conflict between knowing and willing, thinking and doing, wanting and living.

What do you know more deeply than anything else? What do you know that has the greatest influence on how you live? What's at your heart? Attempt in this day, pray in this day, that you know God and God's way of love and justice more deeply.

When we take the time,
we study the Bible,
we catch some church history, and
we discover our denomination's missional priorities.
We know about some things.
"At heart, know God."

When we survey our lives,
we see how we spend money;
we identify how we fill our time; and
we recognize all those to whom we relate.
We know what matters to us.
"At heart, know God."

When we get to the heart of it all,
what we know most deeply
we express with our lives.
"At heart, know God."

PRAYER: Eternal God, we desire to know you. From our very hearts, we long to express such wonderful knowledge in all the moments of this day. Amen.

Glance over this entire psalm. Psalm 119 is extraordinarily long, 176 verses. Each stanza is a cluster of eight verses. In the original Hebrew, moving through the alphabet, each one of the stanzas begins with a different letter. Then each word that follows in a stanza begins with that particular letter of the alphabet. If it had been first written in English, the first letter of the first stanza would have begun with *A,* as would every verse in that stanza. The next stanza, and every verse of that stanza, would have begun with *B.* The psalm's stanzas progress through the entire Hebrew alphabet with such a pattern. The format is a poetic and complex game of word search.

The form reinforces the focus of the psalm—the word. Throughout the psalm terms point us to the law or will of God. They include *decree, ordinances, commandments, promise, precepts, statutes,* or *ways.* The psalmist, through both form and terms, makes every attempt to point to God's way. Today's reading begins with the question, "How can young people keep their way pure?" and suggests the question, "What do you seek?" Living the psalm, young and old are challenged to seek God's word and way in the midst of the stanzas of our daily lives.

Almighty God,
  at waking, at table,
  at work, study, play, prayer, service—
  all times—we seek your way.

Before caring less,
  before deciding, before forgetting your precepts,
  behind our commitments,
  between beginnings and endings—we seek your way.

Continually,
  consistently, "With my whole heart I seek you;
    do not let me stray from your commandments."

PRAYER: God of compassion, keep us close to you that we may live your precepts with joy and devotion. Amen.

With this Lenten reading from Hebrews, we shift from looking inward to our own need for forgiveness to looking outward to Christ, the cross, and his redemptive suffering. As we gaze on Christ described in Hebrews, we see a priest who offers up and is offered up. The high priests in Jewish tradition were both very human and very holy.

The writer of Hebrews knew people would understand a priestly figure, and the writer placed Christ within that tradition. Here Jesus does not avoid human suffering but, consistent with his faithfulness, embraces it. Being the child of God did not exempt him even from death. He does not separate himself from the people, but his suffering itself exhibits in a holy and ultimate way his redemptive work.

O Christ, Human One,
>   you are a priest forever;
>   you suffer as we suffer.

You go before us and
>   know our human anguish
>   of sin, death, and despair.

We look to you. We look to God.
Teach us faithfulness and hope.
You before us, redeem us.

O Christ, Holy One,
>   you are a priest forever;
>   you take suffering and bring healing.

You offer up more than suffering,
>   more than even your very self—
>   you offer everlasting deliverance.

We look to you. We look to God.
Teach us faithfulness and hope.
You before us, redeem us.

PRAYER: Suffering and redeeming God, in a suffering world may we offer hope through faithful living. In Christ's name. Amen.

Meditate on the cross. Recall all the places and all the forms in which you have seen it rendered. Imagine wooden, silver, gold, or crayon-drawn. Visualize the crude, simple, exquisite, or ornate. Recall crosses in the front of cathedrals or your sanctuary, alongside roads, hanging around necks or waists, or hidden in pockets. What is so compelling about the image? Why might we be drawn to the ultimate Christian symbol?

The cross in the Gospel of John becomes the doorway by which the world enters the way of Christ. Jesus' historical ministry was located in the ancient Near East lands of Judea, Samaria, and Galilee and at a particular moment in time. John's Gospel, however, addresses a later time and an audience more diverse than the Jews of the ancient Near East. Christ's redemptive work, his glory through cross and resurrection, lifts him beyond place and time.

"I, when lifted up, will draw all people to myself."
Look up, world.
You who are poor, despairing, hungry, homeless,
Christ of the cross embraces you.

"I, when lifted up, will draw all people to myself."
Look up, world.
You who are diseased, victims of violence and war,
Christ of the cross embraces you.

"I, when lifted up, will draw all people to myself."
Look up, world.
You of many nations, tongues, and cultures,
Christ of the cross embraces you.

"I, when lifted up, will draw all people to myself."
Look up, world.
You—but not only you—but all,
Christ of the cross embraces you.

PRAYER: God of cross and God of glory, draw us to you and to all those whom you embrace. Amen.

Who Is This King of Glory?

April 7–13, 2003 • *Flora Slosson Wuellner*[‡]

MONDAY, APRIL 7 • Read Philippians 2:5-8

Through this hymn of the early Christian church, we enter into what has been traditionally known as Passion Week. For centuries this week was set apart, along with Holy Week, as the culmination of Lenten devotions.

During these two final weeks of Jesus' life, he emphasized prayer and works of compassion for the poor. Many early Christian leaders even released some slaves and prisoners during these days in the spirit of Jesus who sets all free.

Scripture indicates that Jesus' teachings and healings intensify as he approaches Jerusalem for the last time: blessing the children, healing the blind and those with leprosy, casting out unclean spirits, raising Lazarus from death, experiencing union with God on the Mount of Transfiguration.

Through these culminating experiences as he turns his face toward Jerusalem, as indeed through his whole life, Jesus longs to reveal to us the heart of God, which had so deeply enfolded and shone within his own heart. What do our weekly scripture readings show us this week about the heart of God that was one with Jesus' heart?

"Who is this king of glory?" asks Psalm 24. The psalm gives one answer. Our scripture reading from Philippians seems to show another aspect. What answer do we begin to see and feel as we draw closer to God?

PRAYER: God of mercy, God of healing, help me in my reflections and experiences of this day to see into your heart more fully and to respond to the mystery of your love more deeply. In the name and light of Jesus. Amen.

[‡]United Church of Christ minister; specialized ministry in spiritual renewal that includes authorship, teaching, retreat leading; Fair Oaks, California.

As we approach Passion/Palm Sunday, we traditionally reflect not only on Jesus' healings and teachings but also on the suffering and death that await him. Psalm 118 is one of the most significant lections for this period. If we read the whole psalm, we see intertwined with the exultant praise and confidence in God the definite signs of the hostility and conflict that will confront the bold children of God.

Jesus, of course, would have known this psalm well. Perhaps he found it often on his lips and in his heart as he moved toward Jerusalem, knowing that rejection and danger awaited him there along with the triumph and welcome. But while realistic, the psalm is clearly *not* the lament of a victim moving toward doom. It is a song of strength empowered by God's hand, God's heart.

As Christians we are often called to encounter conflict along with joy, but our loving and suffering were never meant to be a victim stance. God, who rides to the gates of our hearts and who rides with us through "the gates of righteousness," does not force or compel us as slaves. God sets us free to choose our risks of love.

Jesus is never a victim; he makes every choice in freedom. His eyes are open and he sees clearly, even as did the psalmist, that the choice of love is costly. But when we choose to enter our gates of righteousness, we enter them enfolded by God. The vulnerability to which we are invited is an empowered vulnerability.

"The LORD is God, and he has given us light."

PRAYER: God of our strength, God of our peace, as I enter into whatever gates of righteousness open to me today, as I make my choices, help me face the risks of love knowing that your heart holds me forever. Amen.

This scripture opens with Isaiah's wonder and gratitude over the rich gifts God has given him: the depth and eloquence of a true teacher, the healing power to renew those who are weary, and the openness that hears what God says to the heart. But then he speaks of the underlying empowerment without which these gifts would be useless.

"I was not rebellious, I did not turn backward." With each gift, the risks and cost of love intensify. Without God's strength to keep moving forward, our gifts atrophy. Anyone who loves, anyone who serves, knows that as we use our gifts we will experience times of antagonism and hostility as well as times of love and appreciation. Our scripture reading refers to insults, blows, and spitting in scorn. There are many ways of being struck or spat upon, and often they are not bodily attacks. Verbal, emotional, or competitive attacks can inflict deeper wounds than bodily ones.

But we are asked to keep moving forward. Our first reading of this scripture seems to imply that we are urged to submit passively to abuse. A more careful reading gives a totally different picture. As I read the passage, I remember the poignant, powerful television pictures in 2001 of the school children in Ireland surrounded, embraced, supported by parents and neighbors and walking forward steadily to their school each morning for many weeks through the shouts and insults of the angry crowd hostile to their religion.

This picture is not one of passivity to abuse but of a forward motion of immense power, going through one's chosen gates with both face and back vulnerable, knowing that God does not promise safety but limitless strength.

PRAYER: God of our peace, God of our empowerment, as I meet today's challenges, may I walk forward as Jesus did, not as a victim but as a child within your light. Amen.

"Jesus made no further reply, so that Pilate was amazed." We too are amazed. Why didn't Jesus give Pilate, the priests, the crowd a final deathless discourse comparable to the Sermon on the Mount or the Last Supper discourses in John's Gospel? Some of the most sublime speeches of history have been made by those condemned to die.

As I reflect on Jesus' silence, I see something far deeper than the silence of one who just wants to get it over without more words. I see a divine act of *release*, a choice to release everyone around him to their own free choices.

Jesus has already told them who he is. Far beyond words he has also shown them throughout his whole life who he is and the nature of his kingdom. Who he is has been there all along for them to see through his healings, his stories, his compassionate mercy, his clear and decisive discernments, his empowered stance of love. More words will add nothing. He never forces or indoctrinates anyone. When people turn away, he does not run after them with pleas or threats, for his is a love that set others free. Now as he faces death, he makes this supreme act of silent release of his disciples, Pilate, the priests, the crowd. They see him. Now they must choose.

This silence is a great mystery of God's heart. We are confused and angry when God seems silent. We batter God with our perplexities, demands, and accusations. Even the psalms—those great love songs to God—are full of complaint about God's silences. Why doesn't God answer, explain, and tell us exactly, step-by-step, what to do?

But God has already answered us. God has already told us who we are and what God longs for. God's silences in the midst of our furious demands are not God's absence or indifference but acts of love and release. We are released, set free to choose.

PRAYER: God, your love is a love that sets me free. Help me not to fear my freedom but to hear your answer within your unfailing love. Amen.

We want to turn away. We haven't yet reached Palm Sunday! Why are we asked to preview all the terrible anguish to come? We will have to face it, read it again next Friday, Good Friday, which comes all too soon.

Mark's account of the crucifixion is incredibly, almost unbearably, stark compared with the accounts in some of the other Gospels. It hurts with its brief, blinding intensity. Nevertheless, the lectionary invites us to see the full dimension of the story, to see the triumph of Palm Sunday through the eyes of the crucifixion to come. But lest we despair, let us remember that the story of the crucifixion was written by those who had also seen the Resurrection.

It is the same in our personal lives. We understand our suffering more deeply when we see it and share it through the eyes of our healing. Likewise when in the midst of suffering, we value all the more poignantly the precious love given to us. We see love through the eyes of pain; we see pain through the eyes of love.

On the day of Jesus' crucifixion as he faced the hostile crowds, I do not believe that his thoughts were bitter as he recalled Palm Sunday of five days earlier. Perhaps he remembered the eyes of those who genuinely loved him in the welcoming crowd and found that memory precious. Seeing those same eyes now weeping for him, perhaps he found that their love strengthened him.

We are invited to this blended vision that is not the same as the vertigo of double vision. God's watchful heart breaks through to us as we read the crucifixion story through the eyes both of Palm Sunday and the Easter to come. The blended vision is held together in the loving gaze of God's heart.

PRAYER: Open the eyes of my heart this day, O God, that I may see both your pain for us and your strong joy in us. Help me to hold both pain and joy in my heart as I relate to others. Surround me with your heart. Amen.

Again we are invited to a blended vision: the struggle and agony of Psalm 31 and the exultation of the Christian hymn in Philippians. How can both be true? The God we see through scripture is a God of polarities but not of polarization. The apparent opposites are held together in God's heart.

Certainly the opposites are held together in Jesus' heart. During his desperate praying in Gethsemane on the evening of his betrayal, he feels all the anguish Psalm 31 describes: the brokenness, the lash of scorn, the desolation of desertion, "the whispering of many—terror all around."

But at the same time Jesus feels, as did the psalmist, the face of God shining steadily on him and the strength of God forever upholding him. Certainly he is thinking of that psalm as he prays one of its early verses at the moment of his death: "Into your hand I commit my spirit" (31:5).

Out of this union of suffering and trust in Jesus' heart rise such Christian hymns as that of Philippians. As I reflect on this hymn, I do *not* sense a scenario of a manipulative God first smiting and crushing Jesus and then raising and exalting him. Rather I see the exaltation of Jesus in the very moment of his humility. He is able to be humbled because he is already exalted.

Humility does not mean feeling apologetic and ashamed. Humility means being open to full humanness. The most truly great and gifted persons I have known are the most human and approachable. Because they have greatness within them, they are not ashamed of laughing, crying, grieving, being angry, loving—all expressions of the full human condition. Likewise Jesus with his immense God-given powers is not ashamed of "being born in human likeness" or of "being found in human form" (Phil. 2:7). In this mingling of giftedness and humanness, we see the mystery of Emmanuel, God with us. We see deeper into God's heart.

PRAYER: O God, show me more fully the mystery of your love that enters our pain and transforms us in your power. Amen.

PASSION / PALM SUNDAY

As we watch Jesus entering Jerusalem with friends and followers waving palms, not swords, we see again into the heart of God.

A significant little detail (often overlooked) noted by Matthew, Mark, and Luke is that Jesus rides into the city on a colt that has never been ridden. An unbroken colt! As student pastor in the Rocky Mountains many years ago, I attended many riding, roping shows and saw what usually happened to people who sat on untamed colts, *especially* in the midst of shouting crowds! I sense an underlying smile here as the writer of Mark's Gospel contemplates this little miracle, less spectacular than stilling a storm or raising the dead but no less significant in its depiction of gentle power. Jesus does not need a warrior's stallion. The untamed young horse makes the point just as well. The power that enters the gates of our hearts does not force or violate but calms, transforms, and guides us.

We read another often overlooked detail in the clamor of Palm Sunday in the last verse of today's reading. At the end of this incredible day, Jesus does not set up a command center in Jerusalem. He leaves the city and goes to the suburb of Bethany, we assume to spend the night with this beloved friends Mary, Martha, and Lazarus. At the height of his triumph, all he wants is to rest in that quiet, loving circle of friendship. We know that extraordinary days of intensity, confrontation, and challenge lie ahead of him. But that first night perhaps what he most needs is the hearts of his friends.

"Who is this King of glory?" All week we have reflected on glimpses of that heart through scripture. The mystery is deep, but we who are bonded to that heart are deepening too. How do we feel more prepared to respond to that ancient question?

PRAYER: God of supreme yet gentle power, I open my heart to you, so that you may enter and be at home with your friend. Amen.

From Darkness to Light

April 14–20, 2003 • *Martin E. Marty*[‡]

MONDAY, APRIL 14 • Read Isaiah 42:1-9

HOLY MONDAY

What we call Holy Week will climax six days from now on the first day of a new week, on the festival of the resurrection of Jesus. We might well call that day "the feast of light" and the days between now and then a "pilgrimage from darkness to light."

We will walk through literal shadows and darkness, as everyone must and does part of every twenty-four hours. We will also walk through the figurative darkness, sometimes alone, in fear; preferably with company, often that of other people, and always, with the one Isaiah calls "God, the LORD."

God speaks to the people, first the people of Israel, a "covenant" people with whom God has an agreement and for whom God takes special care. "I have given you as…a light to the nations," to open blind eyes and bring prisoners who "sit in darkness" to light—the light for vision, the light of freedom.

God speaks to the people again, this time to the people who make up the community of faith in Christ. The New Testament announces that we are now part of the covenant. This community has spread around the world, among the many nations. All the people in them still need the light of freedom, of knowledge.

God speaks to each of us, so that we who have our own darkness to face and overcome become aware today that the covenant, the agreement, continues: We get to see; we are led out of the darkness of the ignorance and evil that imprison us.

PRAYER: Covenanting God, who brings light through Israel, light through Christ, shine in our hearts when darkness shrouds us, so that we become free for what the day will bring. Amen.

[‡]Lutheran pastor; Fairfax M. Cone Distinguished Service Professor Emeritus, University of Chicago, Chicago, Illinois.

HOLY TUESDAY

No one knows for sure what to make of "the Servant" who appears in some chapters in Isaiah, who here appears "as a light to the nations." Bible footnotes indicate that scholars are divided: Is the Servant Israel? Is the Servant an individual promised in Israel's future? Because the New Testament applies the Servant language to Jesus, we also freely apply this language originally intended for Israel to the community of faith in Jesus Christ. We did so yesterday and do today.

Those aware that they belong to a people are often clubby, exclusive. For them, having a covenant means keeping others away. Many in Israel often did so; many who are called Christian still do. When they did and we do, shadows result, leaving others in darkness. Meanwhile, though the light is available to us, we show that we are in darkness, which is not God's intention.

"I will give you as a light to the nations, that my salvation may reach to the end of the earth" is the ancient promise made new this day. Only a few readers of this devotion will be pondering it in today's Israel. The vast majority of us are doing so in faith because the light has reached "to the end of the earth."

Talking about light is not the same thing as realizing it and being in it. In the Book of Acts in the New Testament, two light-bringers, Paul and Barnabas, quote this verse from Isaiah with this intent: to make all glad. And why? For the same reason we are made glad by it: Salvation has come. Salvation means rescue from darkness to light, from fear to freedom, from being self-enclosed to being free to serve others among all nations—beginning, as it were, next door.

Salvation may sound like a word from ancient times or gets sounded among people who overrepeat the question: "Are you saved?" Yet it speaks to our day, our need, our search for light.

PRAYER: Saving God, let your ancient promises live today among the people of Israel, among believers in Christ, and in our ears, to reach our hearts afresh this day. Amen.

HOLY WEDNESDAY

One of the darkest moments in the stories that believers read each Holy Week occurs before the festival of the Passover at a supper we call the Lord's Supper. The occasion was profoundly sad because it was the last on earth at which Jesus would be present with his disciples. But it looked forward toward occasions that inspire happiness: Some call the meal a "foretaste of the feast to come" at which Christ again offers bread, gives himself.

The story takes its sad turn just before the meal, after Jesus has humbly washed the feet of the disciples in a ceremonial act that shows him to be a servant, a gesture that he wants disciples to replicate by adopting his humble, serving ways.

Right after that comes the dramatic episode. The writer records Jesus' saying that not all will share in those loving ways. Not all will accept the gift of his bread, of himself. In that most intimate circle of followers, one will exclude himself. He will even betray Jesus. He is "Judas son of Simon Iscariot," who with the others "received the piece of bread." Unlike the others, he does not eat it. His heart has turned against Jesus, against God's loving acts that include Judas. He receives the bread but immediately goes out. The curtain comes down: And it is night.

While supper back then was eaten in late afternoon, the Passover meal occurred at night. The writer therefore does not need to accentuate that point. But he speaks also of figurative night: Darkness falls around Judas and fills his heart. He is ready to do his evil. Judas is not the last to betray Christ, to have his heart darkened. Aware of that, we pray for light around us, in us.

PRAYER: In a world where people slam the door against you, O God, leaving themselves in the darkness of night, spread the light of your love to recall them, to appeal to all. Amen.

MAUNDY THURSDAY

In the midst of this week of shadows and darkness that we call Holy Week, Jesus, the light of the world, facing the darkness of death, surprises us by saying that he "has been glorified, and God has been glorified in him."

We need that announcement of glory to sustain us as we move through the story to tomorrow's word of Jesus' death. We welcome any word that can bring light today, since it is today that we most crave it. It is today in which we will meet so many things that we might think of as inglorious, lacking glory, radiance, light.

Yes, light. The scriptures so often associate divine glory with light. In the Old Testament *kabod*, that glory, comes when God is revealed, sometimes with lightning flashes, sometimes with dazzling spectacles, sometimes with fire.

So in the New Testament we associate the coming of Jesus with glory, with light. Already in the Christmas story, when shepherds watched their flocks by night, "an angel of the Lord stood before them, and the glory of the Lord shone around them" (Luke 2:9). The light of divine glory that was the Father's now comes with the Son. In one story Jesus is "transfigured" on a mountain, and three disciples see him in glory, a glory that features light.

What is startling about this story in the Gospel of John is that the glory appears when one least expects it: as Jesus faces suffering and death. God is present in and through him, not with a shining halo that artists later provide but under the crown of thorns he is forced to wear on the way to his death for others. Jesus speaks of glory because he is on the verge of finishing the work he has been given to do, the saving work, the light in the darkness.

PRAYER: O God, help us see and know the glory you reveal when everything looks dark and deathly: Let it be among us as a light to guide, inform, and inspire. Amen.

FRIDAY, APRIL 18 • Read John 18:1–19:42

GOOD FRIDAY

In the Gospels of Matthew, Mark, and Luke—not John—we read that as Jesus is dying, there is darkness from noon until three o'clock. Most artists who depict the crucifixion and death of Jesus choose to portray the scene during those hours. Against the background of the darkened sky they concentrate on three crosses, three figures on those crosses, and in the middle, Jesus.

Darkness at noon: So familiar are those other three Gospel stories that we need no reminder that what went on that Friday at the edges of the holy city of Jerusalem was a scene from which light was temporarily excluded.

Executions today—who knows why?—usually occur at night. We picture gas chambers or electric chairs deep in the interior of darkened prisons. Executions back then, when the Romans were in charge, took place in broad daylight. When they crucified someone, they wanted that person to be absolutely humiliated just before death; they wanted crowds to see the power of the state, the power to kill.

This execution, this crucifixion, occurring at midday attracted its own darkness. The Gospel writers could not picture the killing of Jesus as something that belonged to the world of light.

John skips the detail: "So they took Jesus; and carrying the cross by himself, he went out to what is called The Place of the Skull.…There they crucified him." The story ends: "[Jesus] said, 'It is finished.' Then he bowed his head and gave up his spirit."

The story ends in the darkness, real or figurative, of this noon in Jerusalem—in the depth of gloom that those who love someone experience when such persons give up their spirit and die. Yet love is stronger than death, and light outlasts the darkness.

PRAYER: God of light, fill us with the word of promise, the message of hope that lets us look ahead on this dark day to the light that will come with Easter and that can shine on us every day. Amen.

HOLY SATURDAY

"When it was evening, there came a rich man from Arimathea, named Joseph," a disciple of Jesus who asks for the dead body. "So Joseph took the body and…laid it in his own new tomb, which he had hewn in the rock." A stone closes the tomb. No one is left except "Mary Magdalene and the other Mary," who sit there opposite the tomb.

"When it was evening…." The darkness at noon when Jesus is crucified has given way to light and then dusk, and now evening. Suddenly there is a sense of repose, a quieting that comes not too late for readers of the wearying story, for pilgrims who want to follow Christ's path into darkness on the way to hoped-for life. Now not the perhaps miraculous mistimed darkness at crucifixion time or the natural, ordinary, timely dark of night but "evening"—the time when loving people come out of the shadows to act as Joseph did, to keep vigil and mourn as did the Marys.

The final chorus just before the last chorale that ends Johann Sebastian Bach's *St. John Passion* speaks to the moment: "Rest well," the chorus, representing believers, sings to the lifeless Jesus. "Rest well…that I may not further mourn; rest, and bring me to my sleep as well." The singer cannot leave with the somber and stilling word about the "rest" of Jesus and the "sleep" of the believer. No, while the grave has been "prepared for Thee," yet "from need [it] will set Thee free." And that action "will open Heaven wide for me."

Even in this most quiet evening hour those in whom the risen Christ dwells cannot let death and night have the last word. "From need," the grave has to set Jesus free. "From need," says or sings the believer, "the grave" has to let go of me. It has lost its power.

PRAYER: After evening and darkness come morning and light. Anticipating the resurrection, grant us rest on this Holy Saturday and a vision of the hope that will dawn tomorrow. Amen.

EASTER

"Early on the first day of the week, while it was still dark, Mary Magdalene came to the tomb." Those who love and believe in Jesus cannot be confined by the rhythms of the day-and-night as night comes and lasts. They cannot be inconvenienced by the darkness that inhibits action, cannot be left to cower and mourn.

So this Mary, who "while it was still dark" found the stone removed from the tomb and found no body, "ran" to two disciples to tell them the news. Then Peter and the other disciple also ran, until they came to the tomb, went in, "saw and believed."

Mary Magdalene stayed and wept, until a figure she did not recognize spoke with a voice that she did recognize: "Mary!" The light of the new life, the resurrected life, entered her world upon the sound of her name from a voice she knew.

So went the day. One verse beyond today's reading from John 20 tells us of the spread of the light. "When it was evening on that day, the first day of the week," Jesus entered the room where the disciples were mourning. "Peace be with you." Again, it did not take a long talk to convince the disciples to believe and live in a new way. It took only the presence of the risen Lord and a word of greeting.

Between the time "while it was still dark" on the morning we call Easter and "when it was evening" on that same day, disciples must have spent the daylight hours grieving, wondering, puzzling over the word of Mary Magdalene and two disciples. Do they go back to work? Saturday has been their Sabbath, their workless day. Do they on Sunday eat noon meals, buzz around with friends, sit at home and grieve? The way they spend the day leads them to need one another, to gather: They are ready for the word of peace that only their Lord can give them. The room in which the words are spoken is no doubt lit, as rooms then had to be, with dim lamps. Now it becomes light. Jesus is with them.

PRAYER: Be the light among us, O Lord, and let it shine through us as we hear and say to others, "Peace be with you." Amen.

Life Together

April 21–27, 2003 • Elizabeth Canham[‡]

Abundant blessing

During my childhood in England I often heard my mother say, "Eat your greens; they are good for you." Greens did not taste good to me; I craved the pleasant sensation of digging into the heavy suet pudding smothered in golden syrup that was sometimes served for dessert and definitely *not* good for me. Life has taught me that what is good and what is pleasant rarely come together.

The Hebrew psalmist chooses some rich images to convey the blessedness of kindred living together in unity. It is both good *and* pleasant, he says, like the copious anointing oil poured on Aaron's head or the abundant dew covering Mount Hermon in the early morning. This psalm celebrates harmonious relationships and the honoring of life together. God pours blessing upon the community that holds together in faith. Psalm 133 does not address the difficulties inherent in community life or the means for restoring harmony when disunity threatens. Perhaps this good and pleasant ideal can only become reality if we are willing to let go of our preference for what is sweet and satisfying in another and accept those whose personalities do not tickle our palate. Maybe life together involves eating our greens and gradually coming to appreciate their flavor!

PRAYER: **Gracious God, make us a people at peace. Where there is disunity, strengthen our resolve to listen to one another and break bread together. Pour out your blessing upon your family and make us one. Amen.**

[‡]Episcopal priest; author; leader of pilgrimages; founder of Stillpoint Ministries Retreat Center, Black Mountain, North Carolina.

Transforming presence

Waiting can be excruciatingly difficult, especially in a culture that demands instant products and answers. We wait at the bedside of a sick friend, in gridlocked traffic, or through a dry desert phase in our journey with God and feel out of control, anxious, perhaps angry. The followers of Jesus come to an impasse after his death, uncertain about the future despite all his efforts to prepare them for this moment. Fearfully they gather, lock the doors, and wait.

God has a way of stepping into human history at times when expectation has almost gone. "When the fullness of time had come" (Gal.4:4), a young peasant woman hears the incredible announcement that she will bear the Christ, and her "yes" to God changes the world. A soul-thirsty woman at a well meets Jesus, who leads her to the only source of inner refreshment that will transform her life. And tired, wondering, disillusioned disciples fearfully huddled behind locked doors encounter the living Christ who comes with the gift of peace and God's Spirit. Christ comes not to make of them a comfortable clique but people of proclamation. Their task is to widen the circle of believers by sharing their faith in the world.

What are you waiting for God to do in your life at this time? How do you wait? God is full of surprises, coming to us when we least expect it and always changing us. Peace is the gift held out: a peace that sustains us when times are hard, enabling us to bear witness in places that seem hostile. The Spirit blows away fear and binds us together as the community of Christ.

SUGGESTION FOR MEDITATION: **Ponder those times when God has surprised you with joy, and offer thanks.**

Doubts dispelled

God has a way of meeting us where we are.

The disciples of Jesus are filled with expectation when a week after their first encounter with Christ they gather together again. Thomas, previously absent, has joined them and expresses skepticism and disbelief. He demands proof and boldly announces that unless he can see and touch the nail prints and the wound in Jesus' side, he will not believe. The cohesion of the community is inevitably threatened by one who challenges their credibility and earns the title "Doubting Thomas." The gathered community waits and once again experiences the risen Christ in their midst, speaking peace to them and then inviting Thomas to do what his "little faith" demands. Jesus comes to Thomas where he is with his doubts and makes a believer out of him.

The story of Thomas provides encouragement for us to be honest with God and ourselves. I like to think that I am a mature, if battle-scarred, believer whose years of experience and theological education have made of me a person of deep faith. Sometimes I do pray with trust in God's faithfulness when outer circumstances or inner turmoil assault me. But sometimes panic, fear, and impatience move me into a place of doubt; then prayer becomes little more than a child's cry for help. Then I am surprised by the grace of God that comes to meet me in my waywardness, and I can only utter the grateful cry, "My Lord and my God."

PRAYER: Holy One, come to us with your promise of peace, and sustain us in our turmoil. Help us to know our own truth and to pray with integrity, confident that you hear us and love us. Amen.

The infant church

The Acts of the Apostles gives us glimpses of the infant church at its best and its worst. We are told of missionary journeys, bold steps to include those who are marginalized, and a picture of community sharing that leaves no one in want. "Now the whole group of those who believed were of one heart and soul, and no one claimed private ownership" (Acts 4:32). Yet there are also sharp divisions: Paul and Barnabas disagree and go their separate ways; dishonesty and lying lead to the death of two members; and contentious debates rage in Jerusalem between leaders with differing opinions. The story of struggles in the early church bears a close resemblance to those that beset us today.

The harmonious sharing of resources recorded in Acts 4 challenges us to find ways of becoming compassionate and inclusive. Instead of dismissing this passage as hopeless idealism, we can see it as holding out an invitation to consider prayerfully our attitude toward what we have. We may not be called to live the radical poverty of these early Christians or later monastic communities, but we are asked to think of possessions as gifts to be shared. If I can learn to look at the TV, microwave, automobile, home investment account as not "mine" but on temporary loan from the Giver of all, then I will choose wisely and share generously what has been entrusted to me.

SUGGESTION FOR MEDITATION: **Take some time to reflect on the things you own, and identify what you most value. In what ways might others benefit from your willingness to share these resources?**

Joy-filled fellowship

In her book *Kitchen Table Wisdom*, Rachel Naomi Remen reminds us that everyone is a story. We sense excitement at the beginning of First John as the author tells the story of hearing, seeing, and touching Christ. To know and accept this witness, this story, he says, leads to eternal life, an expression that in the Johannine literature refers to a quality of being—a joy, fulfillment, and vibrancy known by believers *now*. Those who know the story tell it in order to lead others into a deep human fellowship rooted in relationship with God. This fellowship and connection are the source of complete joy.

I once attended an AA meeting with a friend and was struck by the warmth, acceptance, and *fellowship* that existed there. During the evening people told their stories, naming the triumphs and failures in their struggle with alcohol. They were drawn together by a common need and found support for the journey. Do our churches offer opportunity and encouragement for storytelling? Are we sometimes so anxious to get newcomers to join our ranks that we fail to give them time to tell their stories? How often do we seek out opportunities to speak of our faith experience and to know completeness of joy? Maybe the greatest gift we can give to others is the willingness to listen to their stories and to share our own, including the highs and lows and the faithfulness of the God who calls us into fellowship with one another.

PRAYER: Listening, loving God, thank you for bringing us into the fellowship of your people. Enable us to listen with our hearts to those whom you would bless through us. Amen.

Reconciled believers

Sometimes when I am gardening, I lift a rock and watch the many creepy-crawlies who live beneath it run for a new hiding place in the dark. The beginning of John's Gospel describes Jesus as the true light, rejected by some but inextinguishable. Those who prefer darkness, like the bugs in my yard, scurry away in search of a hiding place. But the light shines on.

"God is light and in him there is no darkness at all," writes the author of this epistle, and suddenly we become aware of things we would prefer to keep hidden—deeds and words that shame us. Fellowship in the Christian community depends on walking in the light, scrutinizing our motives and actions, and knowing that God sees all. The Christian community to whom this letter is addressed is as imperfect as any other. Sin pollutes the fellowship, and these scriptures are written to guide both individual and community in the life of faith, enabling them to name and avoid sin.

One Ash Wednesday when a group of us met, we lit a large candle symbolizing the light of God's presence and then turned our chairs outward. With the overhead lights extinguished, the candle threw our shadows onto the walls, and we felt keenly our alienation from one another. After silently confessing our sinfulness and hearing words of forgiveness spoken, we re-formed the circle, and hymns of celebration marked the reconciling grace of God. We are children of light and, as people of faith, bearers of light in a darkened world.

SUGGESTION FOR MEDITATION: Light a candle this evening and sit quietly in God's presence. After a few moments of silence, repeat several times, "Be my light in the darkness, O God."

Living under the Word

Life together becomes a vibrant reality when Christians choose faithfulness to God's Word rather than personal preferences. What joins the community in a common purpose is paying attention to the teaching of Jesus, who first and foremost calls us to love—not necessarily to like—one another.

The other disciples probably don't like Thomas very much when he questions their report of meeting with the risen Christ, but they do not expel him from the circle. He is one of them, fallible, questioning, perhaps deeply disillusioned, but he has not given up. He sees Christ and cries out, "My Lord and my God."

The words spoken next offer the greatest encouragement to those of us who today long for a deeper experience of God, for they tell us that we are blessed in our not seeing! Christ is present to us as the Word through the word. We read of Thomas and know we are acceptable with our doubts. We reflect on the Gospels and find ourselves in the followers and falterers, in Jesus' friends and in his critics, in those who need healing and those who sit with him at table.

Life together obliges each one of us to remain open to change by being faithful to daily reflection on the Word. Christ is at the center of this community, and from the many memories of his teaching and life, the author of the Fourth Gospel has selected these that enable us to believe so that through believing we may have life in Christ.

PRAYER: **We are yours, gracious God, and we ask that in the power of your Spirit we may grow more fully into the people of faith whom your son called into being. Amen.**

Living Deeply in God

April 28–May 4, 2003 • *Benoni Reyes Silva-Netto*[‡]

MONDAY, APRIL 28 • **Read Acts 3:12–19**

Peter takes the opportunity to preach the good news. The crippled beggar, a familiar fixture before the gate of the Temple, is jumping for joy and walking. People gather to witness the miracle. And a congregation is ready to listen when Peter issues an invitation to "live deeply" in God (1 John 2:28, THE MESSAGE).

The broken body of the beggar is a metaphor for the "breakdowns" in the lives of those who gather to hear Peter. They too in some ways are "poor in spirit" and crippled in their faith. Perhaps we find ourselves in this crowd.

A story was told of a young man who was frantically working under the hood of his Model T Ford. A car stopped beside him, and a well-dressed gentleman got out and walked toward him to inquire about the problem. The stranger suggested a few minor adjustments to the car's motor. Desperate, the young man followed the stranger's suggestion. "Now," said the stranger, "start your engine." And as the young man cranked the engine, the car started like a new car. Amazed, he asked the stranger who he was and how he knew exactly what to do to make his car run. The stranger replied that he was Henry Ford. He had designed and made the car; he knew everything about it.

Living deeply in God means allowing our Designer and Maker to help us work on our broken-down machines, our shattered hopes and failed dreams, our dysfunctional relationships and meaningless pursuits. Let us turn to God, who wipes away sin and pours out showers of blessings that refresh.

PRAYER: O Lord, may we turn to face you not in fear but in faith, not in grief but in grace, not in hostility but in hospitality. Amen.

[‡]Professor of Pastoral Care and Counseling and United Methodist Studies at the Pacific School of Religion and the American Baptist Seminary of the West/Graduate Theological Union, Berkeley, California.

Being in distress, a "tight place" (THE MESSAGE), is a common experience that normally creates uncomfortable feelings. Like the psalmist, many of us find ourselves in such a situation time and again and, like the psalmist, some of us have the good sense to acknowledge our powerlessness and seek help from others and from the Power greater than we are.

A pastor shared the story of his visit with his parishioner who lived in a small house on a tiny island. The man worked as a shoemaker in a small shop located on the ground floor of his house. The pastor wondered if John didn't feel closed in and confined in such a tiny room.

John responded, "Pastor, when I start feeling that way, I just open this door." And he opened the door from his shop to the outside, which provided him a fantastic view of the ocean. John described how the sky became a magnificent canvas for the unseen master painter who daily painted a moving picture from dawn to dusk. John's small place on that tiny island was connected to the fantastic universe of a myriad of stars, galaxies, and novas far beyond the reaches of sight. And in a real and magnificent way, his life was connected to the Creator of it all. The pastor got the point. Living deeply in God means finding room in the tight, confined places of our lives. The vision of faith can turn the tomb into a tunnel of hope, trash into treasure, hostility into hospitality, problems into prospects, haunts into hopes, crosses into crowns. In his book *Life after God*, one of Douglas Coupland's characters speaks words to this effect: "In spite of all that has happened in my life, I have never lost the sensation of always being on the brink of some magic revelation."

PRAYER: **Help me, O Lord, to be content in whatever state I am in and learn that you are there with me even in the tightest and most uncomfortable situations. You see the larger picture, and you have the power to lead me to the open spaces of your love and grace. Amen.**

There is much truth in the belief that living deeply in God assures "more joy" in our heart (v. 7, RSV). This joy does not free us from the trials and tribulations of living on this earth. Rather it means that in the midst of the normal parts of human existence, we can find profound and authentic joy.

God has set within every heart a persistent hope for that delayed but inevitable day when joy and peace become the reality in the lives of people everywhere. We do not experience the fullness of this hope as yet, but God invites us to live our lives in the constant awareness of God's desire to put more joy in our hearts. This joy springs from more than what material things can provide, "more than when their grain and wine abound."

I grew up in a small farming and fishing village in a rural province north of Manila, Philippines. On many occasions my memory has led me to visit the places of my childhood where simple living provided joy and peace that affluence has not successfully guaranteed. I remember making toys from available material: empty cans and strings to make telephones, or bamboo poles and coconut leaves to design horses, or backyard trees wrapped in green Japanese papers for a Christmas tree. My friends and I enjoyed playing with the toys we made and sharing with others. It didn't cost our parents a penny.

In contrast, the toys of our children's generation are much more expensive due to high-tech complexities. Our children make us feel that they are culturally deprived if we don't buy them the latest gadgets. Yet we must remind ourselves and teach them that true joy comes from living deeply in God.

PRAYER: May we search and find, O Lord, serenity and joy both in sun and in shadow. And may our lives and our labors reflect true happiness found only in the comfort of your presence. Amen.

I've heard grace defined as the "overmuchness of God's love for us." God blesses us despite the fact that we don't deserve to be loved so marvelously and generously. Justice, mercy, and grace are ways we experience the love of God. With justice we get what we deserve; with mercy we get what we don't deserve; through grace we get better than we deserve. In whatever way we experience God's love, we know that it bounds us on all sides. We are never far from the loving arms of God because nothing is ever left untouched by God's redemptive love.

Scientists tell us that we human beings are just a speck of dust in the vast celestial desert and that no substantial reason exists for us to consider ourselves the center of the universe. But the coming of Jesus Christ and the story of his mission point us to the fact that every living thing is precious in God's sight.

My experience of God's love points me to who I am, how I relate to God, and what I may become. My being is radically and significantly transformed by my belonging to God, who empowers my becoming a new creation. As we become aware of this relationship with God, our values, views, visions, and vocation are transformed, making us indeed bloom into those beautiful persons of God's initial intentions.

Christ points to a God whose unconditional love accepts us just as we are, as beloved "children of God." He models a God who has not given up on us and who persists in holding before us God's faith in and high purpose for our humanity. Living deeply in God means knowing that God is love and that "if we love one another, God lives in us, and his love is perfected in us" (1 John 4:12).

PRAYER: Assure us, O God, that deep within your heart there is a sacred and safe place for us. May you find a hospitable dwelling place within the cloistered spaces of our consciousness so that through our lives and relationships others may know that you are love, pure and perfect. Amen.

Members of an adult Sunday school class discussed their definition of the church, as well as views on the church's essential mission. Two common responses emerged in terms of mission: to proclaim the good news of the gospel and to make disciples of Christ. Then the class went on to unpack the meaning of these responses and how they could be translated into action in their daily lives. Most class participants genuinely desired to follow Christ and to model their lives after him. Yet it is hard to pattern our lives after a person who, from a biblical and historical perspective, is perfect.

A visiting novice painter was moved to tears by a master artist's magnificent paintings of sunsets. The artist asked what was the matter, and the young man confessed that the master brought out colors of the setting sun that he had never seen before. He admitted that he could never paint like that. The artist simply responded, "Don't you wish you too could see those colors?" Jesus' model empowers us to see a new reality.

Our culture urges independence, self-reliance, autonomy— a discovery of our own uniqueness. At the same time, many strongly desire a hero after whom we can model our life. Many of us seek "a glistening purity" (3: 3, THE MESSAGE).

For me, Jesus has been that model because he exemplifies through word and work, life and mission, what it means to love. A quotation whose source I cannot recall reminds us that we are called simply to make gentle this bruised and hurting world, to have love and compassion for all, and in the time that is given us to live on this earth to resonate through our lives and our labors the ancient tale of God's redemptive love. Living deeply in God means living like Christ, the love who comes down and lives with us and among us.

PRAYER: Enable us, O Lord, to look at Christ and to see, through his life and ministry, what it means to love. May the glistening purity of his example inspire and encourage us to live our lives in compassion and care. Amen.

Albert Schweitzer once noted that the only certainty we have in this world is that we are surrounded by mystery. Miracles happen all around us every day: Some make newspaper headlines; other silent, gentle events impress us and touch us only when we look more closely. Who among us has not experienced lifting a glass of water to find the vibrant colors of a rainbow reflected through it as sunlight bathes the glass? We find ourselves irresistibly transfixed for a brief instant and know deep within our hearts that we are in the presence of a miracle. Jesus invites his disciples to look more closely at his hands and his feet, to touch him, to look him over from head to toe, and to know that he is really Jesus.

A little girl about five years of age helped serve refreshments at a meeting. Her vibrant spirit, spontaneous laughter, kind hospitality, and sincere willingness to help impressed both me and other participants. As the meeting progressed, a severe storm moved in; rain, thunder, and lightning raged furiously outside the building. Electrical power was momentarily cut off. I reflected that God's presence can be experienced both through the roar of mighty thunder and through the gentleness of a little girl. We can see God if we are willing to look more closely.

Resurrection is happening all around us— even within us— if we will look more closely. We too can witness people who once were blind but now can see, who once were lost but now are found.

A pastor persuaded the congregation to look at its surrounding community more closely, to discern God's presence in unlikely places. The congregation began to relate to its community, identifying and meeting needs; and in a drug-infested, dying community it found resurrection and new life.

PRAYER: **We long for the dawning of a new day; we yearn for the fulfillment of our hopes; we search for the secret of lasting peace; and we dream of the resurrection of life. Help us, O Lord, to rise up and look more closely upon your face and know that we are in the midst of a miracle. Amen.**

"You are witnesses of these things." When Jesus appeared to the disciples, he spoke about the fulfillment of the law and the prophets; however, in verse 44, Jesus also refers to the psalms in connection with the law and the prophets. The other writings testify to God's promises and the history of God's relationship with the people, but the psalms offer a different type of witness. They offer an emotional witness. Our most basic understanding of the Book of Psalms is of praise. Because our feeling levels speak of our inner depths, we can say that the psalms live deeply in God.

"You are witnesses to these things." In that closed room, Jesus opens the disciples' minds and hearts by speaking about the scriptures. We have little record of the spiritual practices of these disciples. Did they spend much time in prayer and fasting? If so, what kind of prayer did they practice? Or did they argue about different ways of becoming open to God?

We know little about the spiritual practices of the disciples, but we know that they became open to God through Jesus' teachings. We know that they listened to Jesus' words and then acted on those words. They proclaimed repentance and forgiveness of sins to all nations, and the message of God's love and forgiveness moved from Jerusalem around the world—even to places as distant as my home in the Philippines. This witness through time and space could be possible only if people listened to Jesus and lived deeply in God.

Listen deeply to Jesus in today's scripture. What do you hear? Where will you witness to Jesus' words? In what ways will your witness praise God and speak of your emotional depths? How will your witness speak of love and forgiveness gained from living deeply in God?

PRAYER: Lord, enable us to experience your love and forgiveness and then to bear witness to others. We pray in the name of Jesus Christ as we remember his life, death, and resurrection. Amen.

Green Pastures, Still Waters

May 5–11, 2003 • *Patricia Barrett[‡] and her Companions*

MONDAY, MAY 5 • Read Psalm 23

We begin this week of readings with the most familiar and beloved of the Psalms. These comforting words rise within us most often in times of trouble and distress. Unlike some other psalms, this one does not address God's mighty power, nor does the psalmist write of hope that God will defeat enemies. Rather here we find images of comfort, nourishment, hospitality, and healing—all in the midst of dark valleys, evil, and enemies.

The young woman had just moved into a new home. Violent tornados had passed through the neighborhood, leaving a path of devastation in their wake. But her home was left intact. During an interview with a local reporter, she said that God had surely blessed her because her home was spared. Another family had lost two children who had died when their home had been destroyed in the storm. Was this family not blessed by God?

Some would have us believe that if our faith is strong, we will be blessed with health, ease, and prosperity. Health or illness, ease or distress, prosperity or want—none is a marker of blessing. The true blessing is God's enduring presence. Whether in green pastures, beside still waters or through dark valleys, God the shepherd leads, restores, guides, accompanies, and nourishes.

Green pastures, still waters, feasting tables, even the Shepherd may lie outside our range of vision if our attention is captured solely by our circumstances and we fail to be attentive to our Companion. "For you are with me...."

PRAYER: Holy God, open the eyes of my heart so that I may know the goodness of your companionship through this day and all my days. Amen.

[‡]Staff member, General Board of Higher Education and Ministry, Section of Chaplains; clergy member of the Greater New Jersey Annual Conference; member, Belmont United Methodist Church, Nashville, Tennessee.

"It's not my job." After a journey through the voice-mail system, I finally reached a human being. My question fit none of the mechanical options, and I expected that a person would be able to guide me to the right place by translating my question into the particular vocabulary of that organization. Instead I encountered someone with a job—and a dead end for me. My next attempt resulted in contact with a pleasant, helpful voice that belonged to a person who quickly resolved my dilemma by connecting me to someone who could meet my need. Clearly on the second attempt I found someone with a vocation.

The hired hand has a job to do, and the job description doesn't include exposure to personal danger or coping with wolves. The shepherd, on the other hand, lives with the sheep, cares for the sheep, protects the sheep, and lays down his life for the sheep. That is vocation.

We can take on the job of being a Christian and prove it with a transformed life. We can obey the rules, avoid the sins, and fulfill our obligations. We can be like the hired hand, meeting the requirements of the job description and expecting reward for our performance.

Or we can respond to the invitation of the Shepherd and live with transformed hearts that transform lives. Compelled by love rather than obligation, we can be like the faithful shepherd.

PRAYER: Gracious God, transform my heart so that I live out the spirit of Jesus, the good shepherd. Amen.

"I know my own and my own know me."

In my voice-mail memory is a recorded message from my husband, Warren. He didn't need to announce himself. The voice was familiar and precious. Even now, more than three years after his death, I know his voice at the first sound. Love, time, intimacy, and living together assure that I know his voice.

And so it is with our relationship with Jesus, the good shepherd. We know him. We know his voice because of our day-to-day loving relationship. Of course, if our relationship is casual and infrequent, if we speak and listen only on occasion or in times of crisis, if we are guarded or shallow in our sharing, perhaps we may mistake the hired hand for the good shepherd.

Hired hands abound. Some tell us what we want to hear, inviting us to what my friend Dennis calls "short-term pleasure with longtime pain." Others point out our failures and fears, promising quick fixes to make us finally good enough for God. Or we may listen to self-satisfying messages about our talents, competence, accomplishments, and self-reliance. Some voices point out how much better we are than others.

Like sheep we wander off, drifting away from the shepherd. But the shepherd speaks to us continually. We just have to learn to recognize the shepherd's substantial voice over the thin, shrill voices of those who do not care for the sheep. Living with God's word, prayerful listening, the companionship of the faithful, watching for God all around us—all these disciplines help us test the voices, sort out the invitations, and step out in faith.

PRAYER: Shepherd God, open the ears of my heart so that I may more fully hear your voice above the noises of my daily life and follow you. Amen.

It made a great deal of sense at the time. Caiaphas, the high priest, determined that it was "better...that one man die for the people than that the whole nation perish" (John 11:49, NIV). A calculated, practical choice. Just another stone rejected by the builders.

We know the story, so we know that Caiaphas is one of the "bad guys." One day while preparing to preach on this text, I encountered a reference to Caiaphas as a "complete bureaucrat," and it stopped me cold. For years my ministry has been in organizations where I've had administrative responsibilities. In short, I'm a bureaucrat. Ever since that day I've developed a wary sympathy for Caiaphas. What would I have done in his place? How would I have viewed Jesus if I had held his position, having to manage the tricky territory between the Jewish people and the Roman oppressors?

It is easy to function out of a spirit of expediency, to do what has to be done according to the rules and regulations, viewing tasks as ends rather than as means to a greater purpose. But God calls us to a spirit of obedience. In this spirit we seek God's presence and God's will in all we do. Each task and every choice are sacred. Nothing lies outside God's concern.

Peter and John healed and preached (Acts 3). Caiaphas elected to hand Jesus over to the Roman authorities. We make choices every day. All that we do testifies to the spirit that shapes us. I keep that quote from Caiaphas ("better...that one man die for the people than that the whole nation perish") on my desk as a reminder of the dangers of a spirit of expediency.

"By what power or by what name did you do this?"

PRAYER: Holy God, be present in all I do this day—in my speaking, in my actions, and in my heart. Amen.

We know love by this, that he laid down his life for us....

Years ago I worked in a county jail as chaplain and counselor. I was in seminary at the time, eager to pass along all the theological and liturgical wisdom I was gleefully absorbing in the classroom. My sermons were marvelously intricate, obscure, and enthusiastic. One day following the service, one of the older prisoners came up to me. Speaking kindly, he said, "It's just words, Pat. Just words. What really matters is whether you can walk the talk." That may have been the most important lesson from my seminary years.

"And we ought to lay down our lives for one another." Certainly we have heard profoundly moving and dramatic instances where lives have been given for others. Perhaps we have wondered whether we could be as courageous should the opportunity come our way. But the opportunities do come—daily, though usually in ways so subtle that we often overlook them.

Faithfulness means that God is at the center of our lives. God at the center of our lives loves through us.

Sometimes my life is like the car I see from time to time. On its dirty, dusty hood someone has written with a finger, "Wash me." Many things drift into the center of my life, and they are mostly about me: my needs, my pride, my fear of getting involved, my certainty that I know best how to meet the needs of others.

Faithful living means laying down arrogance and hesitation and returning to God, the center. Then, attentive to God and to others, we may love "in truth and action."

PRAYER: Loving God, teach me to train the eyes of my heart to you, so that I may be a channel of your love, compassion, and justice. Amen.

The scene is dramatic. All the religious authorities gather together in their dignity to convene an inquiry of two prisoners —all because one man has been healed. The man and his restoration are forgotten and irrelevant. The issue, their issue, is authority: "By what power or by what name did you do this?"

For Peter and John the issue is not permission but loving obedience. Jesus could not be eliminated by execution. Raised by God, fed by the Spirit, the power of love and justice taught by Jesus and caught by his followers spread like wildfire through the city and over the seas.

Those whose lives were touched by Jesus touched the lives of others. The walls of power dividing "us" from "them" were brought down by love. The powerless discovered the power of the Spirit; those who feared to speak out were given voice. This faithful community found their name in the name of Jesus of Nazareth, the cornerstone. And they were known by their love.

The Acts of the Apostles is our earliest church history book, showing us how the power of the Holy Spirit transformed lives and shaped a community of faith, whose legacy we are. It has been said that this is a book without an ending; every day, as faithful followers of Jesus Christ, we write another chapter.

PRAYER: **Thank you, God, for the men and women who had the courage to live as you taught. Grant me the wisdom and courage to follow their example. Amen.**

He makes me lie down in green pastures;
he leads me beside still waters;
he restores my soul.

We hear a lot these days about the importance of stress relief and self-care. We now know that physical health has a strong link to mental health. So we jog, reduce our fat intake, work out, and eat deep-green, leafy vegetables.

But self-care is not Sabbath; diet and exercise will not restore our souls. The psalmist knows that it is God who restores our souls. Douglas Steere*, writing on "The Twenty-third Psalm and the Dialectic of Renewal," stated, "There are few of us who can have our souls restored until we have been brought to lie down."

"I just don't have the time." But we do. Each of us gets twenty-four hours a day. No more, no less. And, like manna, they cannot be stored up. We spend our time, fill our time, waste our time—and then the day is done.

Today is Sabbath, the day set aside for us to remember that God is God, and we are not. Sabbath time is rich and full. It restores our souls because it calls us back to our vocation as children of God and followers of Jesus. Sabbath time restores perception by expanding our vision, enhancing our hearing, equipping our spirits so that we may see and hear and do God's will. In obedience to Sabbath time we allow ourselves to be caught by the God who loves and leads us like a shepherd.

SUGGESTION FOR MEDITATION: Sit quietly with eyes closed, and reflect on the events of the past week. Where have you seen God at work through others? Where have you heard God's voice calling you to reach out in love, to step out in faith? Give thanks to God and ask for a spirit of attentive obedience in the week to come.

---

*Douglas Steere, *Gleanings: A Random Harvest* (Nashville, Tenn.: The Upper Room, 1986), 131ff..

The Assurance of Things Hoped For

May 12–18, 2003 • *Kenneth H. Carter Jr.*[‡]

MONDAY, MAY 12 • **Read 1 John 4:7-11**

Beloved, let us love one another, because love is from God; everyone who loves is born of God and knows God. Whoever does not love does not know God, for God is love.

The greatest gift of God, wrote the apostle Paul to the Corinthians, is love (1 Cor. 13). Love expresses both God's nature and mission: God is love, and God shows that love for us in that while we were yet sinners Christ died for us (Rom. 5:8). To know God's love is more than intellectual assent; true knowing is always characterized by a life of love.

Jesus exemplifies this life of love. At the Passover Feast, he washes the feet of his disciples and then gives them a new commandment: Love one another (John 13:34). If we want to know the source of love, we look to God. If we want to see the expression of love, we look to Jesus. And if we want to know God, we practice love.

In Jesus Christ, God's love took human form. And in the lives of Christians, God's love continues to take human form. To know God is to love others. To withhold love from others is a sign that we do not know God. We often think of the stereotypical atheist as someone who, for intellectual reasons, has no place for God in his or her life. But might it be true that an atheist is a person for whom the love of God has not become a reality?

Whenever we separate belief from love, knowledge from action, faith from life, we miss the point. The greatest challenge to faith may not be intellectual but practical. Knowledge of God is always linked to love for one another.

PRAYER: Give me an integrated life, O God, a life of knowledge and a life of love, through Jesus Christ. Amen.

[‡]Pastor, Mount Tabor United Methodist Church, Winston-Salem, North Carolina; author.

No one has ever seen God; if we love one another, God lives in us, and his love is perfected in us.

Someone has noted that we are all from Missouri! In one way or another, we are all saying "show me!" We want to see, in order that we might believe. Yet the Christian faith, according to the Book of Hebrews, is "the assurance of things hoped for, the conviction of things not seen" (11:1).

Sometimes we have trouble seeing. Maybe our vision is out of focus. At times our obsession with what is right before us prevents our appreciation of the beauty that surrounds us. At other times we are distracted by all that swirls around us, so that we can't see the immediate and the obvious. We believe in God, even the unseen God, but our vision is a bit blurry.

First John begins with these words: "What we have heard, what we have seen with our eyes, what we have looked at and touched with our hands, concerning the word of life…" (1:1). The writer focuses on the practical, the tangible, the authentic.

For those in the far country and for those within the fellowship, for those who are lost and for those who are found, for those who doubt and for those who believe, there is good news in these words: We have never seen God, but this does not mean that God is invisible. God is always present in the lives of those who love. Our richest human experiences are gifts of God, glimpses of God, signs that God lives among us and is not finished with us. Our lives come into focus as we love one another, making the invisible visible.

PRAYER: Help me to see you today, Lord. And let others see your life in me, through Jesus Christ. Amen.

Do you understand what you are reading?...How can I, unless someone guides me?

Philip had met Jesus in Galilee and had responded to his invitation, "Follow me" (John 1:43). Much has happened since that encounter. Jesus the Messiah has taught the disciples, healed the sick, fed the multitudes, and proclaimed God's kingdom. He has opened the scriptures to those who will listen. He has seen in his own life the fulfillment of Isaiah's prophecy, and he has been crucified. His Resurrection has empowered his disciples to tell his story, and their movement has been further confirmed by the gift of God's Spirit, a gift so explosive that it begins to find receptivity among the Gentiles.

Philip, on his way from Jerusalem to Gaza, has another encounter. Philip sees an Ethiopian official reading the prophet Isaiah, and he, perhaps in amazement, asks the question, "Do you understand what you are reading?" The Ethiopian responds, "How can I, unless someone guides me?"

God speaks to us through the scriptures, but God also places us within communities and traditions that help us interpret them. Philip has been with Jesus the rabbi. He knows the life story of Jesus. He also knows the stories that shaped the life of Jesus. Philip also sees himself within the ongoing story of what Jesus is doing in the world. Jesus has commanded his disciples to make other disciples (Matt. 28), and Philip leads the Ethiopian eunuch into an experience of faith through baptism.

Sometimes an inner voice speaks to me in the silence and asks, "Do you understand what you are reading?" And I know that any understanding has come through guides, faithful men and women, past and present: Sunday school teachers, grandparents, preachers, professors, friends. Because of their guidance and instruction, I am part of the ongoing story of Jesus.

SUGGESTION FOR PRAYER: Give thanks for those who have guided you toward an understanding of the scriptures.

Those who say "I love God" and hate their brothers and sisters, are liars; for those who do not love a brother or sister whom they have seen, cannot love God whom they have not seen.

I sometimes think that loving God is easy compared to loving other people. Yet loving others is the test of our love for God: "We know that we have passed from death to life because we love one another" (1 John 3:14). It sometimes seems easy to love God, but what about that neighbor who gets on our nerves?

Here we move from the universal to the particular, from the abstract to the personal. We tend to think of love as a broad generalization that allows us to keep our distance from the cost of love. A brother may be in need of love, yet the demands of response to his particular situation can seem too great. A sister who seems undeserving of love may tempt us to judge or withdraw. While love in the abstract can be sentimental and even idyllic, love in practice is always specific and costly.

In life experiences of disappointment, betrayal, and frustration, we may find it difficult to love the specific persons involved. Sometimes these difficult persons are also people of faith with whom we find ourselves worshiping and serving. Love can require much of us, even within the household of faith.

Yet we number ourselves among those who are loved despite the very faults we see in others. "In this is love," John writes, "not that we loved God but that [God] loved us and sent [the] Son to be the atoning sacrifice for our sins" (4:10). This is the cost of God's love for us. We grasp the depth of that love as we consider the cross, a stumbling block because of its particularity. And because God loves us, in costly and specific ways, we love one another.

PRAYER: O God, help me to find some tangible way to express my love for you today. Amen.

For dominion belongs to the Lord, and he rules over the nations. Posterity will serve him; future generations will be told about the Lord.

Psalm 22 is best known as the source of some of Jesus' last words: "My God, my God, why have you forsaken me?" (Ps. 22:1). Though these words express his sense of abandonment, they also represent an affirmation of faith. In his dying moments Jesus speaks to God, quoting the scriptures, crying out for help. The psalm is an honest and graphic testament to the devastation of suffering; yet the experience of pain is transformed into praise.

God's people have always viewed suffering through the lens of faith. We know that our ancestors experienced persecution and affliction and that God delivered them and led them to freedom. We also believe that God will be praised by those who will come after us, who will also bear witness to the mighty deeds of the Lord.

We all experience some measure of suffering in this life's journey. While each person's suffering is unique, our common experience can be read against the background of this psalm. We name the suffering, and we cry out to God. Here Jesus serves as our model: Our crucified Lord, without sin, bears witness to his pain and his hope. We offer in response our faith and trust. The apostle Paul wrote to the Romans, "I consider that the sufferings of this present time are not worth comparing with the glory about to be revealed to us" (8:18).

Some of our favorite hymns, many of them based upon the psalms, are affirmations of faith in the midst of great difficulty. The good news is that suffering can be redemptive. In the depths of despair we give praise to God, our help in ages past, our hope for years to come.

PRAYER: O God, I will praise you, even in the midst of pain. Amen.

I am the vine, you are the branches.

The imagery of the vine and the branches is one of connection, life and growth, portraying a life rooted in Christ, our beginning point. While there is no one way to discover Christ or meet Christ or receive Christ or accept Christ, there is an essential need for connection to Christ. One of Paul's favorite ways to describe faith is through his use of the phrase *in Christ*: "If anyone is in Christ, there is a new creation: everything old has passed away; see, everything has become new" (2 Cor. 5:17).

Once we lived in a vital connection with the earth. If we worked the ground, cared for the soil, nurtured growth, and supported the vocation of farming, we were blessed with the fruits of the earth. Now we fill our carts with produce and meats and canned goods and beverages. Our plastic cards are placed on scanners, and we have daily bread. If floods come or an ecological disaster or famine strikes, another market is found. There is no longer a vital, visible connection between what blossoms from the earth and what feeds and sustains us.

The vine nourishes the branches and is essential to the growth and life of the branches. In the same way, a relationship with Christ is at the heart of our lives. We draw strength from this relationship as we pray, as we read the scriptures, as we follow him in our daily lives. A relationship with Christ is not a status symbol. Rather, to live "in Christ" is to be a part of a dynamic process of growth. That was, after all, the divine intention: "I came," Jesus said, "that they may have life, and have it abundantly" (John 10:10).

PRAYER: Lord Jesus Christ, you are the way, the truth, the life. Sustain me in all that happens today. Amen.

Those who abide in me and I in them bear much fruit, because apart from me you can do nothing.

We are strong. At least we think we are strong. We like to be in control and at the center. Maybe being strong is about survival, about perseverance, about doing what needs to be done.

But at times we realize that our strength is less than believed; we are not in control. We realize that our center resides not in God but in self. When the illusion of our strength is made plain, we acknowledge our weakness and our need to live by faith. When the illusion of our control becomes apparent, we acknowledge our uncertainty and our need to live by hope. When the illusion of our being at the center of all things is before us, we acknowledge our pride and our need to live by love.

Jesus says, "I am the vine, you are the branches...apart from me you can do nothing." In stark contrast to self-sufficiency or self-help, the Christian life assumes our need for God. To acknowledge Christ as our Savior is to admit our limitations, our failures, our incompleteness, our brokenness.

The good news is that our need for One who can forgive, complete, and save is met, prior to our asking, by God's offer of grace through Jesus Christ. He feeds us with bread, his body. He nourishes us with the cup, his blood. He sustains us with the reminder that both convicts and comforts: "Apart from me you can do nothing."

PRAYER: When I am weak, O God, remind me that you are strong. Keep me connected to your power and presence, through Jesus Christ. Amen.

Join the Club!

May 19–25, 2003 • *Susan Passi-Klaus[‡]*

MONDAY, MAY 19 • **Read Acts 10:44-48**

As a child I loved starting clubs. Whether it was a fan club of Elvis devotees, a gang of girls who shared a crush on the same sixth-grade heartthrob, or a clique filled with kindred spirits, I enjoyed belonging to the chosen few. Whatever the bond that brought club members together, an inevitable problem arose when someone left out of the club wanted "in." Folded notes passed between desks; whispered opinions crossed behind backs; and tallied votes mounted—in or out?

Now that I'm an adult, I don't play those kinds of games—or do I? What groups or activities I am part of exclude others? a country club? a circle of friends? a neighborhood? a private school? a selective social event? Childhood lessons might have taught us the importance of accepting and including others unconditionally. Yet how often as adults do we silently delight in our membership status among the chosen few?

God has a club called the Good News Club. Regular meetings of members convene anywhere people gather in God's name, and all are welcome. God's club labels no one as unworthy, unpopular, or unlikely. Good News Club members know that God's love is not solely possessed by insiders. As Peter learned through the baptism of Cornelius (Acts 10:1-33), God's clubhouse doors swing open to all. God says, "Come and join this club of believers. Come and follow me."

SUGGESTION FOR MEDITATION: Which clubs would I resign from in order to walk the talk? How can I include in my life today someone who feels excluded? How can I welcome others to join God's Good News Club?

[‡]Freelance writer; author and publisher of an inspirational newsletter for women, Brentwood, Tennessee.

As much as I hate to admit it, some of the best teachers of life's lessons have been the people who tested me most. Though my father and I were often at odds, our emotional wrestling matches taught me to turn weakness into strength. And though at times I may have felt misunderstood by those in authority, their rejections inspired me—even dared me—to discover my true talents and calling. And though I have often envied others who appeared to be getting a bigger, tastier piece of life's pie, watching God work through their lives enabled me to see the divine at work in my life as well.

I once attended a lecture by best-selling author M. Scott Peck. Discussing his book *The Road Less Traveled*, Peck talked about the importance of tension in relationships. I understood him to say that the pulling and tugging between human wills, the working through and working out of problems, and the bending and straining to find compromise and balance are necessary for growth. Creative and loving tension is also valuable in our relationships with fellow Christians.

The unlikely connection between Peter, a Jewish Christian teacher, and Cornelius, a Gentile Christian convert (Acts 10:1-33), is yet another lesson in God's use of tension as a spiritual tool. What could the two men have had in common? What gifts could they have shared with each other? What part did each play in helping the other grow closer to God? Peter spoke, and the Holy Spirit fell upon all who heard him. God used the differences—the tensions between Jews and Gentiles, circumcised and uncircumcised—to redefine spiritual boundaries. Peter and Cornelius found a similar end: a unity through blessed tension in the oneness of Jesus Christ.

SUGGESTION FOR MEDITATION: **What lessons have you learned by experiencing tension between yourself and members of your Christian family?**

I have to admit I'm not a big *praiser*. Despite all the attention I try to pay to my Higher Power, I seem to fall short in the spiritual puffery and plaudits department. Sure, I've been known to shout—but rarely for joy. If I clap my hands, it's usually because I liked a performance; and when I sing out, it's for amusement, not adulation. So when it comes to expressing my love for God and my gratitude for God's blessings, I rarely do it with lyres and horns. Often a simple, silent *thank you* is all I can muster.

Perhaps I hold back lest I appear too emotive or theatrical in my expression of faith. Does God really want me to let loose with laudations? I've seen others do it on television. They sway with their hands in the air, and their voices fill sanctuaries with rowdy alleluias and amens. I admit that I usually dismiss these folks as too showy and then think to myself, "I'm glad my congregation is more reserved—though no less devout."

But when I begin to think of all the praise I need as a human being for everything from a job well done to my striking appearance on a special occasion, I wonder why I have a hard time giving God due enthusiasm. After all, as Psalm 98 touts, God has done "wonderful deeds," has created this intricate and awesome world. The Almighty has authored a best-selling plan and has provided unlimited care and love to the creation. For heaven's sake, God certainly deserves more than a pat on the back. God deserves a joyful symphony—and oh, so much more!

So today as I look out my office window into a beautiful world filled with spring's blessings, I'm going to raise my voice above a private thank you and shout, "Well done, Lord! Alleluia! I join all living things in thanking you for your gift of life! I love you, Lord! Amen!"

SUGGESTION FOR MEDITATION: **Let loose with your praise for God today. Don't hold back from giving the credit God is due.**

As much as I love my young daughter, she is not the child I would have chosen if I had had a say in the matter. She is stubborn beyond description. She is pugnacious and sloppy. Though some say she is her mother's daughter, I don't often see the resemblance—except when she is overdramatizing or debating. If the dark truth be told, I expected God to deliver something much different via the stork: something tidier, meeker, and more pliable. As the years continue to reveal the divine plan both for my daughter and me, I'm sure I'll more fully understand why God gave me the child I needed instead of the daughter I thought I ordered.

I wonder if it isn't the same way in God's larger family; God does the pickin' and choosin', and it's up to us to do the loving. Sure, maybe we'd like our Christian brothers and sisters to shape up, be more of this and less of that; to fit an image or fill a void in our lives; to think and act more like we do, but that's not the way God designed it.

Though our differences may outweigh our similarities, our Christian family is bound together by a love for our Creator and the diversity of God's creation. As with many families, our heavenly household may make loving our brothers and sisters in Christ seem like a chore. It's then that we must look at one another through God's eyes, see the greater good, and willingly perform labors of love—not to meet our own expectations but to fulfill God's anticipations.

SUGGESTION FOR MEDITATION: Think about the families God has given to you: both earthly and divine. What issues divide your family of believers? What judgments have you made about your brothers and sisters, parents and children that separate you from your Father/Mother God?

Ever had a song you just can't get out of your head? As I studied these verses in First John, the lyrics to Lynn Anderson's country song repeated continually in my musical memory bank: *I beg your pardon; I never promised you a rose garden.* The song goes on to remind us that with the sunshine we also get rain. I can just imagine God humming along.

The spirit of the song reminds me that although God has promised us a new life in Christ—a transforming experience—we have received no guarantee that practicing what Jesus preached will be easy. In fact, he said the load we carry will be darned heavy and will require self-discipline and hard work on our part. Early on Jesus gave us a grace-full "heads up," so we'd know not to expect immediate results. Nor should we expect the results we assume we have earned and rightly deserve.

How often do we react in this way: "I beg your pardon, God, but didn't you promise happy endings if I was good and followed you? Didn't you say you'd save me from punishment, free me from fear, love away my problems, and give me everything I need to survive being human? God, why didn't you make it a little clearer in the beginning that living life as one of your followers wasn't going to be a piece of cake, a stroll in the park, a downhill ride—or a rose garden, for that matter?"

The truth is that God tells it the way it is. Life is a struggle. And though the bumper sticker may at hard times tell part of the story—"Life's a bummer, and then you die"—it omits the real truth, the whole truth. It doesn't convey God's promise to us: We are not alone. We may at times be burdened by the service our faith requires of us, but Christ can be trusted to help us when the road looks long and the load becomes too heavy. The writer of First John reminds us that living faithfully is "not burdensome."

SUGGESTION FOR MEDITATION: During times of trial and doubt, how have you experienced God's presence with you?

The writer of First John states essentially that loving God means keeping God's commandments, and really that isn't difficult. Excuse me? Whom is he trying to kid? I don't know about you, but for me, following God's rules is easier said than done.

After all, what does this writer know about today's challenges—everything from drugs and date rape to road rage and reality TV? Keeping God's commandments during times of financial temptation, terrorist threat, and terminal diseases—how does the writer expect us to carry those kinds of burdens without falling to our knees?

Perhaps that's it, I remind myself. *It's on my knees that God wants to find me. God doesn't expect me to carry the load alone. By accepting God's outstretched hand, it becomes easier, though not effortless, to rise to my feet and continue my human journey on the Divine's behalf.*

I have an eating disorder. While in treatment for bulimia, I cried one day as I sat and talked with my therapist. "What's wrong with me?" I pouted. "I'm smart, attractive, successful, popular with my peers; yet I cannot seem to control such a simple thing as the amount of food I put into my mouth." My therapist responded with "words from God" that I will never forget: "Susan, your need for control is so great, your defenses so complex, your will so strong that perhaps this is the circumstance in which you will allow God to work in you. Without this burden you might never have realized how much you need your Higher Power and how much your Higher Power needs you."

Since then I have come to welcome "knee time" as an opportunity for spiritual growth. My problems are no fewer, and keeping God's commandments is no easier. What has changed is that I live through each crisis, each challenge, and each day knowing that when I am on my knees, God will lift me up. I am not alone.

SUGGESTION FOR MEDITATION: What circumstances bring you to your knees for God's use?

I'm a little confused. In today's slice of scripture Jesus doesn't refer to himself as my Lord or my Master; instead he calls *me* his friend. Jesus thinks of me as a friend? The very thought rocks my theological resignation.

I wonder if Jesus knows my reputation for poor relationship maintenance: the birthdays I forget, the calls I never return, the lunch invitations I turn down because I'm too busy. Does he know what a terrible listener I can be? Does he know how often I neglect to send thank-you notes? *Surely he doesn't want me for a buddy*, I think to myself.

I'm so much more comfortable being Jesus' servant. It's easier—cut and dried. He's the boss, and I'm the flunky. I can clock in and then clock out of our obligatory relationship. It's just 9 to 5, and all I have to do is follow orders: Love thy neighbor. Thou shalt not kill. Thou shalt not miss church on Sunday mornings.

But make me a friend, and I become a volunteer in the relationship. I put myself at Jesus' disposal because I desire to. I perform without being asked. I love without invitation. I obey out of choice. I communicate out of longing. I sacrifice out of love. Just as Jesus does for me.

My, my, how friendship changes things. Church becomes community, not just a place. Prayer becomes conversation, not just confession. God becomes tangible, not invisible. Our lives become intertwined, instead of separate. We become companions. We become collaborators, helpmates, and confidantes.

Imagine that…Jesus calls me, calls you, a friend.

SUGGESTION FOR MEDITATION: What a friend we have in Jesus, all our sins and griefs to bear! What a privilege to carry everything to God in prayer! O what peace we often forfeit, O what needless pain we bear, all because we do not carry everything to God in prayer.

My Joy Made Complete

May 26–June 1, 2003 • *Hilly Hicks*[‡]

MONDAY, MAY 26 • **Read Acts 1:15-17**

"Peter stood up." I wish the Bible editors had added an exclamation point for special emphasis. That Peter was there in Jerusalem and able to stand up at all was a major moment in religious history and an event worth celebrating by every Christian.

At the Last Supper Jesus had predicted that one of the disciples would betray him and that another would deny him. Peter said, "Lord, I am ready to go with you to prison and to death!" (Luke 22:33). Only a short time later, Peter shamed himself by denying Jesus while Jesus stood trial. Peter left the scene weeping bitterly, his heart torn asunder.

But now we find Peter in Jerusalem, still among the apostles, and not only "among" them but rising to address them as their leader. What happened in those intervening days that gave Peter the courage and confidence to speak as Christ's representative? What mended that terribly broken heart? What enabled him to make such a dramatic comeback?

The Peter who stood before the crowd in Jerusalem and spoke that day was a changed person. He had been with the risen Christ. When we enter the presence of the Savior, we experience his grace, love, forgiveness, and renewal. God's grace can make an apostle out of a tax collector, a "rock" and cornerstone for the church out of a spineless coward, and whatever God wants to make out of you and me in spite of our weaknesses and failures.

PRAYER: Lord God, you can mend broken hearts and warm cold ones. Grant that we might so enter your presence that we will be changed...forever. Amen.

[‡]Producer for United Methodist Communications; ordained American Baptist clergy; member of Hillcrest United Methodist Church, Nashville, Tennessee.

Today's passage records the first ever episcopal election. The candidates Justus and Matthias have equally good credentials. Both have closely followed Jesus' career from the beginning. The fact that each is put forth as a candidate indicates the high regard and esteem in which they are held; both deemed worthy of joining the elite group of Christ's apostles.

Whenever we seek leaders for business or church, we are likely to be found poring over resumes and letters of recommendation. Yet in recent times we have seen persons elevated to high positions who were later discovered to have falsified their academic or professional records. Clearly the criteria that we human beings use to choose our leaders are imperfect and subject to abuse.

When choosing our personal associates, we are sometimes guilty of using the same rather foolish standards of judgment. We consider someone a worthy candidate for marriage because of wealth, position, or sheer physical attractiveness. These standards have been known to deceive men and women throughout the ages, yet we still make this critical mistake.

The best friend is not always the most popular and attractive one. I have a dear friend whom I thought at first to be a little weird. His mannerisms were idiosyncratic, and to look at him—well he just didn't look like somebody with whom I would have much in common. But God moved in both our hearts and led us to begin having lunch with each other on a regular basis. During those lunches we have shared so much about life. And in so many ways he has encouraged and supported me. He has warmed my heart when I have felt low. And today I feel a love for him as if he were my own sibling.

PRAYER: Lord, you are the one who does not read resumés but reads hearts. Guide us to read hearts whenever we exercise the privilege of choice. Amen.

My wife and I enjoy having guests—but for a very selfish reason: We use their visits as an excuse (or perhaps I should say as a motivation) to give the house a good cleaning. Something about the anticipation of guests makes you clean up.

When Jesus comes into our hearts and takes up residence there, we must honor and respect his presence. A powerful new drive within us wants everything to be different from before. In at least three ways we are called to be different in light of this presence:

1. Keep it clean.
"Your body is a temple of the Holy Spirit within you, which you have from God" (1 Cor. 6:19). God's spirit demands the respect of a clean heart and mind. There can be no place made for sin. No evil thoughts can be shoved into a closet or back room. When the Holy Spirit comes in, every part of us is in view. So we must make a clean sweep of the place if we are to entertain the Holy Spirit.

2. Listen and obey.
The responsibility of setting our inner house in order and making it an acceptable dwelling for the Spirit is not ours alone. God takes the lead. All that we must do is yield with our whole heart and do our best to follow God's lead, whose purpose is to save us and make us fit company for paradise. We cannot do that alone.

3. Relax and be confident.
The writer of First John seeks to reassure his readers that they have already been given the gift of eternal life. The presence of the Spirit within us is the best proof or "testimony" to that fact.

The message therefore is to relax and be confident in Jesus. Your victory and salvation are already won!

PRAYER: Spirit of the living God, help me to honor your presence within me today. Amen.

The text from Acts reminds us that our Lord gave instructions. Jesus was a teacher not just in the intellectual, classroom sense. Instruction given in a classroom always has a kind of optional sense to it. But Christ's instructions are of a more serious and urgent order. His instructions more often resemble commands. So the model for our service in Christ is not the student, either in the classroom or at the feet of the guru.

The better image for us may be one of a Christian mission team poised to dispense humanitarian aid to the world. To be sure, this is an all-volunteer group. We have not been conscripted. Nevertheless, by agreeing to serve, we agree to surrender our autonomy and even our very will to the one in whom we have complete trust and confidence.

Thus "the apostles gathered around Jesus and told him all that they had done and taught" (Mark 6:30, NIV). At the end of every day we too ought to report to Jesus on what we have done over the course of the day to carry out his instructions. At the beginning of the day, therefore, we must be intentionally focus on our mission. If we are prayerful, we will receive an infusion of the Holy Spirit that empowers, guides, and teaches us in all things. We have been instructed to go and make disciples of all nations. We do that not by violence and coercion but by bringing light into the world. "Why do you stand looking up toward heaven?"

PRAYER: Lord, let us go forth in Jesus' name, taking every instruction of his as our marching orders, so that at the end of this day we will bring to him a good report. Amen.

When Internet technology first came on the scene, it was hailed as the "information superhighway." Now we know why. At the click of a mouse, information and advice on any subject are right at hand. But with the good has also come the bad. As this information floods into our homes, we may become the victims of misinformation, consumerism, fraud, and hate mongering.

With two teenage daughters in the house, my wife and I have struggled to guide them in their use of the Internet. We have tried to teach them that not all information is good, that everything that is good *to* you is not good *for* you.

Information is key to making us what we are. It comes to us from the outside but forms us on the inside. "In-forming," then, is the process of forming the inner content of the heart and mind. These days "the counsel of the wicked" comes streaming in through the Internet, television, radio, psychic readings, advertising and so on; its aim is the heart and mind.

The psalmist teaches us that the path to happiness involves two things: first, screening out information and advice that tend to lead us away from God. We must watch our spiritual diet with the same diligence that we watch our physical diet. "Keep your heart with all vigilance," says the writer of Proverbs, "for from it flow the springs of life" (Prov. 4:23).

And second, we must discover the "delight" of meditating on God. This activity of the mind and heart produces peace and well-being, helping us navigate the Internet and life in a healthy and prosperous way.

PRAYER: **Lord, be our guide through the confusing complexities of life. Amen.**

In 1992 I traveled to Zimbabwe in South Africa on assignment for United Methodist Communications. Zimbabwe had experienced a terrible drought that year. All along the highway from Bulawayo to Wange, my companions and I saw the devastating results of the lack of rain: the dusty, dried-out fields containing no vegetation, the carcasses of thousands of livestock strewn across the countryside.

However, when we reached the legendary Victoria Falls, I saw an incredible sight. The forest in the immediate vicinity was as luxuriously verdant and lush as anything I had ever seen. I soon learned the reason: The natural spray from the Zambezi River, as it plunges over the deep cliffs of the falls, literally creates a constant "rain" or mist over the area. The result is spectacular foliage.

The presence of that luxuriant rain forest in the midst of such a devastating drought was both shocking and revelatory. Sometimes we too live in the midst of drought, not a drought of water but a drought of compassion, understanding, and love—a drought of the heart. And that inner drought leaves us as thirsty and hopeless as the bony farm animals on the side of the road in Zimbabwe.

The miracle we experience is that even in the midst of a drought God can supply our every need. God ministers to our drought-weary hearts through a song, the kind words of a friend, an unexpected telephone call, or a note sent in the mail. When we are planted and rooted in God, we are in the flow of God's loving spirit. We even become part of the stream ourselves, flowing and nurturing others. By those ever-flowing streams we and others are bathed in the refreshing spray of God's love and care.

PRAYER: Lord, help me to find your life-giving water today. Amen.

As kids we used to sing, "Lord I want to be a Christian in my heart, in my heart." I always thought it was a depressing song—conjuring up images of condemned people slowly marching out to meet some terrible fate. We might also hear the prayer in John 17 in such a negative way. It speaks of being "hated" by the world and the need for protection and sanctification.

Do we really want to be sanctified? There are a lot of cool things about the world. Do we want to be permanently set apart from it in order to be holy? At times I understand why Saint Augustine prayed, "O Lord, help me to be pure, but not yet."

We must overcome this dilemma. Two things can lead us to make a complete commitment to Christ: a history and a future. Our history must revolve around an encounter with Jesus. Have you been lost in despair, totally without hope? I have. From time to time I think back on that experience and on how I prayed to God for help. Then I remember how often I have been rescued and restored. Such a savior is worthy of my highest praise and my most complete devotion.

We are also strengthened by reflecting on our future with Christ. My mother used to say, "There is joy in serving a true and living God." Jesus once compared the kingdom of God to a "treasure hidden in a field. When a man found it, he hid it again, and then in his joy went and sold all he had and bought that field" (Matt. 13:44, NIV).

In today's reading Jesus expresses his great desire for us: "I am coming to you, and I speak these things in the world so that they may have my joy made complete in themselves." The joy that the Lord has promised is worth sacrifice. This is the joy of being fully actualized, fully accepted, and fully committed. I want to be a Christian in my heart.

PRAYER: God, today help me be grateful for your faithfulness and for the joy you give us. Amen.

Breathe, O Breathe Thy Loving Spirit

June 2–8, 2003 • *Blair Gilmer Meeks*[‡]

MONDAY, JUNE 2 • Read Acts 2:1-4

"They were all together in one place." "All of them were filled with the Holy Spirit." Not one person alone. Not a few scattered disciples. All of them. All together.

But who are "they"? Acts 1 lists names: Peter, John, other familiar disciples, "together with certain women, including Mary the mother of Jesus." They waited as Jesus told them, constantly devoting themselves to prayer (Acts 1:14).

A few years ago my theater group decided to revive an old play about Jesus' family, and I thought about taking the role of Mary. The final scene takes place in Mary's home years after Easter; and in the playwright's mind, everything has returned to normal. Mary had a son who died in strange circumstances and that's it. She's sad sometimes; but she has grandchildren now, and she doesn't know why people still talk about that son.

I found I didn't want to play this Mary. It's not the Mary I know from scripture, who sings, "My spirit rejoices in God my Savior" (Luke 1:47). She was there—at the crucifixion and at Pentecost. She knew that Jesus rose and ascended. If Mary had been alone then, she might have dismissed the talk. But she was with the others—praying—ready for the coming of the Spirit with a mighty rush of wind and fire.

A medieval carving in a German church provides an image for Pentecost: the disciples, including Mary, pray together as tongues as of fire rest on each one. When we gather to pray and work for God's reign, we are ready to receive God's gift of the Spirit falling afresh on us all.

PRAYER: God of light and fire, unite me with your gathered people everywhere and prepare me to receive your Spirit. Amen.

[‡]Writer and teacher in the area of worship; author of a new book of prayers for the grieving; Brentwood, Tennessee.

My family once had neighbors whose native language was Slovak. I had never heard Slovak until we invited them to dinner, and the husband translated the conversation for his wife, who spoke no English. I wanted to talk to her directly. She also spoke Czech, but that was no better. I offered to help her shop for groceries, and we discovered that we both spoke German. That was a breakthrough. Despite my limitations we managed to communicate, and she left the store with a full cart.

Listening to the babble of languages the foreigners spoke in Jerusalem must have been like listening to my neighbors speak Slovak—completely unintelligible. When people around you don't speak your language, eventually you stop listening. The problem isn't just with foreign languages. When my sons talk computers, I tune them out as soon as they get past my elementary understanding. But how many conflicts could be resolved if each side refused to tune the other out—and only listened?

One gift of Pentecost is the miracle of hearing: "In our own languages we hear them speaking about God's deeds of power." Pentecost opened the ears of the crowd in Jerusalem. Observers were amazed at this occurrence and began to search for explanations. Peter laughed at the idea that Jesus' followers, who had spent the morning praying, could be accused of drunkenness. Filled with the Spirit, he proclaimed "the coming of the Lord's great and glorious day."

Peter preached that the Holy Spirit breaks down other barriers too. Barriers of age, gender, and economic class come down when God's Spirit leads young and old, women and men, slave and free to dream dreams, see visions, and prophesy together.

PRAYER: **God of all peoples, teach me to listen to those I meet. Open me to their needs, their joys, their sorrows so that I may receive your word. In Jesus' name. Amen.**

One day at the beach I watched two little girls dance their *pas de deux* with the waves. As their toes touched the water they squealed with delight and then backed off. Olga, the older one, was graceful and serene. Tiki was small as a sandpiper, skittering in and out with the foam. Olga urged Tiki to come play in the swells, but Tiki kept retreating to the warmth of the sand. Their mother pointed to dolphins cavorting beyond the breakers: gleaming arched bodies suspended above sun-polished waves.

The sea holds the possibility of elemental fear and exhilaration. Even we occasional beachgoers relearn each time we reach the shore the thrill of catching a wave at the right moment, letting go to cold panic as the water hits, swirling through chaos, and finally sliding over slick sand to safety. Today's psalm uses our fascination with the sea to call us to enter with our whole being into praise of God, who sends forth the Spirit to create and renew all things, "both small and great."

God's glory is greater and wider than the sea, yet God enjoys the sea creature's sport. We feel God's power like pounding waves; the earth trembles and mountains smoke. When God's face seems hidden, we are dismayed; but then God's hand opens before us, and we find it filled with good things. For this "I will sing to the LORD, as long as I live."

When I left the beach, Tiki was in the ocean, fearlessly jumping at waves as tall as she. Olga lay on the sand, wrapped in a towel—self-assured and peaceful, at home in her mother's care.

PRAYER: God of winds and waves, I pray that my meditation will please you. Teach me to sing your praise, to rejoice in you as you rejoice in all your works. In Jesus' name. Amen.

My friend who has seven children says she has two who are "homegrown" and five "exotic imports." She knows well that having children is hard. With two she groaned "in labor," and with five she experienced the painful ins and outs of the adoption process. Paul writes that God knows all about the anguish and joy of having children, for God loves us and wants to adopt us and make us heirs. Adopted children learn that they are special because they were chosen, and we know that God redeems us and chooses us for adoption.

We often think of adoption as an event in the life of one family with the parents and child at the center. But Paul sees our adoption by God as a cosmic event with the whole of creation "groaning in labor pains." With today's problems of pollution and the wasting of natural resources, it's not hard to imagine creation's groaning. We know that God intends the redemption of all creation. God loves the whole world enough to send God's only son to save it.

Waiting for adoption is an agonizing process for all concerned. The children experience pain too, especially the ones who may have to wait for a long time. But Paul says when we "groan inwardly," awaiting the fullness of God's adoption, we already have the "first fruits of the Spirit." While we wait, the Spirit brings hope, and hope teaches us to wait with patience.

Isaiah heard God say this about our redemption: "Do not fear, . . . I have called you by name, you are mine" (Isa. 43:1). These words are music to the ears of God's adopted children.

PRAYER: God of life-giving streams, you brought me through the waters and breathed into me your Spirit. I am thankful today in remembrance of my baptism. In the name of your son. Amen.

I heard a Lutheran pastor interviewed on the radio shortly after TWA Flight 800 went down in July 1996. The high school French Club in the pastor's town had been on that plane. The interviewer asked what the pastor could say to her congregation after such an unthinkable loss. The pastor agreed that there were no adequate words, but she would take as her text Romans 8:26, which reads, "That very Spirit intercedes with sighs too deep for words." There are times when we cannot even pray, but the Spirit intercedes for us.

Paul suggests that even in ordinary circumstances "we do not know how to pray as we ought." We sometimes forget that we pray always with others, mindful of God's love for all humankind. But the Spirit knows how to pray, and God knows "the mind of the Spirit." The spiritual says it clearly: "Every time I feel the Spirit moving in my heart, I will pray." The key is that the Spirit intercedes for us "according to the will of God." We may not always turn ourselves to God's will as we ought, but we know the Spirit can turn us so that we face God.

In the Holy Spirit we have a friend who knows us intimately, searches our hearts, and is concerned for every aspect of our well-being. We also know that this same Spirit groans with creation, longs for the health of all human beings, and knows God's will for saving the world. The Spirit sighs with us and helps us wait on God in this moment where we have the first joys—the appetizer—but not yet the full feast of God's new creation.

PRAYER: God of words and sighs, send your Spirit that I may pray as I ought and present my life as living prayer for those who hunger for your care. In the name of Jesus. Amen.

When our son John was sixteen, he was asked to give the children's sermon on Youth Sunday. The scripture chosen by the planners included John 15:26. While intrigued, John couldn't figure out how to use the image of "Advocate" with children. I told him that older translations used the word *Comforter* instead. John grinned and said, "You mean like the blue comforter on my bed?" I couldn't guess where he was going with that idea.

John's imagination jumped from his blue comforter to an earlier source of comfort: his security blanket. He told the children that when he was small and his parents left him in the care of a baby-sitter, the only thing that made him remember their promise to come back was the familiar feel of the well-worn blanket, given to him when he was a baby by someone who loved him.

No image, of course, is adequate for children or adults to convey the workings of the Spirit, but my son did understand what Jesus was saying to the frightened disciples: "Now I am going to him who sent me....But because I have said these things to you, sorrow has filled your hearts....But if I go, I will send [the Advocate] to you" (John 16:5-7). When someone we love and depend on goes away, as Jesus did, the emptiness is so painful we need comfort, and God sends it in the presence of the Holy Spirit.

The Spirit of truth is our security and comfort but also our Advocate, who calls into question what passes for righteousness and justice and who stands up for us in the face of adversity and loneliness.

PRAYER: God of hope, you are my very present help. Be with me now; give me courage to work for your justice and share the love of Jesus, in whose name I pray. Amen.

Our family once visited Mammoth Cave on vacation. We had small children, so we chose the self-guided short tour. Suddenly, just when we got to the deepest part of our walk, the power supply failed, leaving the four of us standing completely alone in utter darkness. At least it seemed that we were alone, until, very quickly, we saw the steady light of a good lantern coming toward us. A ranger, a woman with lovely long, brown hair, appeared out of the dark to gather a group of frightened tourists and guide us out of the cave. She led the way cheerfully, teaching us about our surroundings as we walked. A few weeks later our four-year-old Douglas told a friend that we had been lost in a dark cave, but an angel came to lead us out; and we weren't afraid any more.

Today's verses come from a section of John sometimes called Jesus' farewell discourse, beginning with John 14:1: "Do not let your hearts be troubled." This theme runs throughout. The community of believers shouldn't be afraid about the future, not just because things will be better by and by, but because Jesus promises to send the Spirit to be with us now. The Spirit's presence emboldens us to live out Jesus' teachings every day. "I need thee every hour," the old hymn declares. "Teach me thy will; and thy rich promises in me fulfill."

The Holy Spirit, for all its mystery and power, has a specific task: to be our guide, to teach us the way. Jesus, our way, our truth, our life, sends the life-giving presence of the Spirit of truth to be our constant companion on the way.

Prayer: God of love, teach me to follow Jesus' way. Send afresh your Spirit that I may show your love in the world your son came to save. In his name. Amen.

Three Aspects of God

June 9–15, 2003 • Alec Gilmore[‡]

MONDAY, JUNE 9 • Read Isaiah 6:1-8

A call without coercion

Some things we instinctively feel to be right regardless of training or culture—like returning love to those who love us or forgiving those who have forgiven us. We may not always do it, but we could never argue against it.

Other things we instinctively know we have to do. Mostly we know we are in control; free will is all-pervading, but every now and then we encounter a set of circumstances from which we feel we have no escape. We know we must. We cannot explain why to ourselves or to others. Something inside tells us.

This is where Isaiah finds himself. A believer with a profound sense of an awesome, all-demanding God, Isaiah's prayer time today is different. Everything around him remains the same, but he senses a fresh voice, a new urge, and a definite challenge. The details don't matter.

Our circumstances are not Isaiah's. What matters is that he finds himself in a situation where he cannot say no. That is "a call"—the moment when we know we cannot say no, but we do still have to say yes. Answering God's call entails a conscious commitment, never coercion.

What holds Isaiah back is his unworthiness. He knows he just hasn't got it in him. He can easily say yes, but he can't deliver. Then he realizes that if the call is right, God will cleanse him of his inadequacy. When he responds, new doors begin to open.

PRAYER: Father, when I sense the call that can only come from you, give me the courage to respond and what it takes to follow through. Amen.

[‡]Baptist minister, writer and lecturer; Chaplain Emeritus, Sussex, England.

The uncontrollable is in control

Underlying this psalm is the fear of the uncontrollable. The Jews always feared that the chaos of the waters would disrupt the harmony of creation, and verses 3-9 read like a thunderstorm coming up from the Mediterranean and thrashing around Lebanon.

Some scholars suggest this is an ancient Canaanite psalm (depicting an ancient storm-god), adopted by the Jews who added their own touches, much as Christians have often adapted secular poetry and music. Verse 8, for example, seems to refer to Sinai, Kadesh lies en route from Egypt to Palestine. "Thunder" (meaning "voice"), "god of storm" and "sons of God" (all Canaanite forms) become "the voice of the LORD," "Yahweh," and "heavenly beings."

The psalmist sees that the uncontrollable powers we often fear are always under the controlling power of God, and for the Jews the God whom the Canaanites feared is the God who is all-powerful and in control.

This understanding came as a direct result of the people's experience. They had seen it all before—a God who cared for God's people, even in their slavery, and exerted power over their enemies (whether harsh rulers like Pharaoh or rival communities like the Canaanites). This God controlled nature (the Red Sea and the Jordan) and the elements.

This God is a great God. Fear, threats to our humanity and civilization, and many forces and events over which we have no control lead us to desire a big and powerful God—not just a deliverer or a savior of the people but a God of the universe, Creator and Liberator.

SUGGESTION FOR MEDITATION: **Isolate one or two of "the uncontrollables" in your life. Recall the experiences that have led you to feel that what is beyond your control is not beyond God's control.**

One with us

We come to Romans and experience the Son, the second person of the Trinity, as well as the work of the Spirit. God's mighty power and presence become fully human in the Son who shares our sufferings and fears and offers healing, comfort, and support to those in need. We may find the God of Isaiah and the psalmist hard to relate to. But Romans affirms that Jesus is one with us; we are joint heirs with Christ.

We cannot deny God's Fatherhood, but we do have to say yes if we are to become God's children and enjoy the benefits of this parental relationship. We say yes when we choose to live "by the Spirit" rather than "according to the flesh."

If we live "according to the flesh," we live without regard for God; symptoms include indifference or contempt for people (God's children), disregard for all values except our own, arrogance over nature, and a feeling of our ultimate control over the universe. Living "by the Spirit" indicates an awareness of awe and respect for everybody and everything, recognizing that the ultimate forces, powers, and values still lie above and beyond our control.

One sign of our acknowledgment (our yes to this relationship) is our readiness to say, "Abba" (Father). At that point the Spirit without and the spirit within bear witness to the fact that we are children of God, which gives us the incentive to live as if we are indeed brothers and sisters of Christ.

The test of our commitment comes in our suffering, because if we behave like God's children (as Jesus did) there is no alternative to sharing in suffering (as Jesus did). Therefore, we might read verse 17 as follows: "If, as is the case, we suffer...we may also be glorified," where the glory is the suffering and not something that comes after it like a reward.

SUGGESTION FOR MEDITATION: If God is always my Father, when did I say yes to that relationship, crying out "Abba"?

The elusive Spirit

The almighty God and the suffering Son here receive fuller complement from the third member of the Trinity—the "face" you never see, the "person" you never fully know or understand, and the "presence" you can never be sure you have recognized correctly. Like wind, the elusive Spirit blows where it will. You only know where it has been or what it has done, and even then very often not until long afterward.

In Greek (*pneuma*), as in Hebrew (*ruach*), we have the same word meaning "wind" and "spirit," so the sentence has a double meaning that we cannot reproduce in English: neither "the wind blows…" nor "the Spirit blows…" adequately translates the phrase, nor is it satisfactory to say that the one is like the other. The Greek can be either or both, leaving the hearer to figure it out, which makes life difficult for those people who have to have everything wrapped up and know "what it really means."

Nicodemus was one such person. No wonder he was puzzled. He knew what he knew. He needed to know where he was. He had invested a lot of time and effort in getting there. He had "arrived." So many issues with which others struggled no longer troubled him. He certainly didn't want his applecart upset now, not even a little; the thought of stopping and starting all over again in a different place was worrisome to say the least. Jesus offered new answers to old, resolved questions—new and astonishing answers that Nicodemus couldn't understand.

SUGGESTION FOR MEDITATION: Go back over your life in the last week. Try to answer the question: Where might I have missed seeing the elusive Spirit?

A chink in the armor

Verse 9 hints at a chink in Nicodemus's armor. Perhaps he is not so sure that he knows what he believes after all. Had he been really sure, he would never have come to see Jesus. His quest for certainty and then for confirmation of his certainty signals his uncertainty (if not insecurity). Perhaps he is beginning to feel a need to expand his understanding of God, to acknowledge that there is more to God than what he has learned thus far. Certainly he believes there is more to God than is coming from this man Jesus, however remarkable he is—but what is it?

What worries Nicodemus is that he can't seem to get a grip on "the more" of God. Jesus' answer seems to be no answer at all. Nicodemus can't tie him down—does Jesus mean "wind," or does he mean "spirit"? He needs to know, and the meaning is unclear. Both concepts are entirely uncertain, unpredictable, and unverifiable.

I can imagine what is going through Nicodemus's mind: *Is he asking us to go back to the beginning of Creation with "a movement over the face of the waters," in all its chaos and confusion and start all over again? Is that what he means by being born a second time? Or does he mean we have got everything wrong and have to scrap the lot and start all over again? That's not practical either! So what does he mean?*

This passage also reflects Jesus' puzzlement. Not only can Nicodemus not understand, but Jesus cannot understand why Nicodemus cannot understand. Are the answers not there in the scriptures? How can a teacher of Israel like Nicodemus not see them? Two men on different planes, seeking understanding.

PRAYER: Heavenly Father, when I have to engage people who seem to live in a totally different world, help me to try and understand myself as well as them. Amen.

Two men on different planes

Jesus tries to move the conversation on. If "flesh" and "spirit" present problems (vv. 5-6), try "earthly things" and "heavenly things." "Earthly things," things that happen on earth, may have a divine origin. "Heavenly things" are the things that happen in heaven, particularly the sending of the Son. "Earthly things" may act as signs or pointers to help us understand the heavenly things.

The gap exists not only between Jesus and Nicodemus. In the Greek in verse 11, the verbs go from singular to plural. Suddenly Jesus is addressing more than Nicodemus. The "singular" gap between Jesus and Nicodemus becomes symptomatic of a wider gap between those aligned with Jesus' teaching and those aligned with Nicodemus (perhaps members of a synagogue). We see evidence of this misunderstanding between different groups of Christians throughout church history as well. The gap occurs between two different ways of seeing religion, faith, and God: the one looking for certainty, the other open to the winds of the Spirit. And it is not possible to have a foot in both camps. One may be open on some issues and closed on others, but it is impossible for a wholly integrated being to be "open" and "closed" at the same time.

Nicodemus lacks openness to the unexpected and impossible. Just as the lifting of the serpent by Moses brought healing to the people, so too does the crucifixion of Jesus bring salvation and eternal life. Once we are prepared to look upward (or outward) from ourselves and our trials to see the world differently, we begin to appreciate the source of a new beginning, whether it be a serpent in the wilderness or a cross on a hill.

SUGGESTION FOR MEDITATION: **Identify the cross in your own experience and use that insight to discover a new understanding of Calvary.**

Online

To discover the new experience of which Jesus speaks is to have eternal life—uninterrupted access to God—not only through the wonders of nature, not only through an enriched understanding of the Word, not even through participation in the sacraments but as a result of an openness to the Spirit. Other ways to God are like Internet service providers; they have their place as a means of making a connection. For many people in many situations they are invaluable, but they are not the only way and are always second best to the continuous, direct access made possible through the Spirit. Think of being "online" to God.

Of course, this direct access can be frightening, if not terrifying. It's great to be online to God; the worrisome part is that God is online to us. In the minds of some people this consciousness of God's pervading presence serves only to increase fear, anxiety, and guilt—nowhere to hide (Psalm 139). Who can stand the pressure of having God there all the time, peering over the shoulder?

But then verse 17 says that God is not there to condemn or arouse guilt but to express love and to create life. And this God is for the whole world, not just for Christians. No longer do we have to gain God's attention or secure divine goodwill. God is just there "24-7"—all around, all the time. We don't even have to attempt to find or talk to God; we simply allow the Divine Internet Service Provider find us—then we learn to listen and to see.

SUGGESTION FOR MEDITATION: Spend some time in silence in a darkened room with your eyes closed. Bask in God's presence. Feel the warmth of God's love.

Freedom from Fear of Giants and Storms

June 16–22, 2003 • *Susan Marie Smith*[‡]

MONDAY, JUNE 16 • **Read 1 Samuel 17:38-49**

David proclaims a central truth for the whole gospel: "The LORD does not save by sword and spear"—or by armor either. A humorous but central moment in the David and Goliath story occurs when David dons Saul's armor and then tries in vain to walk. What a cartoon moment! I see David tripping over himself, waddling, clanking, and squeaking, trying to get his body aligned with the armor so he can walk.

But David comes to realize that moving in Saul's armor is impossible: Protection for the warrior is detrimental, even dangerous, to the shepherd. For David, the saving grace was not social convention or the standard protection that everyone used —but rather the courage to follow his own course. While he invited and considered the wisdom of those around him, he also listened carefully to the deeper wisdom that arose from his personal relationship with God.

What in our lives is the armor we wear to protect us that actually burdens us instead? May we recognize and remove the armor that impedes us and use the gifts and guidance God gives us particularly, for in this is our ministry and in this our salvation.

PRAYER: Holy Lover-Creator, send us forth "to do the work you have given us to do, to love and serve you as faithful witnesses of Christ our Lord,"* through the power of the Holy Spirit. Amen.

**The Book of Common Prayer* (New York: Church Publishing Inc., 1979), 366.

[‡]Episcopal priest; Ph.D. in pastoral liturgy from the Graduate Theological Union in Berkeley; chaplain at Saint Andrew's School, Saratoga, California.

Has someone ever called you courageous, when inside you knew you were scared silly? *Courage* is an "observer" word: It describes the largeness of heart we observe in another who, though frightened, still enters the burning building, faces the armed giant, or tells the truth. If we act, even in the face of danger, it is not because we weigh the risks against our limitations or because we feel brave. Rather it is because we're focused intently upon the urgent need.

This was the case with the man who, after an airliner crashed into the Potomac River years ago, swam into the icy water and led person after person safely to shore before his own limbs stopped working. This was the case with David who did not concern himself with his odds of winning or the enormous difference between Goliath's armored fierceness and his own simply clad vulnerability. Both the swimmer's and David's focused, compassionate urges gave life to many.

What can prepare each of us to respond as part of God's saving work is the ever-present desire to align our lives with God. Through daily devotion and meditation, weekly worship, and small-group study, we become focused, unself-conscious, and "tuned" to the rhythm of love and service for the Lord. May we be faithful in these practices so that, whatever the risks, when we feel the nudge of need around us, we may be open to the song of God's grace. Then courage will take care of itself.

SUGGESTION FOR MEDITATION: **To practice the spiritual art of focusing, sit in silence for five minutes (twenty minutes if you are experienced). Select a sacred word or phrase such as "Come Lord Jesus" or "In you, Lord, I am free." Slowly inhale, breathing half the syllables; slowly exhale the other half. When you feel distracted, simply return your attention to the sacred phrase.**

Fear is the enemy. Fear is the opposite of love, for perfect love casts out fear. We humans may respond to threat with fight, flight, or fright, or with their emotional counterparts: anger (like a lion who fights), terror (like a deer who flees), or depression (like an opossum who plays dead). We know these reactions well.

But Christians are called to a life free from fear. We know that fearful reactions come both from actual danger (the tree is falling on us) and from imagined danger (the tree is falling). The reaction we cultivate is a spiritual–moral choice: to fear all unknowns or to react with calm awareness. David before Goliath exemplifies the second option. He seems to grasp the angel's message to the shepherds in Luke's Gospel, only without the angel: "Do not be afraid" (2:10).

There are death-dealing, evil, fearsome powers in this world. But their serious nature does not require that we succumb to their threat. A Lutheran bishop in occupied Sweden was called before the Nazi officer and commanded to halt his work of hiding Jews and promoting their escape. "Don't you know I have the power of life and death over you?" the officer huffed menacingly. The bishop replied, "I died at my baptism. You have no power over me."

Out of his own grounded faith, David speaks the truth directly to Goliath without fear. In sure and certain knowledge that he is God's whether he lives or dies, David approaches the danger head-on—and by the grace of God, prevails. May we too so focus our life in Christ that we may meet without fear the strange and the devastating with deep trust in the God who upholds us.

SUGGESTION FOR MEDITATION: **Reflect on your union with Christ in death and resurrection now through baptism, and in the world to come through death. Claim the freedom meant for you in knowing that "whether we live or whether we die, we are the Lord's" (Rom. 14:8).**

Now is the acceptable time; see, now is the day of salvation!...and see—we are alive...having nothing, and yet possessing everything....[O]pen wide your hearts also.

Just as the good news of God's redemption shows us the deeper reality beneath appearances—the king of glory bumps along on a donkey, the savior of the world is cradled in a feeding trough, a youth fells the giant with a slingshot—so Paul points out that as servants of Christ, we are treated as imposters, having nothing, even though we actually possess a freedom beyond measure.

My friend Amanda exemplifies the spaciousness of spirit that comes from living in Christ. She lives simply because she is a student. She lives freely because of her faith. Recently, on her way to work from her room in San Francisco's Tenderloin district, she was accosted by a homeless man asking for money. She told the truth: She had none. Yet as in Christ's inversion of reality, Amanda shared her "nothing": She reached out her hand to the man. "My name is Amanda. What's yours?" "Jeffrey." Thereafter she spoke to him by name daily, often stopping to chat.

One noon hour she saw Jeffrey and offered to share a hot dog with him. She took him to her daily hot dog stand and ordered. They sat across from each other; Amanda cut the hot dog, giving half to Jeffrey. They ate and talked. Suddenly Amanda looked up directly into Jeffrey's eyes and said to him, "This is the most delicious hot dog I've ever eaten—because I'm sharing it with you." A huge grin appeared on Jeffrey's face.

Money and hot dogs are no longer ours when we die: We will finally have nothing. But to have friendship and food shared is to possess everything, here on earth and unto eternity.

PRAYER: Holy God, give us, we pray, such wide-open hearts and such freedom in our emptiness that your Spirit may flow through them to connect us, friend and stranger, in your love. Amen.

I recently taught a unit on moral decision making to twelve- and thirteen-year-olds studying *Of Mice and Men*. In Steinbeck's story, Lennie, who has exceptional physical strength but meager mental resources, inadvertently strangles a woman whose hair he is stroking. We know from the context that once apprehended, Lennie will be murdered by an angry mob, even though he is incapable of moral discernment. His companion George agonizes over what to do. George ultimately chooses to be with Lennie in a moment of loving friendship, to call to mind the dreams they shared, and to shield Lennie—and risk his own future—by pulling the trigger himself.

The students struggled with the book's events and with the characters' morality. Some questions that helped them sort out the issues were these: "Whose interest did the character's action serve?" "In the case of George, did it benefit himself or the other?"

Paul reminds the Christians at Corinth—and us—that suffering can be a sign of authenticity, sincerity, integrity. Willingness to endure hardship, sleepless nights, and being misunderstood without complaining or ceasing to love the other commends the love of God to us. If we give up something in order to act, such as care for someone even if our motives are misunderstood, we are living signs of conviction and faith. This is the freedom of the cross: to stand for love of neighbor, even if that stance results in suffering. "And see—we are alive."

PRAYER: Holy God, help us to see the bigger picture today, so that difficulties and painful moments do not distract us from your ever-redemptive, beauty-making, care-giving movement toward your glorious realm of light. We pray through your Eternal Word in the grace of the Holy Spirit. Amen.

My friend Meg flew to join her siblings around the bedside of a dying aunt named Loretta. Meg felt hand-wringing tension when she arrived. A sister looked up and cried, "You're here at last! Loretta wants to pray." Meg took Loretta's hand. "What would you like to pray for?" "I just want to thank Jesus for all the blessings he has given me." So Meg gathered everyone in prayer and thanked Jesus for life's blessings upon Loretta. But back home after Loretta's funeral, she pondered, *All the family members were churchgoers. Why had they waited for her to pray? What giant inhibition stopped them from beginning to pray their aunt across the river of death to Christ?*

We've all been Meg before; but more often we've allowed ourselves to be in the back of the boat with others, hunkering down, crying out for someone else to stand up, step forward, reach out. What holds us back from taking the lead, claiming our authority, acting in faith? Why is it necessary to awaken Jesus to calm the storm when the rest of us are already awake?

God's great gift to us in Christ takes us a lifetime of prayer to receive fully. Christ offers freedom from the faithless fears that stop us from facing the storm. Have we not, in the waters of baptism, already been freed from death and united in resurrection with Christ himself? Like the early disciples, let us daily widen our claim upon this sacred freedom that is already ours and use our authority to command the storms around and within us: "Peace! Be still!"

PRAYER: Holy Love Divine, so dwell, we pray you, in our trembling hearts that we may be filled with your compassion, transformed by your salvation, and empowered to enact your authority in freedom for your glory. Amen.

It is morning on retreat in Hawaii. My family prepares to meditate. Claire scoops up something on a paper, an insect perhaps. She turns to show us. It is a tiny centipede with delicate curved legs whose turquoise color matches the color of the bay—and its own green-blue antennae! She releases it in the garden.

The thought-gifts come and go. Such ironic freedom comes as we acknowledge the insignificance of our human understanding before the tiny mystery of these green-legged creatures that coordinate two dozen legs while looking for food and hiding from humans and that scurry to survive hurricane winds or fifty-foot tsunami waves. I become aware of a great in-filling of pure joy as I witness life I could never have imagined: the six-inch spider that intimidatingly claims a corner of the house, yowling cats that hunt the yellow and spring-green birds nesting in the lanai roof, mango trees that daily drop enough fruit to feed the neighborhood. This is beauty in all its enigmatic wonder.

We are one part of a pattern, a living family of intricate and intimate relationships. Paul's invitation to the Corinthians and to us is to be fully awake, alive, human—and to begin here and now. For this is the day when God will turn the tide, give us a gift, reveal unspeakable love to us. Today is the day of beauty, joy, and salvation. Let us celebrate the wondrous grace of being alive in this particular moment, this relational earth place—and accept our own niche in this intricate creation.

PRAYER: Holy God, open wide our eyes and break open our hearts, that being freed to take our place in your creation and your salvation, we may be changed from glory into glory. Amen.

Do Not Fear, Only Believe

June 23–29, 2003 • *Geoffrey W. Posegate*[‡]

MONDAY, JUNE 23 • **Read Mark 5:21-43**

As a child I loved pools, lakes, any body of water. However, I greatly feared deep water, so my parents enrolled me in swimming lessons. I learned all the skills necessary to handle myself in water over my head. Still I could not let go of my fear enough to push out into the deep.

I confess that when I ask Jesus to remove some fear from my life, I often assume that he will do all the work. I ask; Jesus dissipates my anxiety; and I move ahead boldly. I must remember that when I welcome Christ to the center of my existence and when I invite the Lord to address fear in my heart, he will in turn invite me to make choices and to act in faith, reaching for him.

Mark 5 records the story of a woman who suffers from a hemorrhage. Levitical law required someone in her ritually unclean condition to approach people from behind and to keep her distance. If she acts on the common belief of the day, that a healer's clothing has power, she defies the law.

Still something inspires the woman to reach out and touch Jesus' cloak. She jeopardizes herself to experience Jesus' power. Yet her healing and salvation occur not only because of the power and the proclamation of the one whose clothing she has grasped. Jesus makes it clear to her that her willingness to reach beyond her fear anchors the miracle as well.

While my swimming instructor assured me I had no reason to fear, I had to choose to push off from the side of the pool. Jesus invites our trust and our decision to reach beyond our fears.

SUGGESTION FOR MEDITATION: Envision your specific fears as walls around you. Hear Jesus inviting you to reach over and around them.

[‡]Senior pastor of The United Methodist Church of Belton, Kansas City, Missouri; geriatric social worker.

Consider some common phrases: "We're in deep trouble," or "You're in it deep now, mister!" Often the concept of depth describes rich, well-conceived, and valuable characteristics. But depth can also describe a circumstance of trouble and difficulty. On some occasions people employ the adjective "deep" to describe turmoil they bring upon themselves.

The psalmist speaks from "out of the depths," an image that might reflect personal trouble and resultant alienation from God. Bible scholars regard this particular psalm as a song of individual lament, one of seven penitential psalms in which the writers find themselves in "deep water" of circumstances they themselves have created; hence, their penitent cry to God for help.

Finding ourselves in such difficulty can intensify our fear of God's presence. Not only are we aware of the deep, swirling waters, but we assume that God keeps a strict accounting below each name. Long before Paul of Tarsus noted that "all have sinned and fallen short of the glory of God," the psalmist understood that if God keeps records, there is no hope.

Even in the depths the psalmist does not accept this view of God. Instead he presumes that God's primary characteristic is to have mercy. The word for mercy in this scripture section comes from descriptions of the relationship between a master and a slave. One entity has total power over the other and chooses to exercise that power in a beneficial way. The psalmist trusts in the knowledge that God hears our cries for mercy. Finally he accepts that God's primary nature is to forgive.

Too many times we gauge an experience of the dark deep in life according to how we feel. On that basis we assume that God is far away, that God is punishing us, or both. But in fact, we need to trust the truth: God has mercy on us; God hears our cry; and God forgives us.

SUGGESTION FOR MEDITATION: **What part of your life is like an unfathomable depth right now, especially a depth you created? Imagine God sending Jesus to lift you from that very depth.**

Doris's husband, Curtis, finally died after a long battle with Parkinson's disease. For over fifty years the two of them had been utterly devoted to each other. When Curtis received the diagnosis of his debilitating condition, Doris's already strong commitment had reached heroic new levels. When Curtis breathed his last, Doris felt as though a part of her very being had been torn away. The loss nearly crippled her spirit.

David surely feels the impact of such agony when his close friend Jonathan dies. David has experienced enough turmoil as a renegade outlaw pursued by King Saul. Losing his soul-friend crushes him. In his song of grief David lashes out in anger against Israel's enemy. Anger is an undeniable component of loss, both then and now. David wishes a curse on the mountains of Gilboa for being the setting for death, much as any of us would curse anything that reminds us constantly of those who are no longer with us. David's grief is honest, real, and sharply painful. Perhaps he fears that the pain of the loss will never subside.

There's an empty place in Doris's heart that no one and nothing can fill, just as there was in David's heart. Both cried out for God and to God in their anguish. The hope of David's journey doesn't appear in the text of his lament; it comes through in the sweep of David's walk with God. Somehow the Lord raises the outlaw who would be king from the mire of sadness. Even with the loss of Jonathan, David moves on, secure in his faith.

Doris does not give in to the fear that the darkness will overwhelm her. She keeps an intercessory prayer list and writes notes of encouragement. She does not attach her faith in God to her feelings, for some days she feels blue and empty. She finds her faith in an act of will, choosing to trust a God who stands with her, even when she cries out in agony.

SUGGESTION FOR MEDITATION: **Think of someone you know who has experienced recent loss. Pray for that person to trust the ups and downs to a God who loves him or her no matter what.**

I assembled this meditation in the shadow of September 11, 2001. As a nation the United States of America finds itself in the grip of a new and ominous fear. Unseen adversaries have declared themselves an enemy to us. They have struck a blow on North American soil. This nation now faces a new type of foe whose attacks could come at any time and at any place. In these days it is hard to hear the mandate: "Do not fear, only believe."

In such times our thinking tends to align with that of most nations and cultures under similar circumstances. We assume that our fear will end with the enemy's destruction. Our adversary's death will restore peace and hopefulness to our hearts.

King Saul of Israel has died ingloriously at Gilboa. Saul had pursued David with an unrelenting jealousy. Saul's death might have ended David's fear; David might have rejoiced as any of us would at the destruction of an enemy. However, David fears something more than Saul; he fears his God.

In the end David treats his adversary as a child of God. Rather than gloat over Saul's demise, David prays that the enemies of Israel will not celebrate the king's death. Cursing the place where Saul has perished, David praises Saul's achievements, referring to Saul as "mighty" numerous times. Though Saul had made David's life miserable, David chooses to view Saul through the eyes of God.

The end of fear's domination over us does not come with the destruction of those who stand against us. Anyone can rejoice over the end of an enemy. Fear's domain ends when we choose to see adversaries as children of God, worthy of the death and resurrection of Jesus the Christ because of God's great love. This new way of seeing takes great courage and goes against the flow of human inclination. Yet such a stance is no less than what Jesus has done for each one of us.

SUGGESTION FOR MEDITATION: **Envision someone you might view as an enemy. See yourself escorting that person into Jesus' presence.**

We begin to fear the loss of our accumulated resources. We arm our homes with security systems, seek protected but lucrative investment options, and clamp "the club" to the steering wheels of our cars. We chain our wallets to our belts. What we gain we aim to keep, and we look over our shoulders, fearing the next attempt to separate us from our wealth.

The founder and director of an urban ministry for the homeless spoke in worship shortly after the terrorist attacks of September 11. This mission leader, while clearly supporting the relief efforts directed to the victims in New York City, Washington, D.C., and Pennsylvania, observed that donations to helping ministries like his had dropped dramatically.

Certainly Christians might find it easier to give money to support ministry when the events of the day are stable and when extra funds abound. Fear and unsettled days will tempt us to circle the wagons around the resources we possess.

While not stating as much overtly, Paul seems to imply that some of the Christians in Corinth have resisted his collection for the poor of the Jerusalem church. He notes that his apostolic authority empowers him to demand Corinthian support for this mission. However, Paul hopes that the Corinthians will choose to give, following the example of Jesus himself, who gave up the "rich" status of coexistence with God to become poor and to deal with the poverties of the human state.

The director of the homeless mission declared to our congregation that giving to the work of Christ should not decline in troubled times. Indeed, he proclaimed, this will be a time of the most miraculous outpouring of support for the missions of the kingdom. Giving may not be at its best when born of surplus and ease. Miracles come when the body of Christ pleads for the privilege to give in the mode of Christ, even, and especially, when times are uncertain and lean.

SUGGESTION FOR MEDITATION: **What does your current giving say about your faith in Christ?**

A new parishioner recently experienced a unique and devastating form of grief. Her grandfather, the primary caregiver for his wife, who had Parkinson's, took a shotgun and ended his wife's life, then turned the gun on himself. A note explained that neither of them could take the constant pain and burden any longer.

The spirits of many struggle to rise above ongoing circumstances that seem to promise no relief from physical, emotional, mental, or relational pain. When people fear that some chronic ache will never leave, spiritual defeat stalks their hearts.

In today's scripture we see someone facing chronic illness. The woman who reaches for Jesus' garment has been bleeding for twelve years and has depleted her resources.

The woman's hope in Jesus is primitive at best. She acts on a superstitious impulse, hoping that her touch of his clothing will conduct the power that will make her whole. Despite her limited approach, Jesus knows that power has gone forth. He seeks her and proclaims that her faith has made her whole.

Too often, when facing chronic brokenness in our lives, we assume we must cover a number of bases before we seek help from Jesus. Exercising all the options available to our own scope of power, we must fully understand how and why healing and help come from the Lord. We must follow the right leadership, the right liturgy, the right language, and have the right motivation. Sometimes the effort requires so much that we give up and accept our ongoing agony.

Yet this woman's story affirms that even the weakest, most ill-informed reach opens the door to the healing power and presence of Christ. Wholeness may not come in the way we prescribe. A painful situation may leave us, or the Lord may give us the ability to withstand it and receive blessing from it. Either way, Christ and our faith in him can and will make us whole.

SUGGESTION FOR MEDITATION: **What pain causes you to reach for Jesus' cloak?**

Early on Sunday morning Ruth arrived at the church facility to decorate the sanctuary. That Sunday a time of celebration would be the culmination of a stewardship campaign. Ruth had worked hard to coordinate the decor and theme and to arrange a congregational meal to be held at a nearby school facility. Humming happily she completed her church chores and prepared to go work on the meal preparations.

The morning turned sour when Ruth realized she had lost the key to the school. Entrusted with the care of a public facility for this church event, she now had no way to get in. She slumped down at the altar steps and wept in despair.

All week we've examined just a few circumstances in which we find it hard to obey Jesus' admonition, "Don't be afraid, just believe." So often our willingness to obey comes when we've exhausted our abilities and resources or when suddenly circumstances rip control from our grip. Frayed and exhausted, we might simply collapse in tears on the altar.

Ironically, at this point the psalmist seems to buoy us up. Psalm 130 begins with lament and then continues a downward slide into confession. In verses 5 and 6 the singer waits on God. Then the spirit of the song rises with confidence in God's redemption. Life's barriers become venues for hope in the Lord.

Ruth decided simply to throw herself on the mercy of the congregation and the local school officials. For reasons she can't explain, she took one last searching look by an outdoor cross that had been set up for the occasion. At the base of the cross she found the key. Ruth accepts that a logical reason exists for the key's ending up there. However, she embraces the obvious metaphor. When the hour is darkest, hope comes at the foot of the cross through the truth of a crucified and risen Christ.

SUGGESTION FOR MEDITATION: Think of the least likely situations in which miracles might happen in your world and in the world in general. Choose to hope in the Lord in those very circumstances.

Gifts As We Journey

June 30–July 6, 2003 • *Marta Sanfiel*[‡]

MONDAY, JUNE 30 • Read 2 Samuel 5:1-5, 9-10

Emily, my ninety-year-old friend, would tell me about her life. One day she told me about her husband's execution during a civil war in Spain. After his death, she decided to return to Cuba. In shock during the journey, Emily did not remember how she went from Spain to Cuba. She and I agree that it does not matter how she traveled; what we believe matters is that God was with her on this journey.

David is in Hebron when the tribes of Israel ask him to be their king. Samuel has earlier anointed him. As the tribes seek their king, the leaders of the twelve tribes claim two promises of God: David is one of them ("your bone and flesh"), and God has chosen David to rule over Israel. Then David and the leaders make a covenant before God. As we read the remainder of this passage and the later stories of King David, we follow his passionate journey through life. We are aware of the gifts David has received from God and how David uses his gifts on the journey.

God invites us on a journey. We enter into a covenant relationship in which we open ourselves to God's love. We serve God by using our gifts as we travel on our life journeys. As with David, God encourages us to use our gifts for the loving transformation of the world.

Just as my friend Emily found refuge under God's guidance, so we can count on God's promises on our journeys.

PRAYER: O God, as we journey with you, anoint us that we may know your gifts. Amen.

[‡]Retired United Methodist clergy in the Louisiana Conference; living in Lexington, Kentucky.

TUESDAY, JULY 1 • Read 2 Corinthians 12:2–10

Paul begins this passage with the words, "I know a person in Christ..." and then tells of a deep and intimate spiritual experience. The apostle writes of himself. How else would he know the depth of this being "caught up to the third heaven"? Indeed, Paul describes a heavenly experience with God that can only be his own spiritual journey. Nevertheless, Paul maintains a sense of humility while speaking of this experience: "I refrain from it [boasting], so that no one may think better of me."

Contrast Paul's attitude with the more common contemporary attitude in which we celebrate only triumphs and consider only the rich and powerful as role models. Paul was not rich. He journeyed physically as well as spiritually. He may have been a powerful speaker and missionary, but contemporary culture would not feature Paul in any stories about wealth and power.

What gifts did he have on his difficult journey? One gift is this mystery that Paul describes as a thorn in the flesh. We do not normally recognize such a problem as a gift, and yet we do identify with Paul. We each carry a thorn in our own flesh that may remind us of our dependence on God as we journey. The thorn becomes a gift when we remember and speak of our relationship with God. Paul wrote, "I will boast all the more gladly of my weaknesses, so that the power of Christ may dwell in me."

What gift of weakness goes with you and causes you to boast? How do you remember the power of Christ because of this weakness?

SUGGESTION FOR MEDITATION: Consider when in your weakness you have felt the strength of God's grace.

Today look at the first portion of the Gospel lesson. Jesus has traveled through Galilee and now returns home. The Gospel of Mark shows Jesus stilling a storm, healing a demoniac, restoring a young girl to life, and healing a woman on this tour. Home he now goes, and the people of Nazareth "took offense at him." They recall his family history. They remember that Joseph was only a carpenter and that Mary has those other children. Mark even records the names of these siblings as part of the general grumbling. From the text we get the sense that the people of Nazareth are no more impressed with Jesus' family than they are with him. They reject Jesus.

Jesus responds first with a powerfully honest statement about the worth of prophets in their hometowns and among their own families. Then the Gospel records these curious words: "And he could do no deed of power there, except that he laid his hands on a few sick people and cured them. And he was amazed by their unbelief."

I wonder about those "few sick people." Did they tell others in Nazareth about the healing Jesus brought? Did the ones who rejected Jesus reject them as well? What happened? Have the people of Nazareth forgotten that God invites all creation to wholeness and holiness? Have they become locked into a life that no longer vibrates with God's grandeur? Have they forgotten that the journey of faith calls us to see with new eyes?

We would see life afresh each day. We would see Jesus.

PRAYER: Holy God, your love is new every day. Open our hearts each day so we may experience the wonder and the surprise of your redeeming love, a love made powerful in the strength of Jesus. Amen.

Evelyn is five years old. She wants to know the "how" of life. Often she explains the "hows" of what she encounters. She invents explanations that she shares with others. Then she goes out to play, completely satisfied with her own explication.

Many of us journey in search of the "how": "How could this have happened?" or "How can I succeed?"

The writer of Second Samuel explains David's success. David "became greater and greater, for the LORD, the God of hosts, was with him." Recall that David, identified as a great king, lived with many failures and failings. What do we mean by great?

Many people equate greatness with success, and success seemingly indicates the degree of being a good Christian. The many books of the Bible warn against such a perverted understanding of success and greatness. The biblical measure of greatness involves an active and passionate spirituality, expressed in caring for widows and orphans and the least in society, and in taking stands against injustice and oppression.

This biblical measure of greatness looks at David's failures and failings but also takes into account his deep yearning for God. David's journey is marked by terrible brokenness, but from his failings David repented deeply. He remained open to God and tried to live in accordance with his understanding of the covenant.

God invites us to journey passionately so that our deep yearnings for God will be filled and so that the measure of our love for God will counteract evil and oppression. That is the "how" of becoming greater and greater.

PRAYER: Loving God, forgive our sins and help us to grow in your love. Encourage us to witness to your standards of success and to challenge false standards. In Jesus' name we pray. Amen.

As I reflect on Psalm 48, I remember many in church history who have seized upon this vision of the city of God. Augustine of Hippo wrote of the city of God even as the great city of Rome crumbled. John Calvin sought the city of God among the elect in Geneva. Others struggled to establish an orderly city of God on earth. These efforts share a history of failure.

Is that failure the failure of institutionalization? Or does such failure happen because these attempts stagnate and limit God's creative gifts?

Verses 12-13 of Psalm 48 stick in my memory. Here I find gifts and challenges for the journey. How might I "walk about Zion, go all around it, count its towers, consider well its ramparts"? I walk as a pilgrim in my day-to-day activities, and I remember God's graciousness.

I remember that God strengthened and encouraged me in my life in Cuba and then in the United States. I call to mind God's gifts of family and friends, of ministerial colleagues and laity who shared the journey. I remember quiet times and joyful times, times of loss and grief as well as celebration. In all these experiences, I recall God's gracious love.

I remember not for the sake of nostalgia but that I "may tell the next generation" about God's love. I may be retired, but I continue to share the good news. Unless I tell the next generations, little children like Evelyn (Thursday's meditation) will not know the gifts of God, and their journeys may have an emptiness. One gift as you journey is the gift you leave behind for those who follow.

PRAYER: O Lord, you are great and greatly to be praised! Be our guide forever. Amen.

When my first granddaughter was born, a friend gave me a book to guide me in preserving stories and memories for the new generation. I have enjoyed this gift and hope that what I pass down will be remembered even when I am gone. For many of us it is important to leave a message for the next generation—and even to those not yet born. Why else would people in the past create and fill time capsules for others to open a hundred years later? Why did so many people create "memory boxes" as we prepared for the year 2000? Maybe these time capsules and records will contain gifts to help others on life's journey.

"Walk about Zion, go all around it, count its towers, consider well its ramparts, go through its citadels...." Before we arrive at Psalm 48:12, we read a condensed history of Israel. Between the lines of this psalm, we understand references to the establishment of God's covenant with the people. We understand that this covenantal relationship has withstood many challenges, such as the efforts by Pharaoh to destroy the will of the Hebrew people. In all these challenges, the enemies of God panicked and abandoned the fight.

As you recall your spiritual journey, what times do you remember in which oppressors stood against you? What temptations did you experience? What gifts of God helped you to stand fast? How were you delivered from these trials?

What will you tell others about those times in your spiritual journey?

PRAYER: **Gracious God, we ponder your steadfast love. We remember times of oppression and hostility, times when we clung to your mercy. Let our story be told to others so they may know the gracious mystery of your love made known to us in Jesus Christ. Amen.**

Despite the rejection Jesus experiences in Nazareth, he persists in his ministry among the villages. He also sends out the twelve in mission, giving them a set of instructions that seems an odd set of gifts.

Sending disciples in pairs reminds us that we are not alone and not intended to go alone. Power exists in community. Our invitation to mission and ministry today is to a small company, as small as two.

"[Jesus] ordered them to take nothing for their journey except a staff." These words remind the disciples of their dependence upon God. They take what they need to walk—a staff and sandals—and no more! Maybe we exercise a spiritual equivalent to staff and sandals when we spend time reflecting on scripture and opening ourselves to God. I know that refugees who have fled oppressive situations carried with them only a Bible and the clothes on their back, yet they experienced God's grace and joy!

Jesus also offers instructions about visiting others. He bids the twelve to stay as long as the people are receptive. If not, move on! Don't engage in disputation or needless debate. Simply move on; go to people who are open to God's love.

As I read Mark's version of Jesus' words about shaking off the dust from the sandals, I imagine that Jesus knew that others would follow the first group of disciples. Perhaps the second or third group might be the ones to communicate the gospel to those who were not at first receptive.

Receive God's gifts as you journey!

PRAYER: **Almighty, all-emptying God, in you we live and move and have our being. Help us recognize the gifts you lay before us for the journey. Amen.**

Being Real in the Worship of God

July 7–13, 2003 • *Helen Price Walters*[‡]

MONDAY, JULY 7 • **Read Ephesians 1:3-14**

Years ago I heard a story that touched me deeply. A young man had received a Bible from his grandfather. He hatefully tossed it aside, resentful and disappointed at not being given cash. Years passed. One day he casually flipped through the pages of the Bible while sorting through his belongings. To his amazement and horror, a check for a large sum of money—enough to buy a new car—fell out of the crisp pages of the never-opened book. His grandfather had died a long time back; the bank account on which the check was written was long closed. Tears stung the man's eyes as he realized how ugly and foolish his behavior had been. He had not been appreciative of a devoted grandfather. He had missed out on many opportunities, not only for a new car but, more important, for a warm and caring relationship with someone who loved him dearly.

Often we are like the ungrateful man in the story. God blesses us with all we could ever want or need. But we stumble about, either complacent or self-centered, searching for instant though fleeting gratification. And what a wonderful inheritance awaits us! Verses 3 and 11 promise us more than we could ever hope for: eternal life and the ever-present companionship of our loving Savior throughout this earthly life.

PRAYER: Gracious and loving God, give me the strength and the self-discipline to praise you sincerely, frequently, and reverently. Amen.

[‡]Educator in the Dallas public schools; lifelong member of the Episcopal Church of the Incarnation, Dallas, Texas.

Who among us does not want to "belong," to be loved and cherished? Verse one says it all: "The earth is the LORD's and all that is in it, / the world, and those who live in it." It tells us who's in control, who we are, and who we are in relation to the One in control.

We live in a world created for relationship, yet many people sit alone facing a computer throughout the day only to come home at night and do the same. Others work in hospitals or classrooms with little support from other adults. While we may feel cut off from nurturing relationships, this psalm affirms that we are loved by God and belong to a community that encompasses all of creation. We find ourselves secure within the expanse of God's all-accepting, all-inclusive love.

We belong to God, regardless of our human strengths and frailties. We are not on loan. No hidden clauses exist in the contract. We are simply—yet wonderfully—God's.

Verse 3 asks, "Who shall ascend the hill of the LORD? And who shall stand in his holy place?" We might rephrase that as "Who will live in relationship to God, under God's reign?" And the answer resounds, "Those who have clean hands and pure hearts"—an inward and outward emphasis with appropriate relationship both to God and neighbor.

Let us consider with joyful ecstasy the prospect of being in God's "holy place." Yet are we not already there, here in this place—the earth, the world? As we live daily in right relationship to God and neighbor, our conduct conveys our joy in belonging to God. To keep our hands, hearts, and tongues—our very souls—clean and pure takes strength and courage in a world bent on self-gratification and self-centered isolation. All we have to do is remember to whom we belong.

PRAYER: Father of all creation, help me stand in your holy place, maintaining a relationship with you, with neighbor, and all created things. Help me to remember that I am yours. Amen.

Verse 3 raises questions that verses 4 through 6 not only answer but assure us of a promise: access to the holy place, blessing, and God's company. Seeking the face of God can both delight and frighten. We know that God loves us and that we belong to God. Yet we also know that God is all-powerful, commanding respect and requiring obedience.

Where do you see disrespect and disobedience in your life? Often they clothe themselves in the guises of selfishness, gluttony, overindulgence, avarice, jealousy, and resentment. In what ways does your disrespect or disobedience not only block you from God's presence but keep you from seeking God's face?

I often see the face of God when I look outward rather than inward. Reflection and introspection are valuable, but when I concentrate only on self, my thoughts can turn negative and self-serving. When I work for and love others, I receive blessing and vindication.

As a classroom teacher for many years, I once observed an older woman struggle valiantly to raise five young grandchildren for whom she had full custody. This woman sought God moment to moment as she worked to salvage five young lives in what should have been a period of rest and reflection—her twilight years. I could not help but admire her strength and determination as I prayed for her.

When have you earnestly desired to seek the face of God? Seeking God is probably one of the easiest things a human can do. It costs nothing but honest desire and the willingness to allow God space and time to come into your life. When do you offer God that space? How might you become more willing to make that offer?

PRAYER: God, for your infinite goodness I give thanks and pray to see your face. Amen.

How easy it is to become complacent! The sun rises each morning, goes down each evening. Rain falls, crops grow; and we scurry about, oblivious to life's daily blessings. Do we make room for the "King of glory"? Do we pencil in time for God in our engagement book? Where do we find a place for glory in our busy lives?

I often go from day to day reasonably content, crying out to God only when trouble or illness rears its ugly head. When the sun shines, the birds sing, and the flowers bloom, I often forget God entirely.

Yet like the psalmist, we feel a cry go up in our heart when we acknowledge our relationship to all creation: "Who is the King of glory?" And we reply, "The Lord, strong and mighty." Is this acknowledgment, this affirmation, a source of praise?

Think about one day of your life. Where do you see God's glory? What gives evidence to God's strength and might? What elicits praise of God from your lips?

This King of glory is my life's companion and worthy of praise. Who shall stand in God's holy place? To whom will the gates open? How will clean hands and pure heart affect how we live in the world? Praise, yes, but with more than words. Visits to the lonely in nursing homes, surprise flowers for a loved one, anonymous donations to a struggling family, kind words to a desolate teenager, frequent prayers for world peace—all these actions are forms of praise.

Who shall ascend the hill of the Lord? Those who understand that "the earth is the LORD's" and who live accordingly.

PRAYER: King of glory, for the earth and my relationship to you, neighbor, and all created things, I give you thanks. Amen.

FRIDAY, JULY 11 • Read 2 Samuel 6:1-5, 12b-19

With thirty thousand men behind him, King David is exuberant as he transports the ark of God to Jerusalem, thereby transferring political power to its new center and opening the way for new understandings of the relationship of God to public power. "David and all the house of Israel were dancing before the LORD with all their might." His great joy brings a smile to our lips. Is David sincere in his show of religiosity or is it simply good public relations? All Jerusalem seems to celebrate in the streets. Only verse 16 lets us know that not *everyone* is celebrating. David's wife Michal watches the festivities from her window.

How often we feel contempt for others when they do not respond in what we think is a fitting manner! Michal "daughter of Saul" despises David's behavior. In the verse that follows today's lection, we learn more about Michal's disapproval. She seems wrapped up in the notion of *What will the neighbors think?* Yet David asserts his right and his desire to "celebrate before the LORD" (6:21, NIV). Verse 23 adds this closing line to thoughts of Michal: "Michal the daughter of Saul had no child to the day of her death." The lineage of Saul has come to an end, but not before David has successfully established Jerusalem as the hub of political and spiritual power.

We do not know David's motivation; we cannot understand what Michal might have experienced. But God knows what is in our hearts. David, while far from perfect, expressed a sincere love for God and was not afraid of showing that love to his subjects. May that same love empower us to dance before the Lord without shame.

PRAYER: Dear God, remind me that I live not to please others but to please you. Give me the open and honest love for you that shows itself in my daily life. Amen.

Growing up we learn that if we make a promise we keep it. A handshake is as good as a signed contract. Our word should be as good as gold.

King Herod solemnly swears to his daughter Herodias, "Whatever you ask me, I will give you, even half of my kingdom." At her mother's urging Herodias asks for the head of John the Baptist. Her request horrifies King Herod, yet he remains loyal to his oath in order to save face before his guests. At a terrible price, he insists that the murderous act take place—an extreme response to a promise made.

One lesson to be learned from today's scripture is to be careful when making a promise—can we keep our word and honor the commitment of our words? Promises are easy to make but often hard to keep. When making promises we need to avoid the entrapment into which King Herod fell. A rash promise resulted in death for John the Baptist. While we often emphasize the keeping of promises, they too—when entered into lightly or ill-advisedly—can lead to death. The physical body, hopes, dreams, and goals can all die when rash promises become reality. So the matter of making a promise becomes all the more important.

Regular prayer and patient listening to God's will for us may ensure that we will make promises that we can keep. Through the reading of scripture and quiet meditation we become receptive to God's will and thereby free our thinking. If we base our promise making on prayerful thought, we can honor them with integrity.

PRAYER: Father, I implore your guidance so that I may honor you in kind treatment of others and refrain from making unwise promises. Amen.

We come full circle in our reading. The epistle writer and the psalmist share much in common. Both believe the salvation of all creation is part of God's plan and the response of the creature to the Creator is praise. Epistle writer and psalmist affirm a promise of blessing.

We are charged with a pledge of our inheritance toward redemption—a pledge to the praise of God's glory. What a small price to pay for forgiveness and life in God's presence! Through Jesus Christ we are surrounded by God's glorious grace, freely bestowed. No earthly inheritance can come near.

In heavy freeway traffic I thought of a close relative who was unable to find work. Another relative was experiencing financial problems. A dear friend was struggling through a messy divorce. A coworker with four children had just learned she was expecting twins. Everywhere my thoughts traveled, I encountered difficulties and obstacles. Then grace kicked in; the heavy traffic became less an obstacle and more a positive force that caused me to slow down. The extended travel time gave me ample opportunity for prayerful thought.

The grace of God surrounds us, turning obstacles into opportunities. Our trespasses and transgressions are forgiven and forgotten. Throughout the soft swirls of God's loving grace, our inheritance always awaits us. We simply fulfill a pledge to praise our God—so easy, so nonthreatening, so truly delightful if we will but do it.

Keeping promises. Honoring pledges. Being real in the worship of God is our loving charge.

PRAYER: To be loved and accepted by you, gracious God—I could not ask for more. All praise and glory be to you. Amen.

Christ Our Peace

July 14–20, 2003 • *Annie Grace Zimondi*[‡]

MONDAY, JULY 14 • Read Ephesians 2:11-13

We human beings can easily forget our own sinful ways, but we don't seem to forget the sins of other people. Their transgressions become topics for discussion, and at times we even remind them of how they have messed up and how sinful they have been. When we achieve something in our lives, be it leadership positions or ordination or serving on important committees, we often tend to view ourselves as better than everyone else. In many cases we tend to think that all our achievements are a result of our brilliance, education, luck, or perfection. Paul reminds us of an important aspect of our faith journeys: "But now in Christ Jesus you who once were far off have been brought near by the blood of Christ." If where we are today is the result of Christ's sacrifice on our behalf, that fact should surely humble us even when we seem to have achieved so much.

Our human focus on achievement or failure rather than on the reconciliation brought about by the blood of Jesus continues to create barriers in our societies. Even in this second millennium in which globalization seems to be realized and Christianity has spread to most parts of the world, human beings struggle with barriers of difference. We view persons who are not like us with suspicion. Before I treat others as different, I always remind myself that I too, an African, a woman, a Methodist, I too am different.

PRAYER: Gracious and loving God, when we feel near while others are still far away, humble us and never allow us to forget that we too were once poor, uneducated, unknown but were brought near by the blood of our Lord Jesus Christ. Amen.

[‡]Ordained elder, Zimbabwe Central Conference; Vanderbilt Divinity School student; pastor, St. James-St. John charge, Lawrenceburg, Tennessee.

With all the differences that continue to keep us apart—First World and Third World, traditional and conservative, straight and gay, rich and poor—one wonders what can bring us together. In verses 14-16, the writer of Ephesians notes what must be destroyed: the dividing wall, the law with its commandments and ordinances, and hostility. Yet even the destruction of these elements cannot solve the problems of human enmity. Unity involves reconciliation with God.

While most African churches have little racial segregation, congregations allow tribalism to divide the Christian family. Folks want a pastor who is from their tribe; pastors want to have district superintendents and bishops who are from their tribes.

A church member of one of the urban churches I served in Harare, Zimbabwe, came to me after my first service and said, "I am glad the bishop finally appointed a *zezuru* pastor to this congregation." I wondered what church members from other subtribes felt about me. I had hoped that people would simply accept me as a messenger of God rather than as a representative of any tribe. Tribal conflicts of this nature are true for people all over the world. Some white congregations may resent ministers or clergy of color. Ethnic congregations often expect to receive ethnic preachers.

What then can bring us together? How do we break down the dividing walls? Today's scripture provides an answer to these questions: "For he is our peace; in his flesh he has made both groups into one and has broken down the dividing wall, that is, the hostility between us." Christ extends this peace to us and to those who seemingly do not fit in our human-created categories. In Jesus we find our peace and unity.

PRAYER: Triune God, we know you as our unity. Help us admit our divisions. Let this be our confession, so that you may unite us with your peace. Amen.

During the completion of my final year at United Theological College in Harare, Zimbabwe, in 1993, the members of one of my study groups began a conversation that centered on the untrustworthiness of human beings. One group member stated, "I don't trust anybody—not even my mother." Another group member responded, "My God is trustworthy. My Lord Jesus Christ will never let me down."

Which statement above is truer in your experience? Whom do you trust? Today's scripture reading reveals a mutual trust between God and David, the first representative of the monarchy. The psalm affirms God's promises to David: "My faithfulness and steadfast love shall be with him." Through the position of king, God attempted to create an institution that would secure justice and righteousness for all. Yet somehow this divinely inspired institution lost the trust of the people. They then faced the question: Can an earthly king serve the ends of justice and righteousness?

We in contemporary society witness untrustworthiness in all areas and institutions of our lives: our marriages, our churches, our friendships, our investment plans, our educational systems, our companies, and even our inner selves. Whom can we trust? Sometimes we have lost reason to trust even those designated as keepers of justice and equity. Yet the failed monarchy led to the expectation of another anointed one, the messiah. That one continued and evidenced the ongoing faithfulness and steadfast love of God, the kind of faith we can depend on.

PRAYER: O God, when people and institutions fail us, remind us of your steadfast love and faithfulness that endures forever. Amen.

I am a village girl, raised in the communal area of Wedza in Zimbabwe. In my growing-up years only one bus operated between the capital city of Harare and my village of Wedza, which are eighty-two miles apart. The bus stop was about a mile away from our homestead, so we could see the bus when it loaded and unloaded people at the bus stop. The children in my family would try to identify who was getting off the bus. We always hoped it would be my uncles, workers in the city, coming home for a rare visit. If an uncle happened to be on the bus, we would recognize him from afar and run to meet him.

We enjoyed having the uncles come because then we would have meat for dinner, and tea and bread for breakfast for the next three days or so. The memories are still fresh in me as I recall how happy we would be to have visitors from the city.

When Jesus comes to the land of Gennesaret, he is quickly recognized by the people, and they respond to his arrival in a fascinating way. They go around spreading the good news that the Messiah is in town and bring to him all who need healing. What do I bring to people who are close to me and those who are not, to people who love me and those who don't, to people I know well and to strangers I know very little?

As I travel this faith journey, I like to pause once in a while and take an inventory of my life. How do I impact other people? What kind of healing do I bring to this broken world?

PRAYER: Almighty God, help me realize that my presence can be blessing enough if I learn from you. Amen.

Today's scripture presents David as a king who has been protected and blessed by God and therefore thinks it would be a good idea to build a house for the ark of God, which at that time remained in a tent. Nathan, a court prophet and advisor to the king, quickly responds to David's plan and gives him the go-ahead. In his capacity as a prophet Nathan supposedly advises the king to move in the direction of God's desire. But after his hasty response to David's request, Nathan hears from the Lord. God does not want David to build a house, and now Nathan has to break the news to the king.

Nathan does the Lord's bidding, although it must be embarrassing to go back to the king to reverse Nathan's earlier decision. At the very least, Nathan will find the situation uncomfortable.

We often find ourselves trapped when confronted with issues that require our quick response. We respond without praying about those issues, only later realizing that we have made a terrible mistake. Some people avoid quick answers by promising to go and pray about the issues—but they forget to pray.

What do we do when God confronts us and lets us know that what we said or did was wrong? We want people to think that we are smart, capable, and always right. Thus we resist correction. We may not be prophetic leaders or kings, but God has called us to some endeavor. However, we all have our excuses for resisting that call. May we, like Nathan, respond readily to the Lord's admonition. We may fear hurting other people's feelings; but by avoiding that responsibility, we may hurt their souls.

PRAYER: God, may we always turn to you in times of decision making. When we miss the mark, help us accept correction. Amen.

Choosing church leaders used to be a big event in Zimbabwe. Election time was prayer time for most congregations that strongly believed God would choose the leaders. So the church members felt a need to pray for God's guidance as they elected congregational leaders.

In our contemporary culture much seems to have changed. Prayer has been replaced by human choices based on education, popularity, gender, tribe, sexual orientation, and race. Consider the issues we deal with every day in our global world: the need to recount votes, the need to have people outside a given country monitor elections, conflicts that arise among episcopal candidates and their supporters.

Particularly in countries that do not operate as democratic republics, persons or groups that come to power rarely want to leave those positions. After they achieved independence from the colonial governments, most African people thought their political problems were over. Little did they know that those elected to power would never want to step down.

Within our churches members may often wonder if leaders serve under the guidance of the Holy Spirit or if they act out of a need for control and desire to dominate others. The issue becomes more confusing when some of these power-hungry leaders claim that, like David, they have been chosen.

We in the church affirm that the same God who chooses a few to lead is the God of all humanity. Leadership positions entail responsibility for others, not abuse of them. Perhaps it is time to revisit the power of prayer for God's guidance as we elect those who will serve as leaders. Perhaps then the church might stand as "an enduring witness" to all.

PRAYER: God, direct us and intervene in the election of our leaders. Amen.

The notion of resting for a while is fraught with negative connotations. Both clergy and laity fill their lives to overflowing. Most people fill in the months, weeks, days, and hours of their calendars with appointments. One of my close colleagues in ministry once said, "Pastors operate like gas stations; they are open twenty-four hours a day." Especially in the African culture pastors can be called any time of the day and are expected to welcome visitors at a moment's notice.

My colleague's insight scares me when I realize that I still have twenty or more years in the Christian ministry. If I make myself available and work twenty-four hours a day, will I be able to make it? Are full-to-the-brim schedules and calendars the best way to do ministry?

After the disciples have been out working hard, Jesus sees the need for them to take a rest. Have times and physical needs changed so much from Jesus' day? Currently the economy is bad in many countries, which forces people to work extra hours to make ends meet. Why does it surprise us to realize that stress, depression, heart problems, and burnout now characterize people in our world?

After performing their duties, the disciples are told by Jesus that they need to rest. He calls them to "come away to a deserted place all by yourselves and rest a while." We need to hear this message today. In the midst of our busy days with phone calls, E-mails, faxes, papers to write, and presentations to give, we need to leave them for a while and take a time to rest. To my clergy colleagues, take a rest from those hospital visits, sermon preparations, and committee meetings. Hear the Lord calling to you, "Come away to a deserted place all by yourself and rest a while."

PRAYER: Lord, enable me to take and make Sabbath. Amen.

Days of Light and Thunder

July 21–27, 2003 • Gail Smith Chesson[‡]

MONDAY, JULY 21 • Read 2 Samuel 11:1-15

Spring brings new life and wondrous beauty. Winter becomes a memory as everything comes to life, made new in the world again. Ripe strawberries leave a cool sweetness upon our tongues and remind us life can be easy and good. Yet we know hidden storms can lurk behind those puffy white clouds that sail across the sky. A time of sunlight and thunder marks spring days. The sun and the storms participate in the drama that is spring.

David has had a springtime like this—a springtime of wonder and beauty, of thunder and storms. God has given him everything he needs—strong warriors, armies to defeat old enemies, a kingdom, a throne, but it isn't enough. David wants more, and he takes it without thought to the consequences. But David is not alone in this drama of spring storms.

Consider faithful Uriah, who dies in battle, striving to be a good soldier and servant. Consider Bathsheba, who must go with David since he is her king. Their lives are torn apart in the most violent of storms. As surely as the thunderheads build up, the pressure grows; and David must manipulate events to try to balance the wrongness of his actions.

David has forgotten God and has relied upon his own thinking and action rather than stopping to consider God's will. With that forgetting he lets loose a torrent of events, much like the roaring of a spring storm: thunder, lightning, and furious torrents flooding everything.

Are you in the midst of a summer ripe with opportunity? How will you use it?

PRAYER: God, help me to recognize those opportunities to do your work and not mine. Amen.

[‡]Educational and curriculum development writer; short story writer; member of Pullen Memorial Baptist Church, Apex, North Carolina.

This strong first verse condemns those who say there is no God. Initially this verse seems to invite us in for calm reflection. Can you feel the force of the anger? Has there been disappointment? Some betrayal or misjudgment, an experience of misplaced trust? Whatever the reason, the psalmist cries out and points at those who "are corrupt, they do abominable deeds; there is no one who does good."

The psalmist may also be asking us to look to our hearts. What is our relationship with God? Are we without blame? Have we mistreated another or denied God through our actions? We may find it difficult to look in the mirror and actually examine our own actions with regard to one another and to ourselves.

We often define our relationship with God by our treatment of others. Sometimes our actions take on a darker reflection of who we really are. When taking advantage of another's weakness, we lie rather than face the truth or confront conflict or discomfort. We don't say out loud that there is no God, but our actions do not reflect God's purpose in the world.

We often deny God through our thoughts about ourselves, choosing to believe we are stupid, inept, unworthy; or we don't like our bodies or our jobs. Ignoring our gifts from God in order to point out our imperfections, we forget we are God's creation to be light in the world. We fail to see that God offers an ongoing, life-giving relationship every day, every moment of our lives.

SUGGESTION FOR MEDITATION: **Take time today to let the love of God flow over you and into your heart. Allow God's love, like a cooling rain on a hot day, to shower you with peace and forgiveness. Then let the forgiveness flow out of you to those who have been involved in wrongdoing; ask forgiveness for them and for yourself, remembering how God loves us all.**

At the end of all these words of anger and dire consequences we come to the hope of the psalmist: "When the LORD restores the fortunes of his people...." After all the anger, anguish, and despair, the psalmist reveals the heart's true desire in these words. The phrase *the Lord will restore* is surely music to our ears. What a wonderful promise! *We* won't restore; *the world* won't restore. *God alone* will restore what has been lost. This restoration is a sure thing: The writer doesn't say *if*; the writer says *when*.

Think for a moment of all those empty places you carry inside yourself, all those empty places in the heart that you attempt to fill with food, drink, careless actions, and hurtful words. Do you have to strive to correct these problems? Yes, but the first step is to trust that God will restore.

We often fear any outcome but the one we plan. Yet if we can trust, we will find God's care better than our own. With trust comes hope like that of the psalmist.

Hope comes to us as a summer breeze, wished for but through no power on our part to make it happen. Suddenly there is a rustle of leaves, a slight bending of the flowers in the garden; and the unseen breeze cools our faces. We feel a moment of ease in the face of our dis-ease with ourselves. How much lighter our burden if we would rely upon the words *when the Lord restores* and know that we are cared for in the deepest sense of those words. God's care restores us much more than we ever could imagine. When God restores us, we can rejoice and be glad.

PRAYER: God of summer breezes, hold me in your love. Let me remember how you can fill my heart so that I need nothing else. Allow my trust in you to become fully formed, as is the fruit in summer. Amen.

Huge black clouds preceded the late-afternoon storm. Then the fury of the July storm pounded my garden. Storms can wreak havoc in a summer garden. Only plants with strong roots survive.

I went out to check on the garden. The weaker stems in a couple of the flowers had broken. Several heavy-headed sunflowers had been uprooted, but the rest of the flowers remained intact. I had propped up the plants that were a little tall or top-heavy. I had taken care to plant the seeds and the plants at the right depth. Giving my plants a fighting chance in the summer storms seemed to be my responsibility as a gardener.

The writer of these verses in Ephesians desires that we be strong in our inner being, rooted and grounded in love. This writer knows the importance of being strongly supported and properly placed when storms of a human nature come to uproot us. Our firm grounding in Christ and our strong inner being can help us weather life's storms.

How do we stay "rooted and grounded in love" as the world pounds us one way and another? The writer tells us that we may be strengthened through the Spirit—not our own spirit but God's spirit. Our own weaknesses fall before God's strength. We must rely upon God's strength, just as the plant relies upon the gardener to plant the seed deep enough so the roots are strong and deep. If God is planted within us, we will be strong enough to face the storms of life.

PRAYER: O God, we ask that you tend us as we go through the storms of our lives. As the Loving Gardener, plant us deeply in your love. Amen.

Have you stood in the dusk and watched the glory of the sunset? Have you wondered how so many colors could come forth from a blue sky? Once-white clouds turn mauve and purple; streaks of orange flare across the horizon and slowly turn to deep coral. Navy blue and a deepening green layer themselves across the lighter bands of color. Does that moment fill you with a sense of a power that is larger than your imagination can name?

We are told that "the power at work within us is able to accomplish abundantly far more than all we can ask or imagine." My imaginings are built on my experience: "I know what I know." Yet I continue to imagine, invent, and produce new ideas.

As human beings, we intuitively know our limitations. We know we, not the holy one, operate in the human realm. One look at the evening sky immediately reminds us of our limitations. We can appreciate its beauty, but had we been given the task of painting a sunset, would the scene before us have been the end result?

We'll never know. We can simply enjoy the sunset. Sometimes, though, we feel that we will not know this love "that surpasses knowledge" that God offers us. We want to know it but don't know how to know it. Unable to measure or reproduce it, we learn that what truly matters is how God's power is and will always be at work, doing far more than can even be imagined. God will fill us with a fullness of God, not a fullness of ourselves, working through us so that we may also do things beyond our experience or imagining. As the summer evening reflects the brilliant colors, we will reflect God's love and the power of that love.

PRAYER: O Creator of beauty in the world, thank you for inspiring us with nature's canvas. Thank you for the life we have and the ways in which you move within it. Amen.

This story of the loaves and fish makes me wonder: Is this story about hunger and being fed or about making do with what we have? An impossible request is made or a difficult situation is pointed out to Jesus, and then all wait to see what will happen. Will Jesus have an answer?

The story starts out simply enough. Thousands of people have gather in the grass, the sea air perhaps stirring appetites. As people watch Jesus heal and listen to his stories, the day grows late. The evening cool descends, and the disciples worry that there is no town nearby where someone can be sent for food. Jesus becomes the practical one. Have the people sit down and count them, he says. Then a miracle occurs with the few loaves and fishes from a boy's basket.

If you had read this parable with no knowledge of its outcome, what might you have expected? Would you have believed that a boy with five loaves and a few fish would suffice?

Yet if we are honest, we acknowledge that we often receive nurture from unexpected places and sources. An impromptu summer's picnic can find us in the meadow without quite everything we need, but the experience is so enjoyable we don't dwell on the lack but on the goodness we experience. Our lives can be filled with miraculous surprises if we pay attention to the moments of grace.

Jesus constantly surprises us with love and grace when we have no expectation of its happening to us. We think we'll be without; yet all the while the basket of loaves and fishes is nearby, blessed and waiting.

PRAYER: Jesus, we want, always want. Open our eyes to what we have and help us to share our goodness with others. Remind us of how deeply loved we are. Amen.

It is evening by the sea. We can imagine the cool, salty tang in the air and the first evening star in the sky. We can imagine the disciples getting in the boat to go to Capernaum, tired but glad to have fed the crowd. Jesus has had to break away from them all and has gone to pray.

Then the Gospel recounts a startling story. After one miracle of feeding huge crowds with bits of loaves and fishes, we immediately get one that defies our imagination. The story grips us with its drama, yanking us out of complacency by the end of the story. We can handle the great picnic and the miraculous feeding—but walking on water? The message we must hear is that of the great love and compassion offered to us at the precise moment we need it.

Take a closer look at the elements of the entire story. What needs does the story present? People hunger and must be fed. Friends at risk must be helped. Jesus' response to both dilemmas is simple: food and shelter. Notice the lack of hesitation in these responses. Gather food and feed the hungry. Calm fears and find shelter. There is no waiting to see if either action is right or appropriate or if all deserve such grace.

Jesus comes to the aid of friends in a small boat on a stormy sea and directs them to safety. Yet his unexpected appearance causes confusion among the disciples. They don't recognize Jesus, so he tells them, "It is I; do not be afraid." What better words to hear in the midst of a storm-tossed sea?

Jesus tells us no matter how great our hunger or our fear, his love for us will be enough. What about that inner emptiness we seek to fill or that unknown fear we try to conquer? Jesus says, "I will fill you up and steady the rolling waves of your life."

PRAYER: Lord, you are with us in our best and worst moments. As in the summer days of light and thunder, your redeeming love stays with us in calm and storm. We give thanks for the love that you give us in those times. Amen.

Our Sin, God's Righteousness

July 28–August 3, 2003 • *Hyeon Sik Hong*[‡]

MONDAY, JULY 28 • **Read 2 Samuel 11:26–12:6**

We were created by God with and in goodness, so where does our sin come from? Many times we sin because of greed and selfishness generated by evil thoughts of the mind. In Chinese the word *evil* literally translated means "self-centered mind," namely "my own mind."

Evil comes about when we try to live under the direction of our self-centered mind. The nature of sin lies in "my own mind." And whenever our mind is drawn by greed, we stand against God's mind and will. We turn our face from the spiritual consciousness with which God endowed us.

David the king sinned when he followed his own desires, thereby ignoring his spiritual consciousness and God's mind. His self-centeredness made him greedy. Blinded to his spiritual consciousness, David could not recognize or acknowledge his own sin. As Nathan told the story of the poor man, David immediately recognized the wrongdoing of the rich man and pronounced a judgment on his sin.

People who do not waken to their spiritual consciousness are easily tempted to sin. Each successive sin closes off our consciousness a little more. One sin brings another, and the result of sin is death. David killed Uriah, and as Nathan reminded David, "The sword shall never depart from your house" (12:10).

SUGGESTION FOR MEDITATION: Is human nature evil or good? Whenever we become greedy for something or someone, how do we take care of ourselves? Do we depend on our own self-centered mind or on God's mind?

[‡]Pastor, Tulip Street United Methodist Church, Nashville, Tennessee.

A greedy mind will always separate us from the truth of God. Our spiritual eyes, which see the right, become blind whenever we turn our eyes from the truth of God and shut the door to our spiritual consciousness.

A tiny greed can bring a huge evil. Greed invites evil, accompanies it, and works with it. And ultimately it causes sin. Sin is by nature secretive. We try to hide our sinful acts, not wanting them out in the open before God and others. We want to keep them secret forever. Eventually sin separates us from God and from God's truth revealed for us through the Word.

The nature of sin is separation. In Chinese, the meaning of *sin* comes through the image of two birds trying to escape from a net by flying in opposite directions. They turn their backs on each other and try to fly off, even though the net holds them. That is the nature of sin, which brings with it the sufferings of separation, loneliness, guilt, fear, and anxiety. We cannot escape the suffering of separation caused by sin without repentance.

David promptly confesses his sin and repents, "I have sinned against the LORD." How honest and courageous he is! Once he repents of his sin, God's forgiveness immediately follows: "Now the LORD has put away your sin." How gracious and merciful our God is! When we lay bare our secret sins, we receive God's forgiving grace and fly free from the net.

SUGGESTION FOR MEDITATION: What secret sins do you harbor? What would encourage you to open your heart and mind to lay those sins before God? Recall a time when you've confessed and repented of a sin. How did that make you feel?

Now David repents. The first step down the path of true repentance is to acknowledge that what we did wrong, to admit our guilt. Only in the light of God's righteousness can we see our guilt, acknowledge our wrongdoing, and repent.

When we repent of our sins within the forgiving grace of God, our sins are forgiven. As loving children of God, we find that with our repentance God blots out sin and iniquity; and we stand before God and one another washed and cleansed.

Only by the righteousness of God are we regarded as righteous. We can open our mouths to praise God's name and to proclaim God's truth, but repentance is not a simple change of outward behavior. It is, rather, a total change of the inner heart that brings about the change in our outer behaviors.

David is blessed again by God. His sincere and honest admission of transgression, his firm and thorough surrender to God's will, and his genuine repentance of sin move David in the direction of God's mind. When David acted from his self-centered mind, he was filled with greed and avarice; and he sinned. But when he realized his sins, he confessed them. He emptied his self-centered mind and looked for the mercy and grace of the forgiving God. Now his mind moves toward being more God-centered.

Repentance is a transitional process from self-centeredness to God-centeredness. God accepts David's sincere repentance and David's sin is forgiven. David experiences new life in God's grace and mercy.

SUGGESTION FOR MEDITATION: **How do you repent? After repenting does your mind feel more God-centered or self-centered?**

Looking for Jesus! One of the most spiritual desires of the Christian life is to look for Jesus, to ask continually, "Where are you, Lord?"

But why and for what? Why do we look for Jesus? Why are we so eager to be with him? We often pray for his presence; we would like to keep him forever. But we look for Jesus with many different intentions.

The crowd in today's lesson eagerly seeks Jesus. The people get into a boat, go to Capernaum, and find him on the other side of the sea. They put forth a lot of effort, but unfortunately they seek Jesus because they need a miracle worker who can multiply loaves.

Wonderful truths from heaven proclaimed by the Son of God fill the spirits of the crowd. There is such a great revelation of God's grace and mercy through Jesus, with precious promises of eternal life and salvation. The crowd has sought him to eat their fill of the physical loaves he indeed provides, but those wonderful spiritual loaves feed their souls.

This crowd of people looks for Jesus—not for everlasting spiritual nourishment but for temporal gluttony. To them Jesus is a great loaves provider, a good and benevolent magician. The crowd looks to satisfy its own greed.

Jesus invites us to look for the eternal food that does not perish: Jesus Christ. Let us not fill our minds with things that perish. Let us empty our minds and fill them with the things eternal. In the way of true Christian discipleship, looking for Jesus is important, but the intent of our looking is even more so.

SUGGESTION FOR MEDITATION: Why are you looking for Jesus? What type of bread do you desire? How will it fill you?

Still the crowd's concern centers on having "bread." They are spiritually malnourished yet do not understand Jesus' reference to the true bread. They simply want to fill their stomachs. So they cry, "Sir, give us this bread always." Often we allow physical desire to surpass ultimate things. But Jesus said in Matthew 6:33, "Strive first for the kingdom of God and his righteousness, and all these things will be given to you as well."

Jesus' response to the people's question shows a clear difference between his interest and theirs. Jesus talks about the bread that gives true life to the world, the life that belongs to the kingdom of God and God's righteousness: the life in Jesus Christ the Savior, the bread of life. If we come to him, we will never be hungry. If we believe in him, we will never be thirsty.

When we focus on ultimate things, salvation and eternal life through Jesus, our once primary concerns about earthly things become secondary. Our constraints in the earthly life no longer burden or worry us. The bread of life changes the focus of our concern, and we are always thankful to God. We thirst and hunger no more.

Faith in Jesus Christ leads to righteousness, and those who are righteous work for God. God's grace also challenges us. Through the wonderful grace of God we have the bread of heaven, the bread of life. We also have a responsibility and duty to share the bread with others. As Jesus works for us to give us eternal life, we also need to share that bread with others. As Jesus himself is the bread to feed others, we also need to be the bread of life, giving ourselves to others.

SUGGESTION FOR MEDITATION: **Just as we need bread for our daily physical life, we also need heavenly bread to nurture our spiritual life. Just as Jesus became bread for us, we need to become bread for others. In what ways are you sharing your bread with others?**

Christians are people called by God. We did not choose God; God chose us and called us to ministry. Because God called us, we are called God's children. What a wonderful privilege!

As the children of God, we need to know what God wants us to do. What does God call us to do?

God arranged all the various parts of creation in unity, harmony and oneness in which only peace exists. Through the Incarnation God came to the world to call all people into that oneness and unity, which Christ manifested on the cross. The cross restored the relationship between God and humans and the relationship among humans as well. Both relationships are united in the nature of love. We demonstrate our love toward God through our love toward others.

God calls us for the purpose of unity:"There is one body and one Spirit...one Lord, one faith, one baptism, one God and Father of all, who is above all and through all and in all." Our calling from God commands us to work for peace, which is the essence of unity. We are called to create oneness and to bring the world's many differences into unity.

This is the identity of Christians: ones who work for unity. This is the responsibility of Christians: to work for unity "with all humility and gentleness, with patience, bearing with one another in love." As we respond to God's calling, we understand the privilege of being called God's children.

SUGGESTION FOR MEDITATION: How do you interpret your calling from God? How does your calling to be a servant of God make you feel? In your role as peacemaker, what differing elements have you brought into unity and harmony?

Who we are often determines what we do. Therefore our identity as Christians is perhaps most clearly understood by our actions. We do what God desires and wills for us because we are the people of God.

By doing God's ministry together, we build up the body of Christ, which is the goal and purpose of Christian life. As we work for Christ, we ultimately achieve unity, maturity, and a measure of the full stature of Christ by God's righteousness. We grow up in every way into Christ, which is sanctification. And finally we reach Christian perfection. This is the process of Christian life to which we are called by God.

We do not stay in a status-quo state. God asks us to grow and to promote the body's growth as we move toward Christian perfection. All Christians work together for one reason and goal: unity in the body of Christ, the completion of love. Unity cannot become a reality without love. As we grow, we realize our goal of unity in love, which is Jesus Christ himself. That is the completion of love.

Called by God, Christians are newly born and justified. Our work is to grow toward sanctification, building the body of Christ in the unity of love. By our actions we will be known. Finally we will be glorified.

SUGGESTION FOR MEDITATION: **As a person called by God, where do you stand on your journey of faith? Do you find yourself at the beginning stage of your Christian growth, or are you growing now to reach the completion of love?**

Dearly Loved Children of God

August 4–10, 2003 • *Anne F. Grizzle*[‡]

MONDAY, AUGUST 4 • **Read Psalm 130:1-2**

I no longer have very young children, but I recently took my fifth-grader to the pediatrician. Outside the waiting room door I could hear the cries of sick children within. I recalled the sound that is regularly heard in a home with babies, even well-loved babies. When babies need something, they don't carefully choose their words or wait until they are sure they have an emergency. They cry as soon as they experience a need, sense a wrong, or feel any pain. A cry is not a polite request or thoughtful suggestion but a deep wail that arises out of the hope and even the expectation of a caring response. (Children without caring adults often no longer cry because they realize no response will come.)

As adults we cry less often, yet in the depths of pain or grief we too cry. Like babies, we cry out in the hope and expectation of an immediate, caring response. The psalmist in his depths cries out to the Lord to hear, to be attentive, to show mercy.

What have been your depths, and what is your depth today? What would your cries sound like if you were to cry to the Lord with an inner urgency and pleading hope?

As dearly loved children of God, we are encouraged to cry out, whether in our everyday need or in the midst of our depths. God listens attentively to the cries of God's children.

SUGGESTION FOR MEDITATION: Imagine one of your depths, whether that be an adult agony or childlike need. Fashion a personal cry for attentive listening and mercy, and in your deepest moment of this day, cry out to God.

[‡]Family therapist; author; speaker; member, St. John the Divine Episcopal Church, Houston, Texas.

In our world of fast food, cell phones, and multi-tasking, we find the act of waiting a difficult practice. Yet the psalmist here speaks of his soul's waiting diligently for the Lord. We hear the word *wait* several times in these two verses. The word comes alive as we imagine a night watchman whose whole job is to wait and watch in the long, dark hours before morning.

Several years ago I heard about monks who rose in the early morning hours for prayerful waiting and the keeping of night watch. While not a morning person, I accepted the challenge to taste these times that I had heard were among the sweetest. I did not attempt a daily rising at 3 A.M. as the monks do but adapted the idea to my modern life by choosing one morning to rise two hours early and simply sit in the night and watch. I brought only my open soul to this watchful time, simply repeating these verses from Psalm 130 and waiting for the Lord.

So amazing was my first morning (a full moon set while a mockingbird regaled me) that I began a weekly Sabbath night watch, which has become my spiritual oasis. I have learned to see and hear life in new ways, have discovered new colors in the sky's palette, have caught snatches of the subtle tunes in nature's music, and have glimpsed the poetry in my own soul. And in the midst of magical silence, God's still small voice has sounded crystal clear. Like new richness springing from ground left fallow, creative new life invariably flows from seemingly insignificant mornings of "wasted" waiting time.

Follow the psalmist's lead sometime and take a few minutes simply to wait for the Lord. Or be a watcher and wait for God over long hours, preferably dark night hours. Don't be surprised by the subtle or blazing dawn colors you discover deep in your soul and God's heart. You might find yourself making night watch a habit or a Sabbath practice.

SUGGESTION FOR MEDITATION: Carve out some still time today or this week and live these verses through quiet waiting. Sometime in the next month, rise before dawn and try a night watch.

I really enjoy bread. A friend who knows me well and loves me deeply once brought me one of the best birthday presents ever. She arrived not with a decorated cake but with a basket filled with a warm, homemade loaf of bread. Her gift delighted me, not because it was elaborate but because it so creatively came from a special knowledge and love of me.

Jesus knows us well and loves us deeply. He has brought us living bread for our journey in this life and into the next. In verse 51 Jesus states, "The bread that I will give for the life of the world is my flesh."

How do we partake of and claim this bread of life? Most visibly, we can gather with hungry hearts around Jesus' Communion table to feast on this bread that sustains our souls. As we wait on God there, we join the disciples who believed Jesus was not simply the son of Joseph but the Son of God and our Savior. At that table Jesus is present with us, nourishing our bodies with spiritual life and hope. Our gathering reminds us of another gift: We are part of a great communion that extends beyond the grave, a communion that will still include us even after our bodies die.

How do we continue to chew and digest the nourishment of this bread after we leave that Communion table? We might choose to use a simple Jesus prayer, repeating the name of Jesus with each breath or heartbeat throughout the normal wakings and walkings of our day. This prayer reminds us that we are not alone but known and loved deeply. As we say the name Jesus, we feast on the bread of his life breathed into ours, allowing the yeast of Christ to rise within us.

SUGGESTION FOR MEDITATION: Meditate in your heart on the last time you feasted on the bread of life at Jesus' Communion table. Bring that image up on the screen of your heart today by saying the name of Jesus. Enjoy the feast.

Absalom was no easy child for his father David to live with. Absalom had killed his older brother Amnon for raping his sister Tamar, after which Absalom fled to Geshur for three years. (Read 2 Samuel 13.) David eventually longs to see Absalom, so he sends for him to return to Jerusalem. (Read 2 Samuel 14.)

However, Absalom then conspires with the people of Israel against his father, an act that forces David to flee Jerusalem. In today's passage, King David sends men to fight the rebelling Israelites led by Absalom. But despite his position as king fighting against Absalom, David retains a tender heart for the son of his flesh. He tells his army commanders to be gentle with Absalom. But Joab, David's commander, is not about to let the enemy leader get away, so he kills Absalom (18:14) and throws his body into a pit.

When David receives news of victory over the rebels, his response comes from the heart of a father not the head of a king. He cannot rejoice at his army's great victory, for his grief at his son's death overwhelms him. His cry "O my son Absalom…! Would I had died instead of you, O Absalom, my son, my son!" is the desperately pained cry of a parent for a child. This cry of love and grief goes so much deeper than any anger at ungrateful behavior and impudent rebellion.

Here we have the Old Testament's picture of the love of a father for his prodigal son. With it we can sit amazed at the love that our heavenly Father must have for us even when we fight against God. The heavenly Father's deep heart desire is one of love, a desire for us to live even at the cost of the Father's own life.

SUGGESTION FOR MEDITATION: **Recall your worst feelings toward or acts of rebellion against God. Imagine God's sending an army to get you in line but with the deep wish for you to live. Imagine God calling your name in the phrase of verse 33: O my child _____! …Would I had died instead of you, O _____, my child, my child!"**

At dinner one evening I gave my three-year-old son a piece of bread (one of the few foods he enjoys eating). As the rest of us went about serving and beginning our meal, he was carefully breaking his bread into pieces. Then he offered a piece to one and then another of us saying, "One for you, and one for you, and one for you." We realized he was imitating what he had experienced so many times at Communion, and he was making our family meal a Communion table.

Loved children naturally imitate their parents. We have seen a loved child welcome visitors with arms flung open wide like those that have embraced her, a woman speaking with the same kind words and tone of her mother, or a man helping out a driver with a flat tire just as his father did many years ago.

At heart God wants us to know we are dearly loved children in the kingdom with its wide communion. Christ loved us enough to give his life, his body as our bread and a sacrifice for us that we would know a deep, broad parental love.

Once we have this love imprinted in our hearts through waiting on God, hoping in God's word, feasting on Christ's bread, God wants us to become imitators of this loving, sacrificial way of being and relating. To imitate, we must know someone well. Let us wait, eat, be embraced so that we can in turn reach out to those at table or at work or across the world who need to experience themselves as dearly loved children.

SUGGESTION FOR MEDITATION: **Imagine yourself as a dearly loved child whose parent has just sacrificed greatly for you. Now walk through your day—your tasks, your conversations, your attitude—as if you are a dearly loved child imitating your heavenly parent.**

As a family therapist, I love working with people, but I don't like record keeping. I'm grateful to discover in this psalm that the Lord has those same propensities.

I can imagine having a heart-to-heart conversation with God in which I bring up my worst faults and sins from past to present. And I can see God listening with great love and tenderness, embracing me while pronouncing forgiveness. Before we part, I picture God laughing and saying, "In my business we don't keep record of these things. Can we move on?"

Our faith is not based on the expectation that we will live perfect lives but rather that we have a God whose forgiveness and mercy are broad enough to cover all our failings. Beyond forgiving and forgetting, we read that we can expect full redemption. Redemption begins with something messed up and then mysteriously works something good from it.

Often people come to see me in great crisis and pain that force them to face hard feelings and to work through tough issues. I often tell them, "If you have to experience so much pain, let's be sure you gain some fruit from it." I watch people gain new self-understanding, develop a stronger relationship than before a blowup, and come to enjoy life more freely than ever before. Imagine an example of such redemption in your own life or that of a friend. Now place a current situation of difficulty before God for forgiveness and even redemption.

SUGGESTION FOR PRAYER: Converse about your sins with a forgiving God who keeps no records. Pray for full redemption.

I took great pleasure in my cousin's motto: "A clean house is the sure sign of a wasted life," because I am not a great housekeeper. Despite my cousin's motto, clean houses are sometimes signs of lives in great order. While all of us might have differing opinions on the value of cleanliness, this passage makes clear that our behavior and inner attitudes as Christians definitely require regular housecleaning.

This cleaning begins with a review of our behavior for any slips in telling the truth, controlling our temper, and working hard. We should pay special attention to examining the content of our conversation—not only for untruths but for anything that does not build others up. A friend mentioned the image of how hard it is to clean up after engaging in gossip: like trying to collect feathers emptied out of a pillow from a tall tower. Beyond our outward behavior, this scripture encourages us to go through the inner closets of our emotions, emptying out any anger, bitterness, unforgiveness, or malice.

Perhaps we can let our housecleaning pile up for a few weeks or months, but I find it helpful to do my temple-of-the-Spirit cleaning each evening. The ancient practice of the examen of consciousness calls for this daily review with accompanying thanks and confession. Fortunately we have a God of great forgiveness, who keeps no record of sins and loves us as dear children while we seek to grow in this high calling of Christ.

Suggestion for meditation: Take time this evening to do a brief review of the day. Try to clean out any daily dirt with God or others before putting your head on the pillow.

The Bread of Life

August 11–17, 2003 • *Steven Christopher*[‡]

MONDAY, AUGUST 11 • Read 1 Kings 2:10-12; 3:3-14

Solomon asks for an "understanding mind" so that in his role as king he may make decisions about the ordering of Israelite society consistent with God's intentions. This choice pleases God, and Solomon is granted his request. While we are not kings, we also have an obligation to consider how we can bring about God's vision for peace and justice in the world.

The prospect of making our voice as disciples heard in the world of politics, economics, and social relations is frightening. Often it is unclear which policy decisions would be consistent with God's intentions. Many circles equate the voice of religion with ignorance and superstition. If we make our voice heard as disciples, we may face ridicule; we may make the wrong decisions and support the wrong causes.

Today's text reminds us of three aspects of our relationship with God. First, God is concerned about the ordering of world societies. God was interested in Solomon's choices, and God is interested in our decisions as well. Second, God wants us to be coworkers in making peace and justice a reality. Third, God promises to be with us as we consider how to order our collective relationships in a manner consistent with God's purposes. God's promise of wisdom to Solomon is offered to us as well. If we turn to God in prayer, God will grant us discernment; then we can enter the world of politics, economics, and social relations with boldness and effect justice in the world.

SUGGESTION FOR MEDITATION: Consider how God may be calling you to make a difference in the world. What issues and causes are you passionate about? How have you responded to God's call to make peace and justice manifest?

[‡]Ordained elder, The United Methodist Church; student working toward Juris Doctor degree, Harvard Law School, Cambridge, Massachusetts.

This psalm is a song of thanksgiving in which the psalmist thanks God for God's action in human history on Israel's behalf. Central to the theology of ancient Israel was the notion that God *has acted* in history and that God *acts* in history with the purpose of bringing about justice and peace. The Israelites believed that God's acting in history brought about the world's creation, the calling of Abraham, the deliverance from Egypt, and the entry into the Promised Land.

At the time they occurred, all these events might have sounded like unpleasant, frightening, unfamiliar, and uncomfortable undertakings. When the Israelites had the opportunity to escape from bondage in Egypt, many of them probably regarded this option with fear rather than praise. The Israelites faced enormous risks in leaving: being captured and executed or starving to death in the desert. Even after escaping Pharaoh's soldiers and surviving in the desert, many of the Israelites longed for the "fleshpots" of Egypt. Only in retrospect over the long haul of history could they see God's grace and mercy fully revealed through the exodus from Egypt.

As Christians we believe that God has acted in history through Christ to bring about the redemption of the world. We can learn from the ancient Israelites to be willing to follow God's call, even when God calls us to frightening endeavors. Following God's call requires faith to step from the familiar into the unfamiliar, from certainty into uncertainty. Discipleship also requires a willingness to acknowledge that we may see God's grace and mercy only in retrospect. May we be willing to risk and follow God's call, assured of God's grace and mercy.

PRAYER: God of grace and mercy, we yearn for your presence during times of trial. Help us see that you are present with us, that your Spirit surrounds us, and that in Christ you have redeemed us. Allow us to be instruments through which you bring about justice and peace. Amen.

The psalmist draws a correlation between the fear of God and wisdom. A few years ago a theologian suggested that the contemporary mainline church change the title of the hymn "Holy, Holy, Holy" to "Nice, Nice, Nice," since mainline Protestant congregations exhibited no sense of the fear of God. In many ways, the God of the mainline churches has become an innocuous figure who doesn't do much besides gently encourage congregants to repent and turn to God—and that only as long as it doesn't unduly inconvenience them. Biblical texts suggesting God's loving and gracious nature are still quoted with enthusiasm. But texts that allude to God's anger or wrath are politely avoided, viewed as the product of an outdated theology. The notion of being afraid of God seems to be associated with fear and ignorance rather than wisdom.

There are compelling reasons to reject the notion of encouraging disciples to fear God. For some, the fear of God evokes expressions of Christianity that used the threat of God's wrath to scare persons into belief and Christian practice. In my Wesleyan tradition, the appropriate focus on God's grace and love seems to preclude the notion that God is one to be feared.

I believe the psalmist's association of wisdom with the fear of God is true for several reasons. Most important, the biblical image of God suggests a Being who, while gracious and loving, also will call us to accountability for our deeds and will judge us in the end. There are consequences to be feared when we turn away from God and do not live as disciples. When we turn away from God, we alienate ourselves from God's transforming work within us and prevent God from making us into a new creation in the image of Christ.

SUGGESTION FOR MEDITATION: Consider your own evaluation of the psalmist's message. In what possible ways do you understand the meaning of the statement that the fear of God is the beginning of wisdom?

During my days as a full-time pastor, I conversed with a parishioner who was a landlord in the community. This parishioner had a tenant who was several months behind on her rent. The tenant, an unemployed single parent, could not afford child care. She had no family to turn to for financial assistance; her only form of income came from public assistance. The landlord had to decide whether to evict the tenant or to grant an extension on the lease agreement, a genuinely disturbing moral dilemma. We had a long conversation and considered through prayer and reflection the appropriate response of a disciple.

Choosing the appropriate course of action in this situation required the discipline of wisdom. On the surface, the landlord's course of action seemed obvious—grant the tenant an extension on the rent. Yet doing so would create potential difficulties for the landlord; the landlord needed the tenant's rent to cover basic expenses, property taxes, and other costs. While that single tenant's rent would not bankrupt the landlord, setting such a precedent could have led other tenants to make similar claims of economic duress. Finally the landlord decided to grant a limited extension to the tenant.

There is a need to act with wisdom in the world. Sometimes the church downplays the value of wisdom, when in actuality the church should be a place where we are imbued with wisdom to face life in a complicated world that requires wisdom to decide rightly. The church should also be a place where we challenge one another to grow in wisdom and discernment. Through God's grace, we can act with wisdom and face the difficult dilemmas and decisions that confront us.

PRAYER: **Almighty and everlasting God, grant us wisdom to face the difficult decisions that confront us every day. May we act decisively and boldly to proclaim your reign in the world. Through Christ we pray. Amen.**

The writer tells the Ephesians that they have the responsibility of living as wise people, surrounded by an unwise world. The citizens of Ephesus who receive this letter know that fact all too well. The early Christians faced the formidable task of living out a system of belief and practice that fundamentally differed from the surrounding Greek culture.

These verses convey important advice for the Ephesians as they attempt to develop wisdom and insight. Verse 19 instructs them to "sing psalms and hymns and spiritual songs among yourselves, singing and making melody to the Lord in your hearts." On the surface, this suggestion for what disciples do when they enter into community appears innocuous. The casual observer would have been unclear as to how singing songs would necessarily lead to wisdom and discernment. Certainly this approach seems less effective than reading, pondering, or listening to one of the philosophers in the marketplace.

But this suggestion to the Ephesians affords good advice. Singing provides a mechanism that communicates to us the meaning and significance of the faith. Singing the words of hymns and reflecting on them can form faith within us. In addition, by singing the hymns together in community with other disciples, we strengthen the bonds of the community and gain strength to live as disciples in the world.

One of the greatest testaments to the value of gathering in community to sing is the long-standing nature of this practice, which was already centuries old in the Jewish tradition. It has been practiced for thousands of years in the Christian tradition. Today millions of Christians voluntarily gather to worship and sing together. The vitality of the practice itself suggests its value, worth, and efficacy.

SUGGESTION FOR MEDITATION: How often do you gather to sing the hymns of the faith? In what ways does this singing affect your moods and attitudes? How has music influenced your faith?

Jesus makes some serious claims about himself that would have startled his listeners. Many more may have been offended or outraged. Ancient Jewish tradition considered the notion of digesting flesh offensive and irreligious. It also clearly violated the law of Moses as established in the Torah.

Jesus' lofty self-perception would have also shocked the average Jewish listener. Jesus appears to be a Mediterranean Jewish peasant, yet throughout the Gospels he implicitly suggests that he preempts the Jewish rulers, the Roman state, and even Moses. No wonder many of Jesus' listeners dismiss him as an egomaniac or lunatic. Mark's Gospel tells us that even his family thought he was mentally unstable.

Consider your reaction if, having had no previous exposure to Christianity, you passed by Jesus as he spoke these words on a busy street corner. I like to think that if I were one of the original listeners, his words would have intrigued rather than offended, and I would have found myself compelled to listen further. Yet with no previous exposure to Jesus, I would have had no more reason to believe the truth of his words than any other prophet I had heard. I might have merely walked away, preoccupied with other concerns.

An important lesson for disciples today is this: Don't be afraid to preach Jesus' message, even though the words sound increasingly odd to the world. Like Jesus, we face the task of bringing God's word to a culture that will probably find the message strange, offensive, and irrational. We face the prospect of rejection, just like Jesus. However, Jesus didn't fear rejection or puzzled looks—nor should we.

PRAYER: Creator God, who has been revealed to us in Christ, lead us to the Christ and give us understanding and patience to see the Christ in the world and in others. Let us be Christ for the world. Amen.

The bread of life discourse indicates John's Christology. John conceived of the Christ as having the single objective of becoming incarnate in order to bring about redemption. If we look closely at the way Jesus speaks of himself through the image of bread, we see that the bread has a single function: to be ingested in order to bring life. Nothing indicates that the bread has any other role or exists for any other purpose.

The discourse suggests that Jesus is concerned with bringing about the world's redemption rather than seeking his own interests. Throughout John's Gospel, Jesus focuses upon this single purpose, speaks almost exclusively about it, and is willing to die to effect it. Even after death, Christ continues to act in the world selflessly in order to effect the redemption of the world.

The bread of life discourse is also indicative of John's vision of discipleship. The image of the believer's literally ingesting Jesus himself suggests the radically all-consuming nature of discipleship: to be transformed into the image of Christ himself. Applying the bread of life discourse to the task of discipleship means giving Jesus our souls, allowing Christ to enter our hearts and transform them.

The Wesleyan tradition upholds the belief that church attendance, good works, and participation in the Eucharist are means to an end rather than ends in themselves. They are means of grace that unite us with Christ. However, the bread of life discourse also implies that disciples are to be Christ for the world, to effect redemption in the world, and to be ultimately concerned for the world's welfare. The text suggests that discipleship is a long process through which we transform ourselves into the likeness of Christ.

SUGGESTION FOR MEDITATION: **Consider how the bread of life discourse impacts your understanding of God, of Christ. How do these understandings affect your life as a disciple in the world?**

The Yearning Soul

August 18–24, 2003 • Elesha J. Coffman[‡]

MONDAY, AUGUST 18 • Read Psalm 84

I spent the summer after my freshman year in college working at a camp in Wisconsin. As I daily labored to the point of exhaustion in the horse barn, I also struggled to make new friendships and establish a faith independent of my family or the routines of my home church. Sometimes it all weighed me down.

When I just wanted to think, I'd walk a mile down the lane to the boulder that marked the camp's driveway. I'd press my hand against the rough, cool surface for a few seconds before heading back to face the rest of my day.

I've visited the camp several times since that summer, and as I wind through the woods on my way, I eagerly watch for that boulder. I've met God there, and I want to meet God there again. The place itself rejuvenates my spirit.

The author of Psalm 84 pines for a spiritual place too—the temple in Jerusalem. He writes, "My soul yearns, even faints, for the courts of the Lord; / my heart and my flesh cry out for the living God" (NIV). Some circumstance is keeping him from the Temple, but he would rather spend one day there "than a thousand elsewhere."

Spending time in places that have special meaning to us can move us closer to God, not because those places have magical qualities but because they focus our spiritual longings. Being in that special place matters because we first yearn to be there. Maps can't lead us to God, but thirsty souls know the way.

PRAYER: With the psalmist we declare, "O LORD of hosts, my King and my God. / Happy are those who live in your house, ever singing your praise." Amen.

[‡]Former managing editor of *Christian History* magazine; current doctoral student in American religious history, Duke University, Durham, North Carolina.

A congregation's priorities usually find concrete expression in its sanctuary. Baptism seems to have been particularly important in the early church—baptismal fonts are often archaeologists' only clues that a crumbled structure was once a place of worship. Because Roman Catholics highly revere the Eucharist, they traditionally position the altar as the focal point of their churches. Most Protestants situate the pulpit front and center. One of the founding principles of Protestantism is "Scripture alone," so the place from which God's word is read and expounded receives the most attention.

No church, however, contains what Solomon's Temple had: the ark of the covenant of the Lord. This ark was not, as the Indiana Jones movie suggested, a box with the power to create thunderstorms and kill Nazis. In a way we cannot fully understand, the ark actually held God's holiness. That's why Solomon made such a big production of bringing it up from Zion and why it rested in the elaborately isolated Holy of Holies. A person who trifled with the ark could end up dead. (See 2 Sam. 6:6-7.)

Everyone who worshiped at Solomon's Temple knew that down a corridor, behind a curtain, and between two massive sculpted angels lived, somehow, the God of the universe. The thought must have set their hearts racing. But—and this is crucial—ordinary folks couldn't go near the ark. God was so close, and yet impossibly far away.

We marvel at the idea of God's living right around the corner. How much more would someone at Solomon's ceremony have marveled at the idea of God's living inside mere mortals!

PRAYER: Eternal God, it is almost too much to imagine that you would come to earth and then come even to me. Help me respond to the gift of your holiness touching my life. Amen.

On a junior-high church retreat the youth pastor asked each of us to define *love*. Of all the probably preposterous answers, I only remember my definition: "total preoccupation." Leave it to a thirteen-year-old girl to come up with that answer.

In a way, I still stand by my answer. By definition a preoccupation comes before other tasks and routines. It constantly runs in the back of the mind, popping up in moments of reflection or decision making. Sometimes it may seem forgotten, but it never completely goes away. Love really is like that.

Today's passage may not seem to have much to do with love. In many Old Testament scriptures, the priests' job comes across as rote, rigid, complicated, and more than a little gory. Priests sacrificed, prayed, and performed other ceremonies because Israel's spiritual health depended on their prayers and actions. We rarely glimpse priests' thoughts or emotions. But we know that humanity was created to love God and that worship is meant to be a tangible expression of that love. Thus a priest's preoccupation—the job before the job—must have been to love.

Perhaps that is why the cloud in the Temple overwhelmed the priests. They might also have felt fear, plus some awe and unworthiness; but more than anything else these priests suddenly met the object of their deepest, strongest love. No wonder they were speechless. The glory of the living Lord has that effect on those who love God.

PRAYER: Ever-present God, give me a taste of your glory. Nurture in me a love so intense that the thought of you erases all my distractions and gives me the strength to do your will. Amen.

"But will God indeed dwell on the earth?" Solomon asks in verse 27. Dedicating a house for God, the king wants to believe that the answer is yes! Still, it seems impossible. "Even heaven and the highest heaven cannot contain you, much less this house that I have built!"

"Will God indeed dwell on the earth?" Jesus' incarnation should have settled the question once and for all. Yet people had a hard time swallowing the truth about Jesus too. In the first centuries after Jesus, a group called the Docetists argued that Jesus was God, but he only seemed to be human—the deity would never stoop so low as to drink our water and breathe our air, let alone experience our death.

Another group, called the Ebionites, believed that because Jesus did not fit the profile of the God of Hebrew Scriptures, he must have been just a specially blessed prophet. A third group, the Apollinarians, suggested that a divine mind guided Jesus' fleshly body, but the two natures never mixed. None of these groups could handle the idea that, in Jesus, God's feet touched the ground—and got dusty in the process.

It's easy to get lost in the details of Jesus' human and divine natures. We can't completely figure him out, because God is still bigger than the heavens and far bigger than our brains. But we know something Solomon, the world's wisest person, could scarcely fathom. God did indeed dwell on earth!

SUGGESTION FOR MEDITATION: What does God's incarnation in Jesus mean to you? How has this truth affected your life?

No human being was ever physically closer to Jesus than his mother Mary. She carried him within her body for the first nine months of his earthly life. She felt him kick, punch, hiccup, and stretch. In turn, he felt her heartbeat. For those months he and she were one.

Even with the Holy Spirit living inside us, we cannot recreate that physical experience. The closest approximation we have is Communion, during which we partake of the "real food" of Jesus' body and the "real drink" of his blood.

Christians over the centuries have debated, sometimes viciously, what Jesus meant in speeches such as today's passage. Some believe that Jesus meant the bread and wine (or grape juice) truly become his body and blood, though human senses cannot perceive the change. Some believe that Jesus spoke symbolically, as he did when comparing himself to a vine or his kingdom to a mustard seed. Either way, this passage has the same message: Communion joins us to God.

Different churches have different ways of administering the elements too. My church distributes tiny cups and wafers to everyone in the congregation. It's not the most historical or elegant system, but I love holding my own cup for one reason: If I sit still and peer intently enough, I can see the liquid pulse in time with my heartbeat. The same rhythm rippling his blood and mine—that's how close I want to be to Jesus.

SUGGESTION FOR MEDITATION: What does it mean to have a heart that beats with the heart of Jesus? How does that closeness color your decisions, your worship, the way you interact with people around you?

Especially since the terrorist attacks on America, security sells. Television ads promise burglar-proof homes, recession-proof investments, crash-proof cars, and theft-proof credit cards. Americans are buying too. An influx of new business helped insurance companies offset huge claims from individuals and companies who suffered on September 11.

Defenses like home security systems, bank accounts, and air bags can avert some disasters. But money cannot buy total protection from the worst that life has to offer. Today's passage speaks of "the devil's schemes" (NIV). Key codes and 401K plans aren't going to stop the devilish schemes.

We need to face the fact that we can't control the world. Even more important, we need to remember who can. Besides providing only faulty protection against life's real problems, commercial comforts can insulate us from God. Whenever we place more trust in our own brilliant defenses than in our all-powerful God, we've actually unlocked a door for the intruder.

Today's verses don't just shake our defenses; they offer better ones. God promises full armor: righteousness, faith, and salvation to guard us; truth to help us stand; the gospel to get us going; and scripture to keep us in the battle.

This armor wouldn't sell well on TV, because it won't ward off all earthly problems. The epistle writer, "an ambassador in chains," is probably writing from a prison, and he doesn't know if he'll survive the experience. But the writer knows that God is on his side, so he has nothing to fear. When we drop our desperate grip on provisional defenses and put on the armor of God, we need not fear evil either.

PRAYER: Sovereign God, thank you for the promise of true protection. Help me to remember that you are always closer than my fears. Amen.

The famous Great Commission at the end of the Gospel of Matthew comes well after today's passage. Jews in Solomon's day operated with a different commission, claiming God's promise to their father Abraham: "Through your offspring all nations on earth will be blessed" (Gen. 22:18, NIV). The Israelites didn't always know what that meant, and they didn't always follow through on what they did know. However, when they hit the target, it resembled Solomon's speech in today's verses.

Solomon's Temple was one of the most magnificent structures of its day. Since rulers from surrounding kingdoms had provided building materials, the place was famous before its completion. Solomon wanted every tourist, every gawker, every trader who merely heard tales of the Temple to know of the God who lived there. He asked the participants at his assembly to spread the word.

Solomon's Temple stood for over four hundred years before Babylonian king Nebuchadnezzar destroyed it in 587 B.C. Many dreams fell with the Temple, but the call to bless all nations on earth remained.

We know from First Corinthians that our bodies are temples of God. We may not attract crowds with glittering gold and sculpted magnificence, but we still have a duty to spread the word about what's really going on inside. God's amazing, indwelling closeness is intended to benefit not just us but everyone around us. Solomon's Temple pointed hearts toward God, a mission that remains with us today.

PRAYER: Lord of all, make me sensitive to those who don't know you. When they turn to me in their search for truth, give me wise words and a welcoming spirit, "so that all the peoples of the earth may know your name and fear you." Amen.

Is Your Heart Really in It?

August 25–31, 2003 • Jim Eastin[‡]

MONDAY, AUGUST 25 • Read Psalm 45:1-2, 6-9

We call it "paying lip service," and the phrase comes from the passage that Jesus quotes in the lection from Mark's Gospel: "These people...honor me with their lips, but their hearts are far from me" (Isa. 29:13, NIV). This week's scripture passages explore different ways of having one's heart in one's words.

The scribes and Pharisees who come to see Jesus have the correct words, but their hearts' intention is to trap Jesus. James teaches the church about the word of truth, which is sometimes "unheard" as a person guards his or her tongue and acts out the belief in the heart. In the Song of Solomon, the two lovers act and speak only with their hearts. Finally, from the psalm we read the lip service of a professional—words of flattery and poetry that celebrate a grand and festive wedding but suggest that the poet may have another motive at heart. In the last verse of the psalm, this person who has praised the king and his bride and who has even arguably at one point called the king "God" [Hebrew *elohim*, v. 6] says, "I will cause your name to be celebrated in all generations." Who is being flattered now?

The words from our lips are powerful tools for good or ill. They can obfuscate or bear witness. They can lie or reveal our heart's deepest desires. In all our conversations with people and with God, we use words. With people we may be able to hide our hearts, but with God we never can. Especially in prayer we must strive for honesty. Our God is a great God and can handle our disappointments and frustrations as well as our praises. We just have to put our hearts into our words.

PRAYER: Christ, create in me a clean heart and help me to translate graciously what is there to my lips. Amen.

[‡]United Methodist minister for nineteen years; now the Program Director for the Gospel Music Television Network, Knoxville, Tennessee.

Like many other teenagers in junior high school, I took up the guitar in the early 1970s. It helped me to express my joy and anger, angst and rebellion, pain and, of course, love. I wrote a joyous "life will always be wonderful" song for every girl I fell in love with and a depressing "life will always be miserable" song every time someone dumped me. Teenagers usually express strong emotion in poetry or song rather than apologetics. Think back to your first significant romance at thirteen or fourteen years of age. Prose may have failed from time to time, but didn't you always have your "special song"?

In our text-driven, English-speaking, Western culture, we easily forget that Hebrew poetry is not meant to be read aloud; it is sung. Whatever the true history of this collection, "Song of Solomon" is a collection of love songs. In verse 8 the voice of the beloved draws the speaker's attention. Like a troubadour serenading below a window, he sings her to himself. May our love for God and others be so deep that prose cannot contain it, forcing us to express it in song.

SUGGESTION FOR MEDITATION: **One does not exegete a song in the same way one does other types of literature: Grammar and vocabulary take second place to emotion and rhythm. Sing the lesson with little concern for the tune or the quality of singing; sing to hear it in a new way. Use a different register for the female singer in verses 8-10a and the male in 10b-13. Sing it five or ten times until the words flow easily; then sing it toward the window as if someone were outside listening. Sing it as two teenagers would. Sing it as two seventy-five-year-olds would. Sing the first part as a prayer and listen for God to sing the other part.**

Pick any interpretation—literal, allegorical, cultic, dramatic, poetic—the lover who invites one to "come away" has a great deal to offer. The magnetic power of one who loves us passionately, devotedly, and expectantly is hard to resist. It puts a silly grin on our faces. It makes us long for the phone to ring even when there is nothing to talk about. How much more exciting if the lover who beckons is the God of Israel or the Christ.

I have trouble using the imagery of "my beloved" in reference to God. It gets mixed up with a concept of the maleness of God from my childhood and with the "otherness" of God from my divinity school days and with the crushing disappointment I suffered as the result of an unfaithful beloved. It has always seemed safer to keep God a little distant, a little formal, a little tentative, lest this relationship fail as well.

Nevertheless the call still comes. The lover still beckons through the song with imagery that speaks of spiritual union as exciting and passionate as lovemaking—imagery echoed in Christian writers from Augustine to Teresa of Avila to Jars of Clay. If God really wants to bring fulfillment to all the failed hopes and expectations we have had for human love, then perhaps this is what it means for the "winter to be past" and the "rains to be gone" from our lives. It is time to move from the disappointment of a distant relationship with God to an intimate and fulfilling companionship with God. It is time to skip through the flowers, hear the birds sing, and walk hand in hand with the beloved who has always called us, loved us, and longed for us to be in love.

PRAYER: O God, your love for us makes our lives fresh and exciting. Keep us in love with you. In the name of the One who calls us to "come away" we pray. Amen.

Mark's Gospel was written for the young Gentile church. He interprets Jewish customs with which his readers may not be familiar, tries hard not to offend the Pharisees who would have been prominent in community synagogues after the destruction of the Temple, and prompts the reader into dialogue with the text by use of the "secrecy motif" and by what I call the "moron motif." The "secret" about Jesus' identity as the Son of God is never a secret to the reader, and any question about Jesus' teaching is always cleared up as Jesus explains things to the thick-headed Twelve.

In this lesson the issue is the Gentile church's relationship to Jewish cleanliness laws. The Jews have accused Jesus' disciples of not obeying the laws of the ancestors. Jesus tells them the weakness of the law: It can only regulate what one does. Jesus challenges people to regulate what they desire. What makes us unclean is not what we touch or eat—what comes from the outside—but what comes from the inside: the evil intentions, the hateful longings, the desire to harm others. This must have been a troubling thought to Jesus' hearers. They had spent much of their lives practicing the rituals of cleanliness. After all, it is so much easier to follow a ritual than to change one's heart.

The challenge is still with us. It is still easier to search for a rule to obey than to regulate what we think, easier to hate someone and still smile at them as we wish for their destruction. No one knows our secret thoughts. No one is the wiser except God and ourselves. The temptation is to continue desiring what we would never openly advocate or admit. Only when we seek Jesus' way and replace those evil desires with loving ones are we truly clean again.

PRAYER: O God, cleanse me this and every day by creating in me a clean heart and renewing a right spirit within me. Amen.

The big-city SWAT (Scribblers, Wet blankets, And Theology) team have come from Jerusalem to shut Jesus' healing ministry down. As the SWAT team members watch the healing miracles take place, they decide that they have to criticize Jesus openly in order to stop him. Will their criticism be about the healing itself? No. Surrounded as they are by the recently healed, that would be a losing and possibly dangerous strategy. Perhaps they will complain that Jesus encourages people to believe he is the messiah. Wrong again. Healing on the Sabbath perhaps. Nope. The best they can come up with is this lame excuse: "Your disciples don't wash their hands properly before they eat."

How can these folks compare healing of the sick to this inconsequential matter of "dipping" hands in water to run off any demons one might accidentally ingest while eating? Perhaps it is a matter of what one believes that is important. Jesus says that the scribes and Pharisees have substituted the commands of the ancestors for the commands of God. Jesus' priority is healing the sick and proclaiming the gospel. The SWAT team attempts to retain authority for themselves.

Things have changed little from that time to this. I have served churches in which the color of the sanctuary carpet or who got to chair a committee became the highest priority. We hear almost weekly about some scandal among clergy or laity who put power, money, prestige, or personal desire above their calling. How different the Gospel story might have been if, after seeing Jesus' work and realizing its importance, the SWAT team had come to Jesus saying, "We would like to talk with you later about some issues; but in the meantime, what can we do to help you with God's work?" How might our stories differ if we approach Jesus that way now?

PRAYER: Lord Jesus, as I go though my day, may I be open to your work and put mine aside to join you in yours. Amen.

They were both good men. I had worked with each of them and liked them equally well, but when I came in that morning the tension between them was palpable. Before the day was over, one had been fired and the other reprimanded. Why? No one was ever sure. A misunderstanding had escalated into angry words, and the damage became irreparable. The future that might have been was lost forever because of angry words.

What would you give to be able to reclaim an angry sentence you've uttered? You know the kind I mean, one that forever darkened your relationship with someone else. I can think of some that, if reclaimed, would change my entire life story. This is why James goes to such great pains to tell us to watch what we say, to "bridle [our] tongues."

Wouldn't you be proud and a little scared if you knew that some of your writing would still be read two thousand years later? I wonder if James had any idea of the lasting impact of his words. If so, would he have said anything different? I don't think so. The first of James's themes in this lection is the control of one's words. He is concerned that Christians speak wisely and not allow angry words to ruin their Christian witness. As children of the Father of lights we are "quick to listen, slow to speak, [and consequently] slow to anger." When we delay our words, the word of truth in us has the chance to speak to others, bringing just the right word in a situation. That word has the power to bring light to our world and also to change the future forever.

PRAYER: O Lord, may all the words of my mouth be acceptable in your sight. Amen.

Our little United Methodist Church in Wingate, North Carolina, had finished a much needed multipurpose building. With dedicated fund-raising and giving, we had paid for the building years ahead of schedule. A question arose about a $5,000 building grant that the Albemarle District had given us. Should we consider those funds spent and close the books, or should we take $5,000 from the church budget to return the grant with our thanks? Either action seemed appropriate since we had used the money for its intended purpose. However, one statement ruled the day. In our business meeting someone said, "It's true that the money was given to us for the fellowship hall, and we did spend it on that. But if we send the district this money back, maybe someone else will have the chance to build a fellowship hall like ours." The treasurer sent a check the next day.

The second of James's themes in this passage is the need for action to accompany belief. Much ink has been spilled over the issue of "faith versus works," which comes up here and in other places in James, but that debate creates a false dichotomy.

James does not say that either is unimportant, but that the combination of the two is Christianity's proper form. James goes on to give an illustration so basic that caring people would surely agree. True religion is about controlling one's mouth, caring for the needy, and keeping one's self from the world's wicked ways. The admonition goes beyond an individual expression of faith to a corporate expression of faith within the faith community. Not only might "I" act in this way, but also "we" should act in this way. The church is not just a collection of persons who take matters to heart but a living body that is also called to act out its beliefs faithfully.

PRAYER: O Christ, I pray that my religion may always demonstrate both belief and action and that the same may be said for the faith community of which I am a part. Amen.

Lessons from the Poor

September 1–7, 2003 • *Virgilio Vazquez-Garza*[‡]

MONDAY, SEPTEMBER 1 • **Read Psalm 125**

Many years ago my family and I were traveling in South America and were driving in the direction of the highest peak in the Andes mountains, Aconcagua. We were driving on relatively flat land, so we could see the mountains on the horizon. As we drove toward them, they seemed to move away from us; then suddenly their awesome size loomed before us. The closer we got, the bigger the mountain. How majestic! How inspiring!

The psalmist uses a beautiful image to describe how those who trust the Lord might experience the Lord's presence. Remembering our time before the high peaks in South America, I understand the comfort the psalmist tries to convey to us. Our God surrounds us in the same way the mountains surround some geographical locations. What an awesome image! What a comforting thought!

We live in a society where the greedy and dishonest seem to thrive, which discourages us. We may believe that doing good and being honest will not amount to much. We begin to question whether such action really makes a difference, whether being faithful to God takes us anywhere.

Remember that God is with God's people. Trust in the ways of God. Remember that sometimes the mountains seem to move away from you, but it is just an illusion. Soon the awesome majesty of the mountain will give comfort.

PRAYER: When I get discouraged and feel like giving up, remind me, O God, that you are with me just as the mountains surround Jerusalem. May I do good even when doing good does not meet the world's expectations. Amen.

[‡]Born in Monterrey, Mexico; pastor of St. Luke's United Methodist Church, Corpus Christi, Texas.

I grew up in a developing country, where poverty and need are part of everyday life. People routinely sit on the sidewalk, stretching out their arms in a gesture for help. Sometimes I might pass four or five in a distance of a few yards. It is not uncommon for the locals to walk past these needy persons without noticing them, even when they almost have to jump over them.

Many of these persons in need congregate around churches, hoping that those attending services will have pity and offer some assistance. A good number of the church attenders do not acknowledge the presence of the needy. Some might drop a coin or two in the outstretched hands. The usual reaction of the recipient is to say, "Thank you; God bless you." The givers usually continue on their way.

One day as I waited for the bus, a man approached the small group of persons requesting alms by a large church. He asked if any of them were hungry. The unanimous response was not a vocal one, but heads nodded yes and faces illumined with hope. The man went to a nearby car, opened the trunk, and took out a large bag filled with sandwiches that he began to hand out. The men and women began to push, but he invited their patience: "There is enough for everybody."

As the folks moved away, eating their sandwiches, several uttered the words *God bless you.* "God bless you," he responded. The man returned to the car, got in, and drove away. As I boarded the bus I thought, *He did not go in the church....*I wonder if he is a religious person.

PRAYER: Lord, help me live the faith. Amen.

In many countries all people don't receive equal treatment. Some men and women are considered inferior because of their skin color, ethnic background, or social class. We create barriers that divide us.

My dad, going through a difficult time financially, accepted odd jobs to help our budget. A wealthy member of our church had asked him to make some repairs at his house. My father conscripted me as his assistant, and I found myself working all day at the huge house of our brother in the faith.

The job took longer than we expected, and we found ourselves near lunchtime still working hard. Mom had placed some "tacos" in a bag in case we did not return in time for lunch. We asked the maids of the house if we could warm up our lunch on the stove, and they agreed. Knowing we were members of the same church as the master of the house, they gave us plates and glasses. We sat in the backyard enjoying our meal.

While we ate, the lady of the house arrived and noticed that we were eating in the backyard. She entered the kitchen and began to question the maids as to why we were using her plates and glasses. Then she ordered them to wash and boil the items we had used.

I remember telling my dad, "I didn't know that poverty was contagious." And my dad replied, "Son, whether we are rich or poor, we are all made from the same clay by the same Creator. Do not hate this person, but love her even more."

PRAYER: Remind me, O God, that you have created me, as well as those whom I find unlikable for whatever reason. Help me to have a heart that is open to all. Amen.

Having grown up poor, I resented the deference paid the rich. It did not matter whether their opinions had any merit. Their wealth made their opinions more valued than the opinions of others—both in the secular society and in the church. I found it particularly upsetting when this deference occurred in the church.

My father, an independent electrical contractor in Mexico, made a modest living and actively participated in our local Methodist church. When the congregation undertook the rebuilding of the sanctuary, he offered several suggestions based on vast experience. But the building committee chose to listen to the suggestions of prominent church members who were wealthy but who had no experience with construction.

I remember how upset I was, and Dad had a conversation with me. He asked that I not forget the experience and hoped that some day I would be in a better financial situation than he. He also cautioned me to remember how it felt to be ignored and set aside because of social status.

These verses from James bring back memories of my father's talk with me about how we choose to imitate prominent people rather than learning from God, how the Mexican revolution produced not new leaders but different oppressors. The poor, once in power, imitated the oppressors.

Perhaps some of us have ignored the poor, but we remember that all persons are children of God regardless of social status, gender, age, or other barriers of our own creation.

PRAYER: Loving God, open my eyes to see others as you see them. Make me a loving and accepting person. Amen.

God has always been on the side of the poor. The Bible shows again and again the concern for the poor and the afflicted. We often try to provide services for the poor but seldom think about other aspects of our lives that may contribute to the exploitation of the poor.

Some of us may hunt for bargains in shoes and clothing without considering that some of the bargains result from cheap labor in other parts of the world. Some of us may invest in stock of companies that participate in the exploitation of children and women in other parts of the world. Some of us may eat food that is harvested by exploited workers somewhere in Latin America.

The United Methodist Church has had a policy of investing in a responsible way and avoiding companies that directly or indirectly support racial discrimination, violation of human rights, gambling, or pornography.

We may not see ourselves as persons who rob the poor or crush the afflicted. We may even consider ourselves good Christians because we write checks for the local food pantries and other charities. But some of our casual attitudes toward the economic reality in which we live may need revision as we responsibly consider the ripple effects of our actions that we have not even imagined.

I just checked my shirt and read, "Made in Mexico." The minimum salary there is less than ten dollars a day. Awareness can help us make more equitable decisions that have worldwide ramifications.

PRAYER: God of justice and love, help me support the poor— not just the ones I see around me but all poor in this global village where we live. Amen.

When I first read this passage as a child, I was appalled by Jesus' response to the Gentile woman. It did not fit my image of Jesus. Then one day a person in a Bible study in a poor neighborhood of Mexico City read this passage. I asked the participants about their reaction to the story.

A quiet elderly woman said, "I see a woman of faith. I see how the woman knew that Jesus had the power to heal her daughter. I see how she had faith and kept butting until her request was granted." Her reference to "butting" puzzled me, so I asked about that term. She replied, "Sometimes the calf has to butt the udder to get the milk."

The woman's insight caught me by surprise. I had tried to find a way to excuse Jesus in this story and had not noticed the faith of the Syrophoenician woman.

My friend in the Bible study went on to explain that Jesus gives a lesson to the disciples about the faith of the Gentiles. "We are like the Gentiles," she explained. "No one wants to touch us or speak to us because we are poor and dirty." She looked at me, pointed a crooked finger my way, and said, "But we have more faith than all of you clean, educated, fancy folks."

I left that day a little more humble, a little wiser. I had been taught by a woman who had learned the Bible by listening to the stories again and again because she could not read. She had given me a profound lesson about faith and acceptance.

PRAYER: God of the wise and the foolish, teach me to read with my heart and not just with my mind. Remind me that you speak to us in many and varied ways. Amen.

"They brought to [Jesus] a deaf man." Who are "they"? "They" are people who believe that Jesus can help this man. "They" have a concern for the deaf person and bring him to Jesus for healing. Notice that "they" beg Jesus to lay his hand on him. People of faith come before Jesus with a sick man.

Jesus, in contrast to modern-day healers who call people to the front and, with great fanfare, touch those seeking wholeness, takes the man aside. The man has already suffered greatly because of his handicapping condition. Jesus respects his dignity and deals with him privately.

Some years ago a person came to my office looking for assistance. It was late; the banks had closed, and I had no cash. I wanted to help the woman, so I called the local rabbi who said he could assist her. I gave the woman directions, and she began her trek toward the synagogue, located about five blocks away.

A few minutes later the rabbi called to ask if the woman was walking. I confirmed his suspicions. He was upset and asked me why I had not mentioned that fact to him. He had expected me to drive the woman to his office. He believed it was wrong to humble those whom we assisted. In helping others we were to protect their dignity.

Jesus heals the man in private and then orders the witnesses not to tell anyone. The man's dignity is as stake as well as Jesus' own integrity. But the Syrophoenician woman and "they" already know who Jesus is and what he can do.

SUGGESTION FOR MEDITATION: Do you know who Jesus is? What could Jesus do for you and others? How do you bring the needy before Christ? How do you share your knowledge about Jesus?

Awakening

September 8–14, 2003 • J. Marshall Jenkins[‡]

MONDAY, SEPTEMBER 8 • Read Psalm 19:1–6

The sun rises, and nothing can conceal color. Nothing can hide design. Everything that sleeps or hides in the darkness evangelizes. Day unfolds like a scroll for all with eyes to read. All things proclaim God's reign. So says the psalm.

My experience says something different. Groaning, I turn off my alarm clock and rise, stretching, scratching, coughing, and squinting in the artificial light over the mirror. I open the window blinds, not seeing. I turn on the TV, not hearing.

"There is no speech, nor are there words; their voice is not heard." I know something of the words but poorly, vaguely, while the psalmist knows so clearly. Do I clasp my hands over my ears? Or do God's hands mercifully shield me from music too beautiful to bear?

"Yet their voice goes out through all the earth, and their words to the end of the world." God spoke into being this morning, that joy, those leaves, you, me, the stranger, our mother, all things. Each created thing echoes the Word that formed it, that shook it free from nothingness. But did God create me unresponsive to the Word that made me?

Or do I choose to see things and miss the words they bear? Do I choose to see a tree but fail to read the message it carries? Do I choose to enjoy its shade in the summer and cut it down for firewood in the winter without ever listening to its sermon? Or do its words hide with God, awaiting the proper time?

PRAYER: Lord, open my ears and eyes. Amen.

[‡]Writer, psychologist, Bible study leader; Director of counseling, Berry College, Rome, Georgia.

With a word, God made me. Created in God's image, I have a tongue.

Alone, I say a word and I hear it. The sound waves dissipate, but I remember it. Did my word create anything besides a private memory?

With a friend, I say a word, and I cannot retrieve it. I can look into my friend's eyes and see a spreading fire or a freezing lake. The word holds too much power for me to bridle and break it. The word can build a bridge of friendship spanning more miles than I ever hoped to travel. Or it can topple a tower we built patiently and faithfully.

I pray and hear the silence. Did I speak alone again? Or did I start a fire, give birth to a star?

Need I pray with words at all? Is God my editor, refining my speech? Is God my inquisitor, ready to strike when my tongue errs? No, God's desire for my heart resembles no other being's desire. If I choose my words in prayer as if addressing someone less than God, the words get in the way.

Created in God's image, I rest my tongue. Do I dare listen for a word from God? If it comes, it could build a ladder from heaven to my feet. It could shatter my world or consume me like a moth in a flame. Do I hear silence because I cannot bear a word from God? Or is God simply silent?

Questions fade, and I abide in the silence of God. When I leave the silence and return to the world of words, I am not the same. God must have spoken.

SUGGESTION FOR PRAYER: Call on God, and listen.

Bull's eye! The archer lowers the bow and smiles, the arrow quivering in the target's dead center. For a moment, everything seems right, and the universe orbits in perfect, synchronized rings around the arrow.

So it was with Peter the moment he got it right like no one else. He looked the long-awaited Messiah in the eye and named him. Everything held together in harmony for that moment.

But the Messiah is not a two-dimensional target of concentric rings. One does not know the Messiah as the archer knows the bull's eye. Seeing his face does not suffice. One must share his sufferings—sufferings Peter cannot yet know.

The archer removes the arrow, consigning the perfect shot to memory. Peter, on the other hand, falls into confusion. Jesus throws Peter off balance with a prediction that the official keepers of the messianic faith will persecute and kill him.

What could anyone do but object? Jesus robs Peter of his bull's eye. He robs all of us of something more, of the god of our dreams, the salvation of our imagining, the life of our highest hopes. He robs us and, like Peter, we must start from scratch and learn how to see him for who he is.

We start from scratch and, like Peter, we return to scratch time and again. Peter will blunder after hitting the bull's eye again and return to scratch. There Jesus waits for him saying, "Follow me." Putting one foot in front of the other and walking with Jesus is all it takes to see him again, to be his companion.

PRAYER: Lord Jesus, stay ever in view, ever within reach as I follow you anew. Amen.

A woman cries out on the street. In ancient Israel, the hearer might have asked: Is she a solitary nonperson or the carrier of a young suitor's highest hopes for family, inheritance, and companionship? Is she a counselor with rare discernment of God's will or an impostor prepared to take anyone who will listen down the fast track to nowhere? Is she God's own wisdom with a human face or a vengeful demon? Ignore her at your peril. Listen to her at your peril.

Woman Folly in Proverbs 9:13–18 mimics Woman Wisdom in Proverbs 1:20–33, but whereas Folly promises privileged pleasures, Wisdom preaches the fear of the Lord. Whereas Madison Avenue successfully shepherds us from store to store using Folly's methods, Wisdom's message scarcely gets more than a handful to church. Little wonder Folly has a six-figure salary and the ear of every Fortune 500 CEO. Little wonder Wisdom sounds angry and lonely.

Refusing the fear of the Lord, we do not hear Wisdom, much less heed her. Refusing the fear of the Lord, we panic when we see no exits on the road down which Woman Folly takes us. Fear of the Lord is the awe and reverence we feel in God's presence. It is our highest joy, and our only exit from Folly's road.

If we fear the Lord, we will listen to the right woman. Whether we find her lovely or angry, mild or abrasive, she offers our highest hopes, divine knowledge, and a face that reveals God.

PRAYER: Lord, fill me with the kind of fear that makes one wise. Amen.

Mark tells so many stories of Jesus' disciples misconstruing their master that one wonders how any of them get it right when he asks, "Who do you say that I am?" Yet Peter passes the test, answering, "You are the Messiah." A few more words reveal that he doesn't really know what he is talking about.

Separated from Jesus by only a few feet, Peter still has to look past a legion of inherited misconceptions and half-truths to see the true man. Separated from Jesus by two millennia, we must look past even more distorted images, not to mention hear his question through modern static of information overload, advertising appeals, and excessive choices. We live and move in a creation filled with windows to eternity, but we go for days, months, sometimes years, without pausing for a single one, so distracted are we with the mirrors and sideshows.

How comforting to know that confused and distracted Peter receives credit for getting it right. We can say the same words and get it right, even if we don't know what we're talking about. We say it best if we admit to having little idea what Jesus' lordship means and if we look forward to an eternity of learning.

Jesus confirms Peter's answer implicitly by instructing his disciples to keep quiet about it. Perhaps he does not want them to spread the word until they have a better idea what it means. They can only learn the hard way, following him, dying daily a death like his, and looking forward to life that they have never imagined.

PRAYER: Lord, your thoughts are not my thoughts, and your ways are not my ways. Yet you sent your Son that I may know you. Give me the wisdom and courage to follow him. Amen.

In this land of freedom, we jealously guard our right to do as we please; we keep the rules few and simple. Yet confronted by school shootings and terrorist attacks, promiscuity and irresponsible parents, lying politicians and greedy evangelists, we plead for more standards, tougher laws, real accountability.

Media and mobility bring us into closer and more frequent contact with people whose standards differ from our own. We respect the freedom of others to follow different rules, but we hope their rules are not too different from ours. We whisper our standards to strangers who resemble us. As our words hang in the air, we wait to see if we built a bridge or burned one.

In such an environment, discussion of laws and standards conjures up anxiety, confusion, frustration, resignation, or anger. Yet the psalmist commends God's laws as "perfect, reviving the soul…sure, making wise the simple…clear, enlightening the eyes…pure, enduring forever….More to be desired are they than gold…sweeter also than honey." If nature reveals God's glory, God's moral precepts prepare us to take it in and enjoy it.

Perhaps we hold our laws and standards fretfully because the highest reason for obedience is the easiest to forget. Yes, God issues commandments to give us order, security, a check on our impulses, a limit to our freedom, and a protection of it. But above all, God issues commandments to prepare our eyes to see, our ears to hear, and our mouths to praise God. If we expect joy as we seek God's will, we will know God's laws and find happiness in them.

PRAYER: Lord, help me to discern your will for me and to obey expectantly. Amen.

Before Jesus, the only way to "taste and see that God is good" was to follow God's laws. With Jesus, God introduced another way: to follow God's man.

In a sense that model made it easier for us Gentiles who did not inherit God's laws as a gift addressed to us. Codes simply do not open the heart like a face can. Laughing during the wedding party, weeping at the grave of a friend, smiling at the children, sneering at the Pharisees, sighing at the disciples, flashing fury at the Temple merchants, tensing up and perspiring at prayer in a garden, crying out from the cross, blinking as he folds his burial clothes, meeting us incognito on a lonely road: It takes this face to open our eyes.

In another sense, nothing can be more difficult. "Deny yourself. Take up your cross, and follow me. Lose your life to save it." It's an oft-repeated refrain, scattered, paraphrased throughout Jesus' teachings, and carried out shockingly on the cross by the teacher himself. Surely he must know that nothing he can say will prepare his disciples for the terror to come.

Yet he expects them—and us— to live it ourselves, to shoulder whatever our particular crosses may be, to follow him down whatever narrow roads God chooses for us. We drop the lives of our own fashioning and free ourselves to embrace the life God offers. Nothing is more difficult, and no one can do it without God's help. It takes more than a lifetime. But God gives us the time and help we need, and there is joy on the other side of this suffering and dying.

PRAYER: Loving God, help me to meet Jesus' challenge so that my suffering and joy may speak of your glory. Amen.

Draw Near to God

September 15–21, 2003 • *Kolya Braun-Greiner*[‡]

MONDAY, SEPTEMBER 15 • **Read Psalm 1:1-3**

Meditate on God's law night and day.

How often are we tempted to follow the advice of others? We may fall prey to the prevailing advice in our society that encourages us to buy more, bigger, better, faster. A high-speed mode of living can cause us to make hasty decisions about buying items, giving no thought to their impact on the producer or on God's creation, our bodies, or our neighbor. The media tell us that a new gadget will make us happy. But does it? "Happy are those who do not follow the advice of the wicked...."

How are we to discern the way to live? The psalmist advises us to meditate on God's law day and night, but that sounds like a daunting task. Having an "attitude of gratitude"allows us to meditate on God's presence in our lives. I have adopted a practice called examen that proposes several questions. On the one hand, we can ask each day, "What gives life?" or "Where did I experience God today?" On the other hand, we can ask, "What diminishes life?" or "Where does God seem absent?" Practicing examen can help us hang on to our true sources of happiness, rather than seek outside sources, things, entertainment.

We can be planted in a way of life like trees that "yield their fruit in its season."We may not actually see the fruits of our lives, but if we hold on to what gives life, then we help sustain life and share this way of life with others.

PRAYER: God of all creation, help us discern and choose a way of life that sustains life rather than destroys it. May our lives inspire others to know your love and healing power. Amen.

[‡]Consultant; freelance writer; immediate past president of the National Farmworker Ministry, an interfaith organization supporting the rights of farmworkers; living in Baldwin, New York.

The way of the wicked will perish.

I feel most discouraged when it seems that acts of injustice continue unabated, and powers of evil prevail. During the 1980s as I read about the torture and murder of hundreds of thousands of indigenous people in Guatemala, I wondered how long it would take for justice to be served. When I hear that the United States releases most of the greenhouse gases that contribute to global warming, yet our nation does not make international commitments to reduce carbon monoxide production, I ask, "How long?" When I've seen the squalid, run-down shanties that serve as homes for farm workers, I ask, "How long…?"

Martin Luther King Jr. stood up to the powers that be, proclaiming the equality of all people in God's sight and asked, "How long? Not long. Because the arm of the moral universe is long but it bends toward justice." It bends toward justice when we respond to evil forces with action: like Rigoberta Menchú, Nobel Peace Prize laureate who wrote about the horrors she experienced as a native woman in Guatemala; like Rachel Carson, who fought to raise awareness of the devastating effects of DDT and other chemicals harmful to the web of life; like Cesar Chavez, farmworker organizer who faced the evils of racism, agro-business, and police brutality; but his message prevailed to bring justice for the "invisible" people who harvest our food.

God watched over these righteous persons who exemplified the spiritual lyric, "Just like a tree that's standing by the water, we shall not be moved." They rooted their lives in the way of justice and righteousness, a way that God promises will triumph over the "way of the wicked." Evil may have its day, but God's way has the last word. How long? Not long.

PRAYER: God of righteousness, renew in me the assurance that your will overcomes evil. Make me a worker in your vineyard, planting justice. Amen.

She opens her mouth with wisdom.

The book of wisdom sayings known as Proverbs portrays God's wisdom in feminine terms; the final chapter is no exception. This acrostic poem (each verse begins with a successive letter in the Hebrew alphabet) depicts God's wisdom embodied in a woman who "opens her mouth with wisdom." Thus Proverbs concludes with the theme with which it began (Prov. 1:7): Loving obedience to God is the beginning of wisdom.

I approached this "Ode to a Capable Wife" with suspicion. I steeled myself for a model of womanhood that portrays a lowly housewife, a pliant servant to her husband and family, with no needs or particular skills beyond the domestic arena. But not this woman! She does serve her family—but with grace, strength, wisdom, and reverence for God. She knows the economics of real-estate purchasing; she has the skills of an agronomist to plant a vineyard; she is a producer of fine linen clothing, which is "profitable merchandise"; and through it all, she retains a vital sense of humor about life.

This woman is not a victim of her circumstances as are many women even today. In many countries women are treated as less than human; girls are valued less than boys. According to UNICEF (United Nations International Children's Emergency Fund), two-thirds of all illiterate children are girls. Where girls are devalued, some suffer malnutrition because the boys in their family receive the first fruits. As girls grow into adults, their work and contribution to society remain undervalued worldwide.

Some of us have come a long way, but we must stand in solidarity with those sisters who are still oppressed and whose human rights are denied. May we too speak with words of wisdom and kindness like the capable wife who reaches out her hands to the needy.

PRAYER: God of women and of men, you created us equal. In reverence to you, help us live out your original intention for us. Amen.

But they did not understand…and were afraid to ask him.

Jesus knows the end of his mortal life is near. He doesn't want anyone to know that he is passing through Galilee. His public ministry there is over, and he needs time to shore up his disciples for what is about to happen. He has already warned them (Mark 8:31 and following) of his imminent suffering, death, and resurrection; but they still don't get it!

We too resist information that is either too much to bear or beyond our comprehension. Sometimes we need to hear it several times before it sinks in. Such was true this week as I prepared these meditations. I heard the horrible news of the attack on the World Trade Towers and the Pentagon. On television it looked like a Hollywood stunt. The event was so unbelievable and horrific that some people needed to see the replay repeatedly just to accept its reality. As we recall this heinous event of September 11, 2001, let us pause for a moment of silence in memory of the thousands of innocent lives that were lost. Let us also pray for the millions of people who need food, shelter, schools, and hospitals.

Jesus' foretelling of his death and resurrection must have been overwhelming and difficult news to the disciples. Hearing it once didn't click. How could it happen that "three days after being killed, he will rise again"? This is so outside their frame of reference that they "did not understand what he was saying." The disciples may have been slow to understand but eventually they did, and they spread this good news so far as to reach us today. The Resurrection remains inconceivable to us, but our faith proclaims a victory of life over death and horrendous evil. Jesus promises us the resurrection too.

PRAYER: God who hears all our questions even when we are "afraid to ask," strengthen us in times of trouble and help us keep our minds and hearts open to your good news of life overcoming death. Amen.

Who [i]s the greatest?…Whoever welcomes one such child in my name.

While on the way to Capernaum Jesus overhears the disciples arguing among themselves about who is the greatest. He waits to confront them on this issue and creates a "teaching moment." First he sits down. In doing so, he physically and visually models equalizing relationships and the lesson of humility that he seeks to impart. Then he speaks of an approach that completely contradicts the way the world thinks and enacts its concept of greatness. The great ones in God's eyes are not those who want to be first in riches or power, but rather those who serve others.

To drive home his point, Jesus places a child among them and admonishes the disciples to welcome children, who were certainly not considered great or given much value, since they weren't viewed as adults or full-fledged members of society. Then, as now, the society often suffered from a kind of "adultism." Our society and many parts of the world are not child friendly: Child labor is used to make expensive running shoes for the global economy; child soldiers are trained to hold and fire guns; military spending takes priority over funding for child care and children's education. And here, in the richest country on earth, one in every five children lives in poverty. These facts certainly imply that children are not welcome.

What if we were evaluated, even judged, on how we welcome and treat children? How would the policies in our church and society change if they were based upon the belief that children are the greatest in the kingdom of God? Jesus calls us to welcome every child in his name. In so doing we have welcomed him.

PRAYER: Loving God, who is father and mother to us all, transform our ways of thinking about greatness. Open our hearts and minds to see the needs of children and to place them first rather than last. Amen.

A harvest of righteousness is sown in peace for those who make peace.

The letter of James has an overarching theme: Practice what you preach! Actions speak louder than words. James challenges us to become wise in faith, not in the ways of this world. This kind of wisdom is akin to "putting on the mind of Christ" in all we do or say. Living Christ's way makes for peace.

In contrast, when we do things born of envy, competition, or bitterness, the wisdom of God does not inspire our actions. Our harried and hurried society tempts us to become so wrapped up in our own ambitions that we can easily ignore the needs of those around us. Too often we forfeit the slow work of building peaceful relationships with neighbors within our community and the broader world in our rush to get ahead, to be financially secure, and to maintain our comfort level and lifestyle.

What if we were to put on the mind of Christ and act out the wisdom of our faith whenever we purchase a new car (considering energy consumption and pollution of the air), vote for elected officials (considering their position on funding for children's programs), watch television (rather than relate to our loved ones), encounter a neighbor (taking time to get to know him or her)? In what other ways may we make our faith manifest in today's world?

James tells us that if we allow "the wisdom from above," or faith in God, to guide us, then we will be full of mercy, peace, and good fruits. Our works will show from whence they came.

PRAYER: God of justice, may our actions be guided by a wisdom born of faith in you. Temper our selfish ambitions so that we too may produce a harvest of righteousness and peace. Amen.

Draw near to God, and [God] will draw near to you.

In contrast to yesterday's little treatise on peace, James now turns to the causes of strife: cravings and covetousness that are "at war within" us. We can be wrenched by longings for things we want but don't really need. When the desire for power or possessions surpasses the needs of our neighbor, the poor, and even our own family, then conflicts, murder, and war arise.

Perhaps the thing we want isn't so bad, but we can be so caught up in our own agenda that we "do not ask"—that is, pray about it. Not asking for what we need is a form of arrogance and pride. We may think: *I can do it all on my own. I don't need anyone else's help* (even God's). It's a seductive temptation to believe that we control everything.

Being in control is in sharp contrast to James's admonition: "Submit yourselves…to God." This means turning our whole selves over to God and letting go of the illusion of control. One of the first steps in twelve-step programs (like Alcoholics Anonymous) is to admit that we are not in control and that we must seek the help of our "higher power." With God's help we can resist evil, temptations, and even overcome addictive behaviors that we engage in to avoid our feelings, like going shopping to make ourselves feel better—"retail therapy." God's filling us can free us from cravings that cannot be fulfilled. By submitting ourselves to God, we can turn away from habitual ways of doing things that harm ourselves, our neighbor, or God's creation.

What to do? Pray! Help is on the way! If we turn our desires, hopes, anxieties, and fears over to God, God is there waiting. God will draw near when we draw near to God.

Prayer: God of grace, give us courage to let go of our control and let you draw nearer to us in all we do. Amen.

Our Help through Crisis

September 22–28, 2003 • Les Dahl[‡]

MONDAY, SEPTEMBER 22 • Read Esther 7:1-6, 9-10

Crisis reveals character. Few of us ever find ourselves in a crisis of national consequence as did Esther, but each of us must pass through the fire. In the crucible, our true mettle shines forth.

Character does not evolve by chance; it is forged by practical decisions made in mundane circumstances of everyday experience. Did Esther awaken one morning full of courage to face head-on the dreaded Haman, murderous enemy of the Jews? Hardly. Was it her lofty position as beloved queen that empowered her to engage such a bold strategy to stem Haman's evil plot? Position and power never shape true character; they only reveal what is already woven in the fabric of one's being.

The seedbed of Esther's character is seen in her upbringing. Without fanfare Esther's tragic childhood is noted. (See Esther 2:6-7.) One would hardly consider this displaced orphan a likely candidate for character, let alone courage, in the face of national crisis. What a profound sense of self-esteem, destiny, and faith Mordecai nurtured in his little cousin whom he raised as his own precious daughter. Parents, whether natural or adoptive, sow the seeds of greatness in children from early in their experience.

Esther's confidence in the midst of crisis was founded upon a secure sense of who she was. Her perseverance against overwhelming odds was fueled by a clear sense of destiny. Courage arose in her heart because she knew and trusted the heavenly Father, whose sovereign hand moves history and circumstance, God's good purposes to perform.

PRAYER: Father, refine in me a sense of my worth in Christ and a vision of my special place in your sovereign purposes on the earth. Amen.

[‡]Missionary; educator; principal, Landmark Academy; pastor in Jamaica for fifteen years; living in St. Ann, Jamaica, West Indies.

Sometimes life is contrary. Criticism rages like a fire out of control. Adverse circumstances swell like a flood. We feel trapped, caught between a rock and a hard place. All evidence to the contrary, the fact remains: The Lord is on our side. God will see us through.

Jehoshaphat's reign of Judah has been peaceful. He has done everything right, and justice prevails in the land. Then, for no apparent reason, neighboring nations turn against him. News arrives that the mighty army of Syria is marching toward Judah. In the face of panic, Jehoshaphat sets himself to seek the Lord and, like Esther, invites his people to fast and pray with him. (See 2 Chron. 20:3 4.) Jahaziel, the prophet, arises with God's answer to the crisis: "Do not fear or be dismayed...the battle is not yours but God's....take your position, stand still, and see the victory of the LORD on your behalf" (vv. 15–17). Victory in crisis begins as we, like Jehoshaphat, take our position and entrench ourselves in this affirmation: God is on our side.

The psalmist reminds us that when crisis overwhelms our soul, the Lord helps us through. What confidence is ours who find our help in the name of the Lord. If God could make heaven and earth by the Word of divine power, God will certainly care for us in the midst of our crises. "But thanks be to God," the apostle Paul writes in his first letter to the Corinthians, "who gives us the victory" (15:57).

PRAYER: **Lord of heaven and earth, you are on my side. You will cause me to triumph in my present crisis. Amen.**

Perspective is a key to victory in times of crisis. On the surface, the fight seems to be against people and circumstances that hinder our advance. The real battle, however, takes place in our soul. Will opposition and adversity overwhelm us and ensnare our soul in a web of pessimism? The choice is ours, determined by our perspective.

In Moses' day, each of the twelve spies witnessed the bounty of the Promised Land. Each scrutinized the well-fortified cities and the menacing giants on patrol. The Bible records these fateful words of the ten who could see only the impossibilities of their situation: "We are not able…, for they are stronger than we.…There we saw the Nephilim (the Anakites come from the Nephilim); and to ourselves we seemed like grasshoppers, and so we seemed to them" (Num. 13:31–33). Their defeat is determined by their perspective on the situation. Joshua and Caleb acknowledge the formidable foe and the imposing fortresses to be overcome, but declare: "Do not fear the people of the land, for they are no more than bread for us; their protection is removed from them, and the LORD is with us" (Num. 14:9). What a difference perspective makes!

Victory is ours not when circumstances change but when we change. Neither adversity nor foe can hold our soul prey when we take our position and declare that the Lord is on our side. Our perspective alone holds us captive in our crisis. Is the Lord who made heaven and earth not able once again to stretch forth a sovereign hand to help us? As we fix our mind on the faithfulness and power of the Lord, our soul escapes the pessimism that so easily ensnares us in crisis and soars in faith to the victory prepared for us.

PRAYER: O God, help me to lift my eyes above my circumstances and beyond my adversaries. With you by my side, victory is sure. Amen.

Prayer is an important vehicle whereby we make our requests known to God. Our first response in crisis should be prayer. The apostle Paul instructs the Philippian believers, "In everything by prayer and supplication…let your requests be made known to God" (Phil. 4:6). Clearly prayer is our hotline to heaven, notifying God of our need. More important, however, is what prayer can accomplish in us, especially during crisis.

The framework of Paul's instruction in Philippians is significant. "Be careful for nothing" (KJV), he begins. Effective prayer arises out of a soul free from anxiety. Worry only exhausts us emotionally and spiritually while accomplishing nothing. We become overwhelmed by encroaching circumstances, unable to see any possible solution. But anxiety flees when our mind nestles in the confidence that the Lord is on our side. "With thanksgiving," the apostle continues. As we reflect upon God's faithfulness to help us in previous times of need, calm assurance dispels present fear and doubt. Our prayer soars on the wings of thanksgiving. Paul concludes, "And the peace of God…will guard your hearts and your minds in Christ Jesus" (4:7). Prayer sustains a positive, confident perspective through crisis.

James makes another encouraging point concerning prayer. Elijah, the mighty prophet who dared to challenge the wicked King Ahab, was "subject to like passions as we are" (KJV). What anxieties, fears, and doubts do you struggle with in the midst of your crisis? Elijah, the man of God whose earnest prayer wrought miraculous results in the heavens, struggled with the selfsame feelings. Answers to prayer depend upon God's faithfulness, not our feelings.

PRAYER: O God, let your peace sweep over my soul as I exchange my anxiety with gratitude and fix my mind upon your faithfulness to me. Amen.

Sin obstructs prayer. The prophet Isaiah reminds us of God's readiness to hear and answer our cries for help, but our iniquities separate us from God; our sins hide God's face and God cannot hear our prayer (59:1-2). James identifies three hindrances to effective prayer: sins, faults (v. 16, KJV), and wandering from God. As these hindrances are removed, our prayer becomes effective.

Sins are deeds that violate God's law. As we acknowledge our transgressions, our sins are forgiven. King David, after committing adultery and murder, prayed, "Cleanse me from my sin....I know my transgressions....Purge me...,and I shall be clean" (Ps. 51:2, 3, 7).

Faults are flaws of character and offenses that obstruct peaceful relationships. Reconciliation comes as we humbly confess our shortcomings to one another. The author of First John writes, "If we walk in the light as [God] is in the light, we have fellowship with one another, and the blood of Jesus his Son cleanses us from all sin" (1:7).

Wandering away from God develops from faulty reasoning. Bad thinking results in bad choices; bad choices produce bad habits. Too often we are blind to the rut in which we are stuck. Therefore it takes the compassionate but firm intervention of a Christian brother or sister to save us from our wandering ways and to steer us back to the truth.

The effective, passionate prayer of the righteous triumphs in crisis. A righteous person is not one without sins, faults, or wandering ways, but rather one who responds appropriately as these shortcomings are exposed.

PRAYER: Father, forgive my transgressions, my weaknesses, and my waywardness. Cleanse me that I might stand righteous through the blood of Jesus Christ. Amen.

A well-known proverb advises, "An ounce of prevention is worth a pound of cure." Crises in our life can be prevented.

"If your hand causes you to stumble...." Some things we do create trouble for us. The crisis that develops is the consequence of our own doing. If we cease doing the things that get us into trouble, crises can be prevented.

"If your foot causes you to stumble...." The company we keep will bring us either blessing or ruin. The psalmist writes,

> Happy are those
>   who do not follow the advice of the wicked,
>   or take the path that sinners tread,
>   or sit in the seat of scoffers. (1:1)

If those with whom we walk are ungodly, their ways sinful, and their attitude negative, we are heading for trouble.

"If your eye causes you to stumble...." Much of what influences our thinking gains access through our eyes. We must choose the things that we allow to shape our thinking. Paul offers the following standard: "Whatever is true, whatever is honorable, whatever is just, whatever is pure, whatever is pleasing, whatever is commendable, if there is any excellence and if there is anything worthy of praise, think about these things" (Phil. 4:8). If what enters through our "eye gate" (or our "ear gate") does not meet this standard, we are well-advised to "tear it out."

Crises can be averted by making some changes. Change is seldom easy, especially when we deal with deep-rooted habits, long-standing associations, and entrenched attitudes. Drastic situations demand decisive action. Whatever causes you to stumble, tear it out or cut it off!

PRAYER: Sustaining God, grant me the courage to be decisive as I scrutinize my conduct, the company I keep, and the influences that shape my attitudes and my thinking. Amen.

"Salt" speaks of character, conviction, and integrity. The "fire" of crisis develops in us "saltiness"—depth and quality of character, conviction, and integrity. Pressure brings out the best or the worst in us. Our response under pressure determines the outcome.

Falsely accused of a crime, a young man faced life imprisonment. The conditions in prison were foul, the convicts surly, and the guards miserable. The lad's talents seemed wasted in such a place, certainly an unlikely forum in which to hone his administrative skills. Studying his hostile circumstances, his reprobate companions, and his heartless captors, the youth formulated a strategy to change his impossible and unbearable lot in life. The young man's skill and leadership so impressed the chief warden that he placed him in charge of the entire prison operation and personnel.

This young man was summoned one day to make sense of the bizarre nightmare of the country's ruler. He responded to Pharaoh with words to this effect: "God alone gives sense and meaning." With the confidence of one who has experienced God's help in a time of crisis, the young man not only unraveled the king's terrifying visions but also laid out a strategy that would save the nation from impending ruin.

Recognizing the character and capability of the one standing before him, Pharaoh made Joseph prime minister of Egypt with full authority to administer the plan that would successfully carry the nation through one of the most severe crises in its history. Joseph embraced the crucible as God prepared him for his great destiny.

PRAYER: God of deliverance, help me trust you to take me through the fire of my crisis. I understand that my character and conviction will be strengthened, even as my integrity is tested. Amen.

The Ways of the Lord

September 29–October 5, 2003 • *Knut Bjarne Jørgensen*[‡]

MONDAY, SEPTEMBER 29 • **Read Job 1:1, 2:1-7a**

This week we will read about God's greatness and love, but we will also be called to an accounting for our actions related to God's love for us. The first question for me is this: Am I willing to handle adversity as graciously as Job? Can I go the distance? Am I willing to give away everything I care for in the trial to prove my love to the eternal God?

Let us take a look at the Book of Job. In the Danish translation the story begins like a fairy tale: Once upon a time.

We know nothing about this man Job. He lives in the land of Uz, a place nobody's ever heard of. A wealthy man with a large family, Job is blameless and upright; he fears God and shuns evil.

In this story we witness a kind of envy taken to extremes. Why else should the angels and Satan ask God to put Job through a second trial? (Read about the first in Job 1:6-22.)

Of course, you may say, "When things are going well it is easy to love and praise God." Why then do many people seek the the support and comfort of the church in times of suffering? The churches in the United States experienced this resurgence of church attendance after September 11, 2001, and in days that followed also—even in my country. A hymn refers to our praying "in such days," which alludes to days of problems, illness, misery, accidents, and so forth.

The story of Job tells us that it is possible to live a life of gratitude and praise even in the face of such adversity.

PRAYER: Eternal God, help me to understand your ways and have the patience to follow them. Amen.

[‡]Pastor of The United Methodist Church, Horsens, Denmark; editor of the Danish edition of *The Upper Room.*

Tuesday, September 30 • Read Job 2:7b–10

Sometimes we do not understand the ways of God. We often ask, "Why did this occur or that happen—and for what reason?" In our anger and despair we cannot perceive the answer. Perhaps we have yet to acknowledge that sometimes there is no answer.

Satan immediately afflicts Job with an illness. People have speculated about the type of illness: leprosy, eczema, a form of bubonic plague. But it doesn't matter. Job experiences severe pain, and other people view it as an abominable illness.

As Job sits among the ashes we meet his wife for the first and only time. She encourages him to condemn God and seems to agree with Satan in the plan to get something for something. You get nothing for your pain; so get rid of God and die.

Only foolish people behave in such a fashion is Job's reply. Psalms 14 and 53 speak of the fool who says there is no God. Job's wife comes close to denying God's existence. But Job sticks to his principle (even if he does not understand it) that we receive from God both blessing and sorrow and pain.

The story of Job reminds us of the following:

1. Whatever we encounter in life will last only for a limited time.
2. When God tries our faith, God will give us strength to persevere.
3. Temptations are sometimes very close to us.
4. Job relied on God's mercy, and we can too.

How do we face problems, illness, and temptation?

Prayer: "Make me to know your ways, O Lord; / teach me your paths. / Lead me in your truth, and teach me, / for you are the God of my salvation; / for you I wait all day long" (Ps. 25:4). Amen.

Psalm 26 proclaims the innocence of the psalmist, a person accused unjustly by someone in the community. This psalm is a prayer attended by a symbolic action of washing the hands and showing them as clean. The psalmist cries out to God for vindication. Rare is the person who has not felt unjustly accused! Sometimes we feel all alone with our problems. We have perhaps experienced accusations of others for things we have not done. And where shall we go? To whom shall we turn for help? This psalm may guide our response.

In such times of trial we, like the psalmist, cry out to God. We seek God's help. We hope for the truth to reverse the situation. When false tales are told about us and we face some personal disaster, we beg God to turn the tide and perhaps even to strike down those who make the false charges.

After petitioning God to act, the psalmist denies wrongdoing and proclaims that he does not associate with hypocrites and evildoers. We see these verses as part of a ritual oath of purification. The words form a confession that contrasts the innocence of the psalmist with those who made the accusations.

"Your steadfast love is before my eyes, / and I walk in faithfulness to you" begins a positive oath formed in verses 3 and 6–12. The hand washing in verse 6 is a ritual act of purification. Because of that rite of cleansing, the psalmist can participate in the worshiping community. The accused can give thanks together with the congregation for God's great and merciful acts. There in worship the psalmist recovers the roots of relationship with God. As the psalm ends, we do not hear anger; we hear affirmation: "in the great congregation I will bless the Lord." So also is the process we experience as we move from woundedness to healing grace—in worship. The ways of God are indeed mysterious!

SUGGESTION FOR MEDITATION: **Think about how often you are set free in the process from woundedness to healing grace. How do you give thanks for God's mercy upon you?**

The writer of Hebrews summarizes the main theological ideas of the letter in these few verses. As if listening to a great musician, we hear—even in translation—the mastery of Greek rhetoric in the letter!

"Long ago God spoke...." So begins this marvelous letter! The epistle writer refers to that long ago time of the prophets, a time much farther away now. Indeed, one difficulty we face as we try to communicate the gospel in contemporary cultures is that the world of Jesus Christ also seems long ago. Communicating the richness of God's grace takes time in a world that does not value rhetoric or theological analysis.

Let us consider these four verses as the prologue to the epistle. In this prologue we find a summary of the history of Israel. We may envision the generations extending from Abraham. We may recall judges and prophets such as Deborah, Samuel, and Nathan. We relive the glory of the Incarnation, the fulfillment of all that the prophets foretold. "In these last days God has spoken to us by a Son." These words speak to the mystery of the Incarnation, a mystery in which we live with the grace of God's love for humanity—for us!

Many people today think of God only as a severe judge. They believe more in the words of popular fiction that portray God taking away some people and leaving others to suffer tremendous harm. Help yourself and help others by focusing on the prologue to Hebrews. Consider the mysterious ways of the Lord. God's glory in Jesus Christ is the glory of self-emptying. God's pathways grow from deep love for us.

SUGGESTION FOR MEDITATION: Consider how to communicate the ways of God's love to those who are uninspired, untutored, unimpressed with the revelation in Jesus Christ.

It is curious, is it not, that our lectionary reading from Hebrews skips the section that contrasts Jesus with angels? What might we gain from this unread section? More people seem to believe in the spirituality of angels than in Jesus. Perhaps the writer's testimony about Jesus may offer a different hope to those who prefer angels.

Hebrews 2 contains several references to the Psalms. The most compelling of these references is to Psalm 8. The psalmist and the epistle writer marvel at God's mindfulness of humans. Here we find a reference to humans who are "for a little while lower than the angels." The writer also describes Jesus, now crowned with glory, who "for a little while was made lower than the angels." What does the epistle writer have in mind with these references to spiritual beings? Is it not, in some ways, to proclaim a word of hope to an oppressed and discouraged people? Is it not to elevate humanity that we might begin to fathom the ways of the Lord?

Images of angels today portray primarily innocence. One popular television program depicts angels as male and female and of different human races. In contemporary presentations, angels are kind, sweet, and safe. Because our world is not kind and safe, we must look for kindness and safety somewhere else.

Angels are not the good news. The writer of Hebrews offers Jesus as the pioneer of salvation and the one whom we should follow. Why do people so much more easily grasp angels? Why do we not open ourselves to Jesus?

PRAYER: Great God, you have made us slightly lower than angels. You have given us Jesus as the pioneer of faith. Open us to receive the embrace of your love through the Christ. Amen.

Some people experience grace in marriage. Others do not. What is your understanding of marriage? That is part of the question asked of Jesus, and also a question asked by contemporary cultures. Many of us, grounded in biblical and theological history, reply that marriage is a male-female covenantal relationship. In this we repeat the teachings of tradition. We may further define marriage as a spiritual blessing. "But what about _____?" someone asks, and we struggle to respond.

The Pharisees pose another question: "Is it lawful for a man to divorce his wife?" The question is simple, but clearly the Pharisees mean to trick Jesus. If he says no they can accuse him of breaking the law. If he says yes they can claim that he encourages promiscuity. In those days a Jewish man could reject his wife. She, on the other hand, did not have permission to leave him.

We still struggle with this question. Marriages break every day. Some marriages receive healing. Sometimes people preserve only outward appearances of marriage to fulfill their understanding of the law. Other marriages die as surely as every human being dies. We struggle with marriage and divorce.

On the surface Jesus seems to support a stricter understanding of marriage than even the legalistic Pharisees. Read closely! Jesus does not answer the Pharisees' question but answers a different one. Jesus speaks to the gift of the marriage partnership. In Jesus' understanding the marriage brings a new relationship not only between two humans but between the humans and the God who joined them together.

Because of God's surprises, divorce and marriage can each set us free to experience God's grace anew. Relationships, whether marriages or friendships, break. Ways of life that seemed familiar and comfortable also die, but we continue to walk in God's paths and experience God's healing love.

SUGGESTION FOR MEDITATION: Recall broken relationships that you have experienced. Bring these before God's healing mercy and grace.

They bring their children to Jesus that he might bless them, but the disciples intercept these adults. Mark gives no reason for the disciples' actions. Perhaps instead of trying to keep the children away, the disciples thought they would help the parents and children behave with a solemnity fit for the occasion. Children and adults differ in their attitudes about special times.

"Don't be childish." Sometimes we hear these words as a rebuke from others when we have done or said something that seems immature. By way of contrast, Jesus invites us to receive the kingdom of God as "a little child." What does it mean for adults to become like children? How might we receive and respond to God's kingdom? Observe pre-kindergarten children at play. Notice their spontaneity, their creative imaginations, their delight in the present moment. Might we too receive God's kingdom if we exhibited these qualities?

Notice in the text that Jesus takes the children in his arms, lays his hands on them, and blesses them. Mark does not record Jesus' words. In contrast to what happens to children in Western culture today, Jesus does not tell the children to hurry and grow up and become like the adults around them. I imagine that Jesus says, "As you grow up, may God's love always be joyful for you."

Then Jesus invites the adults to become like children.

Receive God's love as you walk and play in the pathways of the Lord. Be joyful, for God blesses each of us with the gift of Jesus Christ.

PRAYER: Loving God, we seek your blessing for our children and for our world. Help us learn what it means to be like a child, and guide us to show others the joy we feel in being your child. Amen.

Seeking God's Answer

October 6–12, 2003 • *Ellen Morseth*[‡]

MONDAY, OCTOBER 6 • Read Mark 10:17–25

A rich man who seeks to know what to do to inherit eternal life states that he has followed the commandments since his youth. Jesus responds and adds one costly condition: "Go, sell what you own, and give the money to the poor, and you will have treasure in heaven; then come, follow me." Clearly shocked at hearing such weighty words, the man walks away.

The rich man in this story remains nameless. Could that rich person be you or I? These words of Jesus have perplexed us all at some time in our lives, leading us to wonder if or how we might respond to this message. How could wealth be an impediment to eternal life? Isn't wealth a sign of God's favor? What is wealth anyway? Why should we even consider that this strong teaching of Jesus gives a valuable, if discomforting, message?

Faced with daily decisions for living, we sometimes struggle to let go of our possessions—including privilege and status. During those struggles we may discover our spiritual state of unreadiness. We resist that idea of the camel and the needle.

Following the commandments is not merely a business contract we sign and commit to for a limited time. At their heart is God's invitation to let go of worldly possessions and reach out to others. So why do we busily try to keep a ledger—an eternal balance sheet—which is in God's care? Perhaps we might ask, "What has been possible in our lives that testifies to the riches of God, and to what extent do we share our material and spiritual riches with others?"

PRAYER: Generous God, help me respond freely to others with my spiritual and material gifts, while acknowledging my own poverty of heart. Amen.

[‡]Member, Sisters of Charity, BVM; staff mentor at Worshipful-Work: Center for Transforming Religious Leadership, Kansas City, Missouri.

Would you describe yourself as a successful person? What criteria help determine your answer? Does a consideration of eternal life somehow fit into the equation?

Surrounded by a great crowd, Jesus' popularity at its peak, he issues a most uncompromising challenge in this passage: Discipleship has a price. We're told to "sell what you own, and give the money to the poor" so that we can live with compassion and solidarity with those disciples who have nothing to lose in the first place—the poor, homeless, hungry.

For the rich man this divestment of possessions strikes particularly hard. For those of us with much to lose, Jesus' words seem extreme. Our society spends a lot of time and energy on money issues—some very worthwhile causes and others less than noble, even frivolous. Daily newspapers show us that no matter how our government tries to generate money, budget it and manage it, the money always seems to be managing us. So besides bringing our personal values—gospel-based values—to "money talk" over conference tables and at civic meetings, how might we examine our own attempts to bear this real cost of discipleship?

We might realize that the cost of discipleship affects not only material possessions but our willingness to part with any "treasure" that stands between us and the presence of God in our lives. We might look at our lives to determine if we really follow Jesus the *easy* way (giving just what we are asked to give), the *popular* way (a visible, showy giving that makes us look good), or the *gospel* way (giving from our sustenance, not from what's left over after we've taken care of all our needs and wants). What treasures in addition to money might you need to relinquish if you took Jesus' call to discipleship seriously?

SUGGESTION FOR MEDITATION: **What do I value most in my life? How does that valuing affect my relationship to God and neighbor? What cost of discipleship am I willing to pay?**

It's true, isn't it, that human beings find fulfillment in relationship rather than in autonomy, self-sufficiency, or isolation? Someone who has experienced the fidelity and love of God is often impelled to turn to God even with complaints or questions that require answers. So it is with Job in this passage.

Certainties about God's presence elude Job at the time, and a sense of emptiness pervades his being. We experience these feelings too. We may seem lost, feel bereft of energy for the good things in life, or find that our hearts are bitter. We, like Job, also feel that God is absent, giving no heed to us. Our problems seemingly don't matter to God. But is it possible that these human emotions can indicate new growth, a new in-breaking of God's Spirit into our lives?

Job does not perceive the Spirit through the affliction. He presses God for an answer. The rich man received an answer he could not stomach, and Job is experiencing firsthand the cost of discipleship. What must he relinquish to find himself once more in God's presence?

We too want answers. What will it mean for us when we come to realize that God's presence completely permeates each one of us and everything in this world—even while we suffer the world's pain? Surely we'll understand that the face of God is immutably turned to us in love.

Suggestion for prayer: Pray for the grace to be liberated from fear, to be sensitive only to God's liberating love.

Just as Job experienced God's absence, so too does the psalmist feel forsaken by God. His mind-set is one both of complaint and of faith, seesawing between the bitter complaint of God's absence (vv. 1-2, 6-8, 12-15), on the one hand, and abiding faith that God is able and willing to come to the rescue. How has this been your experience? When have you felt forsaken by God? Where have you experienced God's hand of deliverance? How might complaining keep the psalmist—and you—from seeing a readily available answer?

Praying this psalm has led me into some reflection on what holiness is all about. Enmeshed as we all are in an individualistic society—to whatever extent we choose—an easy temptation is to act as if we are always in charge. We do this until we meet a roadblock or come to the end of our (figurative) rope. Then we may argue with God that we have been abandoned, that our needs have been overlooked. We may even remind God that our ancestors received God's help, that they were rescued from their dire circumstances!

When we think God is far away, we're really involved in the struggle to achieve holiness—an at-homeness with the loving heart of God, a deep believing that God is truly present in seeming absence. While family members, friends, or coworkers may appear to mock or make light of our troubles, those striving for holiness know intrinsically that God understands the nature of human beings: fully frail, yet fully lovable. So the psalm reminds us that God drew us out of our mother's womb and continues to keep us safe.

We are all works in progress.

SUGGESTION FOR PRAYER: Pray the remaining verses of Psalm 22.

Excuses, excuses! Aren't we sometimes like Job? Don't we at times attempt to diminish the scope of our responsibilities and obligations? We're only human, right? Well, God knows us all too well. God knows that we all attempt to blame God when divine presence seems to be absent.

When it comes to complaining, maybe we should take another look at ourselves. God's steadfast love for us is no mere literal and limited business contract—here today, gone tomorrow. It is no instrument of enslavement, no mandate for self-centeredness. God's presence or seeming absence is part and parcel of a rich heritage for everyone who knows God by whichever name(s). In truth, God's ever-present *presence* is our most cherished possession!

"Answer me" is one very human response fostered by our emotions when we fear we're alone. But going a step farther, perhaps our wondering about what God "would say to me" is a wake-up call to pause and reflect on the deeper meaning of God's seeming absence. Maybe we should recognize anew that life is a series of struggles meant to be endured, a succession of challenges from which we are meant to learn. And most important, life is really lived in the presence of a compassionate God who does forgive our questioning and stumbling, while celebrating our sincerity.

SUGGESTION FOR MEDITATION: **How and when has God been seemingly absent in my life? How and when do I consciously name God's presence in my life?**

Note the strong sense of urgency in this passage: We follow Christ today, not tomorrow. Tomorrow is too late. We must not procrastinate, because not to make a decision is also to decide.

If someone spoke these words to us in person, face to face, would we not be tempted to interrupt and ask questions so as to avoid having to explain ourselves?

But then we'd be brought right back to confronting ourselves because of these words: "Let us therefore approach the throne of grace with boldness, so that we may receive mercy and find grace to help in time of need." Sometimes our decision-making processes seem "sharper than any two-edged sword." The struggle we find ourselves in may jolt us out of our complacency if we let it. Our grappling with a matter for decision may force us to choose between our own desire and what God calls us to do if we let it.

We've been told since we were children that who we are and how we live our lives are completely apparent to the eyes of God: We "are naked and laid bare to the eyes of the one to whom we must render an account." Perhaps the rich man, the psalmist, and Job all failed to understand that their questions or complaints could not hide what was in their hearts from God. We, like they, need to be reminded that only God "is able to judge the thoughts and intentions of the heart."

A number of years ago I read a prayer found on the body of a Confederate soldier—one that gave me some degree of comfort. Part of it went something like this: "I asked for riches that I might be happy; I was given poverty that I might be wise." Despite myself, my prayers were answered.

PRAYER: Help me, God, to be authentic in my search for your yearnings in my life. Keep me alert to your ways and aware and confident enough in your mercies to laugh at my own foibles. Amen.

"Indeed, the word of God is living and active," the risen Christ being the ultimate word of God that "is able to judge the thoughts and intentions of the heart."

How many of us grew up with the idea that in judgment after death, God will impose a sentence on our lives? As we've grown older, many of us have come to realize that we also choose who we are before God in the context of God's constant offer of grace to us.

Unfinished persons that we know ourselves to be, we've come to seek knowledge about our God of incomprehensible mystery, and we've come to desire a prayerful collaboration with God in setting the direction for our lives under the guidance of God's Spirit.

We yearn for an ever deeper awareness that the word of God is living and active in our lives, and we want to be visible reminders that God does indeed walk the road of life with us as we decide who we shall become before God.

Life is about experiences, failures, getting up after falling, and growing in wisdom. Life too is a reminder that we receive all we have from a patient God.

SUGGESTION FOR MEDITATION: Consider what event from your life story this passage makes you recall.

A New Perspective

October 13–19, 2003 • R. Gene Lovelace[‡]

MONDAY, OCTOBER 13 • Read Matthew 6:25–33

THANKSGIVING DAY IN CANADA

Matthew has put together his Gospel account with a brief introduction and proclamation, followed by alternating sections of teachings and narrative. In his first teaching section, Matthew collects many of Jesus' greatest and best-known teachings. In today's reading we discover a great but difficult truth.

Jesus offers his followers a new perspective on living: He encourages them not to worry about daily food, shelter, or clothing but to look around them. God the Creator takes care of the created. The birds are fed. The fields display majestic beauty and color. In light of such assurances of God's loving care, Jesus challenges his followers not to fret about their own needs.

Then Jesus lays out the condition: "Strive first for the kingdom of God and his righteousness, and all these things will be given to you as well." How many hours a week do I spend worrying about my finances? How many times have I recalculated my retirement? How often have I estimated exactly when my children's college tuition will finally be paid off? Exactly when will my stocks start to regain the losses of the past years of decline? What keeps me awake at night?

Is this worrying really seeking first the kingdom of God? Should I not worry instead about injustice, violence, hate, prejudice, poverty, and restoration? These seem to be kingdom-seeking concerns.

SUGGESTION FOR PRAYER: Evaluate your worry list. How much of it is self-centered? How much is centered in trust in God and concern for others?

[‡]Senior chaplain at Alive Hospice in Nashville, Tennessee; adjunct professor at Belmont University in Nashville; ordained clergy of the Christian Church (Disciples of Christ).

Have you ever asked for more than was possible? As I reflect on my naive and over-enthusiastic first years on a church staff, I am still haunted by some of my requests. One in particular stands out in my memory.

I had launched an aggressive outreach program, "requiring" all department leaders to attend the kickoff dinner, to be "present and on time." About twenty minutes into the program our preschool coordinator came rushing into the banquet hall, fast food bags in the hands of her two preschoolers. *I can't believe she is so late*, I remember thinking to myself. I made sure that she knew my disappointment at her tardiness. After all, she was a leader and needed to set a good example.

Not until much later in life, after having two children of my own, did I appreciate her efforts. I really did not know what I was asking of a young mother. I had asked her to work all day, pick her kids up at day care, drive across town in Atlanta traffic, pick up dinner, and attend a night meeting at church.

How could I be so critical of her? I did not know what I was asking; I had never faced her challenges.

We might compare the request from James and John to sit at the right and left of Jesus to the offices of secretary of defense and secretary of state. They still assume that Jesus will build a kingdom in Jerusalem; Jesus is the Messiah. They request positions of leadership and honor.

James and John have no idea what the kingdom of Jesus will look like. They cannot know that it will be ruled by a servant, not a king. They sincerely want to be on Jesus' staff, but they have no idea what they are really asking. They have never faced the challenges that loom in Jesus' future.

SUGGESTION FOR PRAYER: **Pray for insight into the realities of your requests and your expectations of others.**

This epistle of encouragement sets as its major theme the perfection of God's revelation in a Son, Jesus the Christ. In verse 4 of today's reading, the writer makes an interesting observation: "One does not presume to take this honor, but takes it only when called by God." Is the writer suggesting that some accept the "honor" or ministry apart from a call by God?

As I reflect on my years at a Christian college and seminary, I can recall many young ministerial students with a "fresh" call to ministry who were easily moved toward another career track. The struggles of the pastorate can be a test by fire. Others discover the financial realities of ministry too great to bear. Servanthood as modeled by Christ seems so contrary to what the world around us models. Other careers don't look as demanding.

A young man in my congregation had just served a tour of duty in our area. Dave took great interest in our congregation as well as in his own faith development. After a singles retreat Dave asked my opinion about his attending a Christian college with the option of attending seminary someday.

Dave shared with the church staff his feeling of a call to the ministry. Staff members spent hours giving him counsel and guidance, but all of us gave him one piece of strong advice: "Dave, if any other career interests you, look there first. Go down this path *only* if you feel sure that it is your *only* option." Dave seriously considered our advice and then began his college studies, followed by seminary, and has now given many years of ministry to congregations.

Several church members questioned our advice to Dave: "You should be encouraging this young man, not asking him to doubt his feelings." But each staff member had already given several years in ministry. Only the call of God can sustain the honor. As Christ's ministry demonstrates, serving God can be difficult—even deadly.

SUGGESTION FOR PRAYER: **Pray for new ministerial students who have received both the call and the honor.**

The prophet Joel announces his prophecy in the midst of extraordinary plagues of locusts and drought. Joel suggests that these plagues come as a warning. God is calling the people to repentance. After this message and the repentance of the people, God promises to restore the land: "Do not fear, O soil;…for the LORD has done great things!" God does restore the people and the land.

Global warming, pollution, and uninformed introduction of exotic species into native forests are forcing humankind to look at the fragile balance of nature. We cannot look to the heavens to place blame. We are responsible for the injustice done to earth through our careless acts of selfishness or misconduct.

Yet when oil spills threaten our oceans, the churning of the seas diminishes the harm. Wildfires clear the land, yet the ash remains to provide a rich nutrient for the new forest floor. Polluted streams clear themselves. Contaminated air, when carried away, becomes harmless. We find God working through the balance of creation to correct our destruction.

According to the primeval stories of Genesis, God created us for several reasons: to honor and praise God, to care for one another, and to care for the good earth and the lower animals. But when we fail to adequately care for the earth, through the mysteries of the universe God does great things. As with the restoration after the plagues, God continues to restore the earth, despite our neglect and poor choices. Be not afraid, O land; the Lord continues to do good things.

SUGGESTION FOR PRAYER: **Pray for courage to participate with the Creator in caring for our earth.**

Has God ever spoken to you in a storm? Not me. I can't say that God has ever spoken to me as of this writing. Yet, as a hospice chaplain, I have dying patients tell me almost daily that they have had mystical encounters with God in ways that they have never experienced God before.

The story of Job is a literary classic. The journey of this righteous servant of God who seems to weather the storms of suffering goes beyond anything I can imagine. Yet Job remains faithful and, as today's reading indicates, God speaks to him.

Most of my hospice patients experience the voice and presence of God in ways they may have never known as they daily move toward the transition of death. Fragile and declined beings, they experience God through dreams, visions, or the presence of "visitors" by their bedside. I ask them about these experiences, "Do they make you afraid?"

"Not at all. It was wonderful," the patients answer. "It was the most unusual thing I have ever known. At first I thought I was losing my mind. But as I reflect on it now, I feel it was a way for God to remind me not to be afraid and to assure me that I would not be alone in my journey."

Their experiences sound a lot like Job's, don't they? Even in the storms of life, God continues to show God's faithfulness and care to God's children.

SUGGESTION FOR PRAYER: Pray that in our intellectual quest for faith, we may be open equally to the mystery of being one of God's children.

This great psalm celebrates the wonders of creation. Its beginning reminds the reader of the organization of the heavens and creation of the earth, water, food, and then the seasons. The psalm closes with a celebration of God the Creator. Praise the Lord!

The complexity of creation amazes me. I remember as a young boy the many summer nights children in my neighborhood spent together playing kick the can. After hours of running through the streets in childhood play, we would lie in the grass exhausted, talking, and looking up to the heavens. As we gazed at the twinkling stars, our conversations would turn to theology—or about as much theology as eight-year-old boys can imagine. I do not remember the discussions that we had, but I do remember the feelings that I had afterward—a power greater than I was at work in my universe.

I enjoy backpacking. Several times a year I take to the trails, live out of my pack, sleep on the ground, and cook over a fire. When hiking with friends, we exchange few words. Most of the time we walk quietly on the trails, taking in the mountain views, the plants, the animals, the majesty of creation. I can put my feet in a clear, cool stream and marvel at all that surrounds me. At night the glow and warmth of the fire are overpowered by the spectacle of stars or the brightness of the moon.

Like the psalmist I too praise God's marvelous order and connected creation. At age forty-six I still lie in the grass, look up at the stars, and receive a message from above. A loving Creator at work in my world provides meaning and order to life.

SUGGESTION FOR MEDITATION: If possible, take a walk this week and marvel at creation.

This section in the book of Hebrews emphasizes Jesus' priestly service. The qualifications for a high priest were well established in the ancient culture. The writer believes Jesus far exceeds those expectations.

The Gospels record many acts of Jesus: teaching, healing, performing miracles, preaching, correcting the religious establishment, affirming the powerless, and praying. Yes, even Jesus the high priest has a reputation among his followers of finding it necessary to offer prayers and petitions.

Daily as a hospice chaplain, I help my patients with their prayers. In their weakened condition, many find it hard to put together the words to express their concern, sadness, fear, or struggle. I see my role not as much to pray for them as to ask them what they would like me to voice on their behalf in prayer. After listening, I voice the things they have told me.

Some patients are afraid; others are sad; most pray for their families as they adjust to their dying. My patients always thank me for helping them voice their struggles. Prayer seems to help them as they move forward on their life-threatening journey.

Yet after a day of praying with others, I easily neglect my own prayer life. According to a worn cliché, sometimes we touch holy things so often that we forget their holiness. But prayer was central in Jesus' life; so may it be for us as well.

SUGGESTION FOR PRAYER: Pray for others but also pray confessionally for yourself today.

God's Restoring Love

October 20–26, 2003 • Karen A. Jones[‡]

MONDAY, OCTOBER 20 • Read Job 42:1-6

Have you ever argued with God? Have you ever yelled at God, screamed "Why?" at the top of your lungs? Have you ever sobbed out accusations, demanded an explanation, held God accountable for the pain you've experienced?

Some Christians say that it's a sin to argue with God. They tell me that I should calmly accept with joy and without question anything that happens to me. They say that questioning God signals doubt, sin, unbelief. They should read Job.

Job is a righteous man—more than righteous. He is pure, generous, loving, wise, obviously blessed and a blessing. So what happens? Does he commit some sin that leads to his downfall? No, the story states that Job loses everything through no fault of his own. Does Job accept the loss with joy? Does he praise God with a thankful heart? No, he cries; he questions God's wisdom, God's love and mercy. Today's passage comes at the end of the story, not the beginning. Job sings this song of praise only after he argues with God.

Job's story offers great comfort. God does not punish Job but welcomes instead his questions, fear, and pain. God honors Job's need for answers. Job expresses great faith in choosing to argue with God, signaling trust and belief in God's love, mercy, and interest in each of us as individuals. Questions can lead to a dialogue with God, opening our eyes and heart to experience God in new ways.

SUGGESTION FOR MEDITATION: What questions would you like to ask God? Imagine God sitting across the table from you, listening and eager to begin the conversation.

[‡]Graduate student at Temple University; member of Salford Mennonite Church; living in Schwenksville, Pennsylvania.

When I first read this passage, I thought, *Oh no, another set of verses telling me that I should always be happy.* After reading about Job, these verses took on a new significance. Yes, they are about praise, but they are also about pain and fear and doubt.

"I sought the LORD, and he answered me, and delivered me from all my fears." The psalm doesn't say that God punishes me for my fears. No, it says God delivers me from them, an important difference. I am human, created with a mind, a body, and emotions. I think, I move, I feel. God wants me to share my thoughts and feelings rather than hide or deny them. God understands them. God in Christ has experienced them.

If a child is important in your life, do you only want to hear about the good things that happen to her? Don't you want to know about the child's sadness, fears, or anger? If the child cries, do you punish her for being sad? If the child is hurt, do you tell him it's his own fault and send him away? No, you comfort her; you care for his wounds. You're glad the child came to you, trusted you enough to share the pain and sorrow.

God responds to us in the same way, listening to our fears and sorrows, to our wounds and pain. God listens and answers and does not shame us or turn away. God saves, hears, and delivers. We can come to God with everything because God loves us.

SUGGESTION FOR MEDITATION: **What have you feared talking to God about? Imagine God holding your hand, listening to your deepest fears and sorrows. Imagine God embracing you and assuring you that you are loved.**

The Lord delivers the righteous from all their troubles. I wish I could take this statement literally and believe that trusting God and doing the right thing assure me of a trouble-free life. That approach certainly makes it easier to judge who is righteous: If I have problems, I obviously am not living right.

Another interpretation tells me that I might have problems, but things will always work out if I trust God. In other words, if there isn't a happy ending, I'm obviously an inferior Christian with inadequate faith.

At times I find it comforting to believe that God will make my problems go away, will wave a magic wand and fix them. Then God takes responsibility for the solutions. I just have to "trust," and God will take care of everything—very simple and tidy.

These views do not fit with my experience of God. Read the verses again: The Lord delivers the righteous from trouble and redeems them. The Lord will not condemn those who take refuge in God. These verses tell me that God will not condemn me for my problems or my limitations. Instead, God offers love, mercy, and justice for me as well as others.

God does not offer a problem-free life. God offers redemption, which may be defined as making something worthwhile. God wants to work with me to make something worthwhile out of the problems, pain and suffering in my life, to redeem my experience. This offer requires my willingness to let go of my solutions, my ideas of justice, my happy ending.

SUGGESTION FOR MEDITATION: How have you experienced redemption in your life? What areas of your life still need God's deliverance, God's redemption?

"What do you want me to do for you?" Close your eyes. Imagine yourself in this scene. Feel the blazing sun beating down on you. You cannot see it. You are blind, but you can feel the heat. And the dust, the dust is everywhere—in your hair, on your clothes, in your breath. The scene is noisy. Animals bray, honk, cluck, whine. People talk, shout, scream, laugh, sing. The heat, the dust, the sounds are familiar to you. They are the sounds of your everyday life. They are the sounds of the road outside Jericho.

Yet today seems different. Something exciting is happening. You can hear the difference in the crowds, in the voices. You can feel the tension in the air. You listen carefully and hear the name, Jesus. Jesus? You grab at the people pushing past and ask impatiently, "Is it Jesus of Nazareth?" Most brush you aside in their hurry to move on, but a few answer, "Yes."

You stop, listening carefully. You hear the crowd going away from you down the road. Now—you must do it now. You might never have another chance.

"Jesus, Son of David, have mercy on me!" You scream the words at the top of your lungs. Your throat is dry and dusty, but you continue calling. People around you yell back, telling you to be quiet. They push at you. They treat you like a stubborn child and respond, "Hush. Jesus is busy. He's on his way to Jerusalem. He doesn't have time to spend with you."

Each one of us calls out to Jesus, longing for healing. Voices tell us that he is too busy for us, that our troubles are not important or, even worse, that *we* are not important enough to deserve his love and attention. Yet Jesus stands still and invites us into his presence.

SUGGESTION FOR MEDITATION: **Take a moment to identify the things that keep you from crying out to God.**

Close your eyes and return to yesterday's scene. You still sit by the roadside and call out to Jesus. The crowd tells you to be quiet. You shake off the restraining hands and yell again, "Son of David, have mercy on me!" You will not stop. "Jesus, have mercy on me." Suddenly the people around you begin shouting a different message. "Get up. Get on your feet. He's calling you." Their voices and hands are urgent, inquisitive, compelling. You stumble as you jump to your feet and are propelled to Jesus.

See yourself standing before Jesus. He asks you, "What do you want me to do for you?" The obvious answer is, "Rabbi, I want to see." Is that the truth? Stop and think for a moment.

Illness, pain, and suffering can become a way of life, comfortable because they are known. Healing is a journey into the unknown. Healing brings more than restored sight; it opens you to a new way of life, a new way of seeing yourself and the world around you.

What is the blindness in your life? Are you ready for healing? What will you see if you are healed? What will change if you gain your sight?

Jesus said, "Your faith has made you well." Faith requires persistence: continued belief even when belief seems irrational. Faith requires courage: courage to go against the crowd, to follow your own path, to face a new way of living. Faith requires trust: trust that God can heal and that you can be made whole.

SUGGESTION FOR MEDITATION: What stands in the way of your healing? Can you believe that God has already given you the faith you need for this moment, for healing at this time?

This is another passage I would like to take literally: God will give back everything that's been taken from me—as long as I didn't lose it through my own sinful ways. Oh, maybe it isn't so comforting after all. Maybe I should skip these verses. Scholars debate whether this last section of Job is part of the original text. Perhaps these verses are the ancient equivalent of Hollywood's "happily ever after" ending.

We might interpret this passage in another way. We can view restoration from the temporal perspective, and the restoration of houses, possessions, family, friends sounds wonderful. What more could we ask? What better sign of God's justice and love? But does this understanding fit with the rest of scripture, with God's vision of the kingdom? Are we to turn to God as our refuge in order to gain power, wealth, friends?

God promises us justice and mercy that far exceed anything we can imagine. If we settle for power, wealth, relationships, we have settled for less, for inferior merchandise. God wants to give us the kingdom, and we ask for a pile of rubble. Material restoration simply allows us to hide from God and ourselves.

This story is not about regaining temporal wealth. This story is about eternal restoration, which involves restoration of ourselves and our relationship with God.

SUGGESTION FOR MEDITATION: **God wants to restore you, to give you a vision of the kingdom and your place in that kingdom. What restoration do you long for?**

The Israelites followed a strict set of laws that governed every aspect of life—not only their worship but their daily life. Food, clothes, illnesses, relationships, business, possessions—all had their prescribed rules and rituals. Breaking the law resulted in alienation from God and from the community. Restoration of the relationship required an act of atonement. Each law had a specific method for atonement, and each act of atonement required the presence of a priest.

The priests, representatives of God, served as mediators between God and the Israelites. They followed an even stricter set of rules for their personal lives as well as ones governing the rituals of worship and atonement. They were held to a higher standard.

The writer of Hebrews presents Jesus as a priest unlike the priests before him who were human. Human priests lived and died, made mistakes and sinned. They needed to atone for their own sins as well as the sins of the community. Jesus is the last priest because Jesus Christ will never die and will always intercede for us.

We no longer need to offer animals or grain to restore our relationship with God. The Holy One asks of us something more profound, simple but not easy. God asks us to believe that God desires a relationship with us, that we are worthy of the sacrifice made on our behalf. God asks us to accept the atonement of Christ and to live in community, in communion with God and God's children. Jesus offered the final atonement for all. Atonement is complete. It is accomplished.

SUGGESTION FOR MEDITATION: Imagine yourself before the cross. Picture Jesus there looking at you with love. Hear him tell you, "You are forgiven. Go in peace."

A Lifetime to Prepare for Eternity

October 27–November 2, 2003 • *Monty Brown*[‡]

MONDAY, OCTOBER 27 • Read Ruth 1:1-18

Naomi must have felt much as many of us do at certain turning points in our lives when we cry out, "Everything has gone wrong!" We have all been to the land of Moab.

Surely Naomi feels that everything has gone wrong—all those deaths. We can almost hear her thoughts: *God has either deserted me or is punishing me. I don't know. I just want to go home. I just want to leave this place of horror and not take any souvenirs. Most of all, I can't handle the responsibility for some remind-me-of-my-pain daughters-in-law. I am spent and useless.*

But the daughter-in-law Ruth hangs on. *What does this woman see in me?* Naomi must wonder. *Why can't she just let go?* Too weary to argue, Naomi concedes.

How often has God, in the midst of our fatigue and emptiness, our failure and lack of confidence, given us one more load to carry in the form of someone who clings to us? Then somehow through this responsibility for which we feel so inadequate, God restores us.

How much do we owe to these forbears in faith who did not feel strong enough to carry the torch but were unable to lay it down? At times we, like they, want so much just to lay the burden down. But in our plodding on, by God's grace, we are restored.

PRAYER: Thank you, Lord, for those who went before. Help me appreciate their effort and reliance on you. Help me realize that it's not all about me, even when I hurt. Amen.

[‡]Sheepdog for the Shepherd (ordained clergy), Barboursville United Methodist Church, Barboursville, West Virginia; writer; spirituality leader; former prosecuting attorney.

The license plate holder on the back of the expensive sport utility vehicle read, "I've got it; you don't; you're the loser." Oh, the pity of small thinking! Small thinking is limited to the life of the flesh. We often eschew the small thinking of a materialistic and consumer-oriented culture, but other ways of small thinking may hold us prisoner.

Becoming ordained as a pastor places a high premium on the education and thinking process. There's nothing wrong with that emphasis as long as we keep it in the right perspective. That perspective came to me one day as I reflected on the death process. When we die, all body functions stop, including brain activity. There is no more thinking. The brain gets buried (or cremated) with the rest of the nonfunctioning remains.

That struck me as a revelation when I realized how much of my relationship with God through Jesus gets lived out in my brain. But what happens when my "breath departs"? Where do my help and my hope reside then?

Jesus said that we are to love God with all our heart, soul, mind, and strength, which means we need to use our mind. But when I reread Jesus' formula, I realized that the mind only factored in at 25 percent of the total. Even when I live out strongly what my mind thinks, my mind's influence remains at 50 percent. If I think that percentage is enough without including my heart and soul, then that's pretty small thinking.

PRAYER: God, grant me the discipline and humility to expand my relationship with you beyond merely thinking. Help me discover the wonderful gifts that elude my meager brain exercise. Amen.

When their breath departs, they return to the earth; on that very day their plans perish. Happy are those whose help is the God of Jacob.

Frank had been my pastor during the tumultuous days of my high school and college years. He was my friend and now, years later, my colleague in ministry. An articulate and brilliant preacher, Frank was more than a mere mentor; he was one of the real saints in my life.

Then during Lent one year, cancer struck him. Treatment put the cancer into remission; but the following Lent, he was afflicted by a stroke. As I sat next to his bed in the hospital, I pondered how this brilliant, articulate preacher would handle the situation if his two greatest gifts—his mind and tongue—never recovered from their present impairment. I couldn't help but ask, "Why?"

It takes a lifetime to prepare a soul for eternity. Each life event can teach a lesson if we allow ourselves to learn.

I remembered when Frank had taken time from his busy, big-church schedule to pound out on his Underwood manual typewriter a three-page response to my letter to him from college. His words had inspired me. Now I understood that his brilliance was not the main quality of his personality. His brilliant mind was only a tool to illuminate the real gift—the love of God within. And no stroke, not even death, could end that.

Frank fully recovered, but in the midst of his illness, I learned about the priority of gifts and their purpose.

PRAYER: Lord, help me pause in my life to learn the lessons you intend without having to wait for the crises to slow me down enough to see your teaching. Amen.

Christ came…[to] purify our conscience from dead works to worship the living God!

Roy told me that he wanted to drop out of the short-term study after the first lesson. He couldn't handle the structure that called for each person to respond to certain questions in front of the whole class. I asked if he would find it helpful to receive the questions to think about ahead of time. He agreed to meet with me to give it a try.

When Roy and I met, we talked about each question and possible answers that he would feel comfortable stating in front of others in the study group. Then Roy shared a childhood experience with me, some remarks his father had made to him about his brother: "See Joey. See how he talks up. I wish you could be like that." That conversation had haunted Roy all these years.

I asked Roy if he thought his father meant to hurt him or to give him such a burden to carry. He was sure that he hadn't; he knew that his dad loved him.

I told Roy that I hoped someday he would be able to forgive his father for those remarks that had caused him to carry the "not good enough" message all these years. Roy said that he didn't need to forgive his father because he certainly had not held that comment against his father.

But forgiveness is more than "not holding a grudge." Forgiveness is letting go—not holding on. Forgiveness is letting dead works die and be buried. Whether the sin is of our own making or the sin of another, the conscience becomes deadly when it serves as more than a warning system, when it serves as a bank of hurtful dead works.

PRAYER: Lord Jesus, you call all who are heavy laden to come to you for rest. I believe; help my unbelief. Empower me to let go of all that keeps me from living abundantly. Amen.

Christ came as a high priest of the good things that have come.

"Just as soon as I finish getting these things done on my 'to do' list, I am really going to settle down to a more disciplined prayer life." "I can't wait until I finish this degree program so that I can set about doing what I have been wanting to do with my life." "In my next appointment, I'm going to make sure that I...."

"Just-as-soon-as-I" thinking is epidemic in our culture. Certainly the church is not exempt. Whether I'm not disciplined enough or I am so much a product of my culture, I always find just one more thing that needs to be done or overcome before I am ready (or the situation is ready) for me to really settle down to what will be meaningful to me vocationally, personally.

Jesus Christ came as the "high priest of the good things that have come"—not the good things that "are yet to come." God created all that exists and said, "It is good; it is very good."

But I spend so much time getting ready, preparing and handling one obstacle after another that I never get around to experiencing present blessings. All the good things that have come and gone unnoticed while I was busy getting ready for some other good thing will one day haunt me. Who am I kidding? They already do.

But I seem so trapped by this way of living. If only I could find a way to break the cycle.

PRAYER: Lord God, forgive me for not even noticing all the good things I receive each day. I need your power to empower me to change how I think, to make me pay attention to *now*. Your will be done—even in my life—now as in heaven. Amen.

ALL SAINTS' DAY

Then I saw a new heaven and a new earth.... "See, I am making all things new."

One of the youth asked me, "Why do you hold your hand like that when you give the benediction?" It took me awhile to understand what he was asking. I finally realized that as I pronounced the benediction I held my fingers up in a particular way—the same way that the pastor of my church as a youth had held his fingers—with the first two fingers upright and slightly separated and the next two fingers slightly bent. As a youth I called that benediction "pose" a loose peace sign. I hadn't realized that his style had become my style as well.

For several weeks I paid close attention to my gestures and my manner of doing things. I discovered that I had unconsciously copied from that pastor and others ways of being and doing. They had, unknown to me, shaped how I do ministry.

A funeral prayer in my denomination's liturgy gives thanks for all of the deceased that continues to live within us. How much we are shaped by the saints who have gone on before!

The picture that the phrase *a new heaven and a new earth* brings to my mind's eye has been shaped by the images and moments of saints who have touched my life. One sage said, "We don't remember days gone by; we remember moments." He's right; but sometimes those moments are only unconsciously remembered and still take root.

Jesus entrusted the transmission of the good news to a bunch of sinful saints and saintly sinners. In every age, the gospel story risks extinction unless that generation passes it on—and it has, in moments that have become indelibly etched in our memories.

PRAYER: Thank you, O God, for all of your son Jesus that has lived on through the saints in precious moments. May these roots bear fruit in my life. Amen.

We so often think of these "great commandments" as laws by which we will one day stand in judgment. The courtroom environment for these laws seems to be our favorite paradigm.

But other kinds of laws exist as well. For example, there is the law of gravity. No one I know has ever been given a ticket or arrested for breaking that law. But we surely pay a consequence if we forget or ignore it.

Since God made us and all of creation and said that it was good, then maybe God's laws are meant to help us enjoy the world's goodness. Then the laws serve as guidelines for abundant life instead of as standards for punishment.

As a former prosecuting attorney, I know how important it is to pay attention to the details of the law. In Jesus' great commandments, he does not say, "Love your neighbor as *you love* yourself." That's how we often view it, instead of Jesus' simpler, "Love your neighbor as yourself."

I broke the law of gravity one time quite by accident. A bowling ball fell right on my big toe. It really hurt! I couldn't say "Ouch! My big toe sure hurts, but the rest of me feels fine." I hurt all over.

When Jesus' law is "Love your neighbor as yourself," then my neighbor is a part of me. She cannot feel pain while I feel fine, any more than the bowling ball falling on my toe can hurt only my toe. Neither can I resent my neighbor's good fortune, wishing that it were mine, when I love my neighbor as myself.

A bowling ball's obeying the law of gravity taught me a stimulating lesson about God's law for the whole body of Christ.

PRAYER: **Help me, God, to see your law as a blueprint for my abundant living. Amen.**

God's Good Purposes

November 3–9, 2003 • *Pamela D. Couture*[‡]

MONDAY, NOVEMBER 3 • **Read Ruth 3:1–5, 4:13–17**

The Book of Ruth is best known for its story of the deep friendship between Naomi, a Hebrew woman, and Ruth, her Moabite daughter-in-law. Their relationship is one of honor, care, and fidelity. Today's reading causes us to contemplate such virtues in the character of Boaz.

Boaz notices Ruth as she gleans in the fields; he allows her to glean among his servants where she will be safe from molestation. Boaz seems to be an older, kindly, and wise man. When Ruth reports to Naomi Boaz's attention, Naomi instructs her on the proper way to let Boaz know of Ruth's willingness to marry him if honorably and legally arranged. Legally Ruth must marry her dead husband's next of kin unless he renounces her and the property she would bring to the marriage. Ruth lets Boaz know she will marry him, and Boaz rejoices. He gains the legal right to Ruth's hand. Their union produces Obed, the grandfather of David.

Each character—Ruth, Naomi, and now Boaz—approaches the other with honor and respect, mutuality and generosity in the midst of a hierarchy of relationships marked by differences of gender, age, and poverty. Too often stories in the morning newspaper remind us of exploitation and betrayal where we would have expected fidelity. The story of Naomi, Ruth, and Boaz offers a reversal that stops our cynicism short: We discover tenderness and care where indifference would have been justified, a sign that goodness is returned with goodness to great ends.

PRAYER: We pray, generous God, that our indifference may open itself to find the good and that when we find it, we may return it with joy. Amen.

[‡]Author; Professor of Practical Theology and Pastoral Care at Colgate Rochester Crozer Divinity School, Rochester, New York.

Some translations paraphrase this psalm by using the word *children* in place of *sons*. The New Revised Standard Version appropriately uses *sons*, the term consistent with the warrior imagery that pervades the psalm. Such rejoicing over sons often corresponds with a parallel dismissal of the importance of daughters. In many places in the world, sons are desired and daughters are not. Data demonstrate that girl children receive fewer of the basics than do boys: They receive less food, especially less protein, and are less likely to be literate. When girls receive less food and less health care than boys, they give birth to underweight babies who may not survive to their first birthdays. Girls with inadequate nutrition become women who die in childbirth or before their children are fully grown.

Are gender selective abortion and female infanticide still practiced? Economists have determined that the ratio of boys and girls is so far from the biologically expected averages of girl births and boy births that clearly some countries are practicing gender selective abortion and female infanticide. Therefore, the United Nations has a continued emphasis on "the girl child" as needing special care and attention in many parts of the world.

With this knowledge we might say that "sons who are a heritage from the Lord" are those who care not only for their fathers but for their mothers, sisters, and daughters. They are those who exhibit the honor of Naomi, Ruth, and Boaz! God made every human being in God's own image and endowed each person with dignity and worth. The same God invites each person to flourish in God's grace!

PRAYER: God of wisdom and justice, we pray for daughters who have less nutrition, health care, and education than the sons in some households. Where girls are deprived when they could have enough, open the eyes of those doing the depriving. Where neither girls nor boys have the basics to flourish, guide us to restore a world in which the fruit of your abundant creation is distributed so that all may share! Amen.

The issues raised by the "sons" and "warriors" of the second half of the psalm circle back to the psalm's initial declaration that "unless the Lord builds the house, those who build it labor in vain." In a world of six billion people, about one third live on less than $2 a day. The largest proportion of those two billion people are children—sons and daughters of God who do not have enough for basic subsistence.

All the countries of the world are deeply interrelated through our political, economic, and social relationships. In many cases, the labor of those who do not have basic food, health care, and education supports the luxury of those who have more than enough. It is easy to find examples of the production of clothing, shoes, rugs, chocolate, and diamonds, where the labor of poor children has contributed to the happiness of the rich. The Lord is the Lord of righteousness. Is the world's economic house one that the Lord is building? Or are we laboring in vain?

I take comfort in reading that God thwarts human efforts that are contrary to God's purposes. All of us engage in a certain amount of anxious toil that is contrary to God's desires. God invites us to let go of that burden, to live simply, and to put our effort toward the purposes of building God's house in which every person is well fed, educated, and cared for.

PRAYER: The suffering of your world overwhelms us, O God. Show us practices that build a house where good nourishment and care are possible for all your people. Relieve our anxiety, O God, about the ways that we knowingly and unknowingly build houses that are not yours. Show us good practices that help us build a world as you would have it to be. Amen.

In Psalm 127 the psalmist speaks of toil contrary to God's purposes that brings anxiety and the work toward God's purposes that brings peace. In today's world, one might translate that idea into the thought, *I need to be about the work of the church rather than engaged in my paid employment.* The writer of the Gospel of Mark stops that confusion in its tracks. In Mark 12:38-40, religious works done from the wrong motivation bring not only anxiety but condemnation! When people engage in practices of piety, including prayer and devotions, for the purpose of status, show, or honor, they are "laboring in vain."

How do we know whether our spiritual practice is genuine? The passage mentions the scribes' use of their prayer life to gain status and attention. Their ostentatious prayers are out of sync with their practices, since the Gospel writer describes the scribes as those who "devour widows' houses and for a show make lengthy prayers" (NIV). Their religious practice should encourage the love of God and neighbor, but they use it to impoverish widows further.

In the sixteenth century Martin Luther challenged the Pope, claiming that the practices of promoting pilgrimages to Rome and selling indulgences among the poor people of Europe enriched Rome's coffers, grossly distorting the purpose of prayer. Protestants are not immune to such distortions: When the Methodist Episcopal church sold tickets for pews and expected fine clothes for worship, the Free Methodist church broke away to establish a purer, freer worship.

The question is not whether our prayer and worship will at times become ill-focused and exploitative; some days, some ways, we will be like scribes, and it will. The question is whether, when we recognize that our prayer and worship serve false ends, we can reestablish their proper purpose: to help us love God with our heart, soul, and mind, and to love our neighbor as ourselves.

PRAYER: **God of integrity, help us to practice what we pray. Amen.**

The honor, fidelity, and generosity of Naomi, Ruth, and Boaz; the single-minded wisdom of the psalmist who builds his house on the foundation of God's purposes; the integrity that Jesus seeks but cannot find in the scribes: All these are gathered up in the image of the widow with two copper coins. The rich who "have contributed out of their abundance" are superceded by her generosity, devotion, and integrity.

Imagine a different scene: Having seen the widow himself and overheard Jesus' approval, the rich man brings all that he has to the next offering. But his motivation is guilt, and resentment fills him. He knows he has missed the point, so he tries to deny his resentment. The next day he comes no more. Acting as the widow acts brings the rich man no closer to God; he needs to experience her motivation, rather than mimic her action.

The widow serves as a spiritual exemplar before she can be a moral exemplar. Her generosity is an end in itself rather than a means toward Jesus' approval or toward some good that her two copper coins will buy. Her spirituality is centered deep in Psalm 127, where the peace of the single-minded pursuit of God replaces the anxiety of those—often the rich—who toil falsely. Her behavior contrasts fully with that of the scribes in 12:38-40. The motivations for her generosity, rather than its effects, are what interest Jesus. Without such motivation, the world will never live in relationships of love and justice.

Does that mean that the effects that result from our giving don't matter? Of course they do, just as Jesus proclaims that the reign of God is at hand. We cannot cooperate with the reign of God unless our motivations, our practices, and the ends they serve are in harmony. Not only are we guided to practice what we pray but to allow both our practice and our prayers to mold us into generous spirits!

PRAYER: Bring us to the wholeness of your peace, O God, from which we pour out ourselves on behalf of others. Amen.

By grace we live to love more perfectly. Loving perfectly is complex, involving motivations, prayers, practices, and actions. Guides testify to generosity and goodness but remind us how easily and inevitably we lose sight of God and go astray.

I wrote this meditation two years before you will read it, but I can say with confidence that God's reign is not realized on earth. The testimony to human waywardness is enormous: Boys and girls still starve, drink contaminated water, die of preventable diseases. Children still suffer the trauma of armed conflict and sexual abuse. Women still die in childbirth in refugee camps, and too many of their babies barely survive to their first birthday. All these events occur in a rich and technologically sophisticated world.

Why do these overwhelming realities come to mind now? In this complicated passage from the Letter to the Hebrews, we hear testimony to the intensity of those forces that lead humanity astray. "The heavenly things themselves"—perhaps referring to fallen angels who influence a wayward humanity—need purification.

Even between the writing and the reading of this meditation, too much blood has been shed; and it is on the hands of us all. But the enormity of Christ's sacrifice meets the intensity of evil that inevitably draws us in. By Christ's sacrifice, we are cleansed; we are forgiven; we are given a new day. Christ empowers us to meet the evil in the world with generosity and fidelity, grace and love.

PRAYER: Dear God, as with Francis of Assisi, where there is evil, let me sow love. Amen.

"Christ, having been offered once to bear the sins of many, will appear a second time, not to deal with sin, but to save those who are eagerly waiting for him." *Eagerly* denotes an attitude that fights despair. We live in hope; in anticipation of a better time, a time of salvation, a time of flourishing. We eagerly await this time when evil no longer has a grip upon the world, but this time is not here. What shall we do in the meantime?

I have taught classes and courses on poverty for many years. People in those classes do not want to abandon the world to destitution; from the beginning of the class, they need "things to do" that allow them to put the energy of their hope into active participation in the reign of God in the world. They are "eager" for the reign of Christ, but they are not passive. They are ready to act when guided to do so.

Eagerness is a wonderful quality in those who wait for Christ's reign on earth. That quality brings us into the company of Ruth and the widow with the two coins.

When we are "eager" we can carry hope for the hopeless, fight for those who are discriminated against or persecuted, accompany those who are isolated, encourage those who have lost their energy.

PRAYER: O God, as we wait, may we wait eagerly, not passively, participating in your good purposes in the world! Amen.

A Sure Foundation

November 10–16, 2003 • David A. deSilva[‡]

MONDAY, NOVEMBER 10 • Read Mark 13:1-2

Anyone who has seen the Western Wall in Jerusalem can appreciate the disciples' jaw-slackened awe upon seeing the Temple. The "large stones" are longer than an adult and taller than a child. The Second Temple was built to last—and to give the impression of permanence. As the center of Jerusalem and the focal point of the hope of Jews throughout the Mediterranean, the Temple's architecture reinforced its symbolic importance.

Jesus makes a poor tour guide for these Galilean tourists. Rather than heighten their experience of the grandeur and impressiveness of the Jerusalem temple, he solemnly promises that it will be destroyed. The focal point, the bedrock, of the hope of so many first-century Jews is unstable after all.

I remember my first trip to New York City as a small boy and my amazement at the grandeur of the concrete world humans had made. More recently, as a responsible adult, I have been advised to build a secure financial future for my family on the bedrock of sound investments. We all want to build our security and hope for the future on something solid and lasting. But Jesus tells us the sober truth—nothing in this world will provide that stability. Our false places of security, those human-poured foundations for hope, need to be broken down so that Jesus can lay the truly stable foundation in our hearts.

PRAYER: Eternal God, lift my eyes from the seemingly solid and sure things of this world. Fix my heart on you and your promises, that in the midst of this world's instability I may have a secure foundation. Amen.

[‡]Professor of New Testament, Ashland Theological Seminary, Ashland, Ohio; ordained clergy of The United Methodist Church; author of twelve books on the New Testament and Intertestamental Period.

TUESDAY, NOVEMBER 11 • **Read Mark 13:3-8**

Struck by their master's declaration, the disciples want to know "when" the disaster will strike and "what" will be the warning signs. Jesus provides an answer at least to the second of these questions through 13:23. His words would prove eerily accurate in the decades that followed his ascension. The Jewish Christian missionaries were subject to persecution (Mark 13:9-13) while fulfilling their commission to spread the gospel; upheavals shook the Roman Empire in the civil wars of A.D. 68–69 (Mark 13:7-8); and the Jewish Revolt broke out amidst false messiahs, violence, and famine from A.D. 66–70 (Mark 13:5-8, 14-23).

Noteworthy is Jesus' interest not merely to inform the disciples of the signs but to prepare them to steer a sure course through the rough seas of deception, hostility, and disaster ahead. He would have them unshaken by the fearsomeness of the events engulfing them, undistracted by the deceptive words of the false messiahs spreading false hopes.

As a remedy for fear, he assures them that, beyond the upheavals that shake the bedrock of civilization, God is working out God's purposes for humankind. The image of labor pains invites the disciples to see these upheavals not as cause for despair but as signs that point to God's good future for humanity. As a remedy for deception, Jesus warns the disciples that no human being will bring about God's future, neither the violence of the Zealot messiah nor the escapism and introversionism of the Qumran messiah.

SUGGESTION FOR MEDITATION: **Wars, earthquakes, famines, and religious deception are commonplace in every generation. How can you bring the genuine hope of God's kingdom to people oppressed by these conditions? How can you stand as a witness to God's good purposes for humanity beside those caught in the birth pangs?**

From the birth pangs of the Jewish Revolt we turn back a millennium to a woman who longed to experience the birth pangs that would give her a child. A woman's honor was especially linked with her sexuality and procreative ability. Virginity before marriage and sexual exclusivity within marriage were essential components of female honor, to which was added the ability to bear strong and healthy children, especially sons. Hannah's husband tries to express his estimation of Hannah's honor by giving her twice as much meat from a sacrifice as he gives to his other wife and to each of his children by her, but it is not enough to counter Peninnah's taunts.

Perhaps the most disturbing part of this passage is the manner of God's presence here: "The LORD had closed her womb." On the one hand, such a statement reminds us that we can view every child not merely as the natural result of copulation but as a specific gift from God, who opens and closes the womb.

On the other hand, this statement strikes hard against the ear of the woman who has longed for a child, has pursued all the avenues that medical science offers and still has never conceived and given birth. "Why, God? Why do you keep this gift from me? Why do you not do what can take away my disgrace, my sorrow, my emptiness?" Hannah may well have wrestled with these questions as she sank into depression (1 Sam. 1:7). The story's great testimony comes in Hannah's keeping faith with God in the face of disappointment—and God's keeping faith with Hannah!

SUGGESTION FOR MEDITATION: **When have you suffered from a crying, unfulfilled yearning such as Hannah's? How has God sustained your faith and your perseverance?**

Thursday, November 13 • Read 1 Samuel 1:9–20

From the depths of her sorrow, Hannah finds the strength to do what we all must. She goes out alone to seek God. Before the Almighty, she pours out her heart and holds nothing back. Hers is not "proper church talk" but open, honest, heart-to-heart communication. The psalms of Hebrew Scriptures teach us much about praying to God. We often find ourselves embarrassed by the many things that the psalmists did not refrain from speaking to God—but our embarrassment says more about us than them.

After opening up completely and unreservedly before God, Hannah makes her plea. It is a strange plea, since she offers, if God gives her a son, to dedicate him to God's service in the Temple. Hannah will, in fact, see Samuel only once each year after he is weaned (1 Sam. 2:19). In her despair she seems to want to know that God cares about her, is mindful of her, and is willing to help her rather than to enjoy the gift itself. She pleads with God in words to this effect: "Give me what I most desire, and I will give it right back to you. Let me experience your kindness and generosity where I need it most, and I will respond in kind with a full heart."

I have been several times where I imagine Hannah was and fortunately have learned to pray as she did. To an onlooker I too may have seemed to rave like a drunkard. In each of those times, God's best gift was the divine presence, assurance of care, and promise that we belonged to each other even in the midst of dismal circumstances.

Suggestion for prayer: Take any need that came to mind in yesterday's reflection, and approach God about it with utter honesty and openness. Press forward boldly, until you sense God's reaching toward you.

Psalm 113 is a fitting response to the God who, mindful of Hannah's plight, made her "the joyous mother of children." The psalm not only affirms that which Hannah never doubted, namely God's rule over the cosmos, but that which she needed to learn so desperately: God cares for each person.

The language of altitude is, of course, merely our human way of giving expression to God's power, authority, and honor above all things created. The psalm celebrates the paradox of a cosmic ruler who can attend to the particular needs and concerns of each one of God's creatures, no matter how marginalized or unimportant it might be in the estimation of the worldly minded.

This psalm proclaims that Hannah's experience reveals God's character and nature as that of a God who regards, stoops, and lifts up the poor person from whom so many people avert their eyes. This God provides a secure place for the barren woman from whose sorrow many people would hide themselves.

In short, God does what James says all true piety, all genuine religion, does—looks at people with eyes that estimate value by God's standards and not the world's (James 2:1-9) and care for the orphan and widow (James 1:27). As we praise God this day for the divine character, let us also pray to be more like this Holy One in character. Whatever heights we attain, let us commit to use our gifts and talents in service to others.

PRAYER: **Thank you, loving and generous God, for being the God enthroned in heaven and for being the companion who walks with me in my time of need and lifts my head! Help me to imitate your heart. Amen.**

We began this week by reading from Mark about the instability and impermanence of all worldly things. We end by reading from the letter to the Hebrews about how Jesus has prepared us, by his death and entrance into the heavenly sanctuary, for our entrance into the unshakable kingdom of God's realm (Heb. 12:26-28).

Throughout Hebrews, Jesus is our forerunner (Heb. 6:19-20), leading us to where he himself has gone (Heb. 2:10), namely into heaven itself, the very throne room of God. Hebrews 9:1–10:18, from which the lectionary excerpts this reading, speaks in detail about this preparation to enter God's presence.

According to the author, the fundamental problem with the levitical priesthood and sacrifices is that they do not enable the people to close the distance between themselves and God (9:6-10). Year after year the people have remained outside the holy places. The fact that the priests have to repeat their sacrifices suggests that animal blood can never make their inner persons sufficiently "clean" to enable them to go into God's inmost shrine (10:1-4). The levitical priesthood and sacrifices were, at best, a holding pattern.

This dilemma gives the author the language by which to talk about the significance of Jesus' death, resurrection, and ascension: Together, these constitute a single, unrepeatable priestly act that decisively cleanses us from all the sins that have kept us from walking into the Holy of Holies. Here, at the conclusion of the argument, the author points to Jesus' sitting at the right hand of God as proof that his priestly work is done and our consecration (the meaning of "perfected" in verse 14) complete.

SUGGESTION FOR MEDITATION: **See all your past sins swept away and your whole being made "clean" again for God by Jesus' priestly work. Pray to be renewed in that cleansing, and give Jesus thanks.**

What direction is your life taking? Where are you heading? The author of Hebrews invites us to see ourselves standing at the threshold of our heavenly country, our permanent Promised Land (4:1-11), prepared by Jesus to make the bold journey into God's real presence. The author invites us to see ourselves as those who are in the process of entering the heavenly Holy of Holies (8:5). Our lives can be marked by the dynamic of "approach," of drawing near to God, our "lasting city" (13:14), and finally entering that rest.

This tremendous privilege was purchased for us at a tremendous cost. The way home to a secure place is through Jesus' flesh, nailed to the cross (10:20). We must show that we understand the value of that gift by allowing it to have complete effect on our lives. Our promise of a place in God's stable, secure city calls us to show stability in our walk (10:23).

Here we find at last the solid foundation for our lives—our trust in the God who is faithful. As long as we move forward unwaveringly in that trust, making all our choices, actions, and investments of ourselves fall in line with the movement of our lives toward God's unshakable kingdom, we will steer a steady course through an unstable sea.

We cannot steer this course as rugged individuals. We need our sisters' and brothers' encouragement and aid, and we need to offer ourselves in love and good deeds to our sisters and brothers (10:24-25). We help one another keep our eyes fixed on the beacon that guides us home.

PRAYER: Faithful God, give me such trust in your promises that I may move unwaveringly toward you, seeking only what pleases you all my days. Amen.

Thy Kingdom Come!

November 17–23, 2003 • *Janet Wolf*[‡]

MONDAY, NOVEMBER 17 • **Read 2 Samuel 23:1-7**

The kingdom of God is often made to sound like some faraway other worldly place yet to come, but biblically it is here and now. This week we explore what it might mean to live in light of the kingdom here and now.

David looks back on his life and considers how, in the end, his rule measures up. In doing so, he does not list military victories, the splendor of his wealth, or his plans for expansion. He asks whether or not he has ruled justly, whether his use of power and resources has been for the people like the hope of dawn splintering the darkness, like the shimmering of sunlight on green leaves soaked by the rain.

What might it mean for churches to examine their faithfulness not by reporting on budgets or buildings or even the number of new members but on their work to seek justice? What if churches were asked to give annual reports on their impact on the community: on the public education system, the creation of affordable housing, equitable access to quality health care, effective treatment programs for addicts, and alternatives to incarceration for nonviolent offenders?

We are a covenant people held accountable for our willingness to embody the kingdom of God. We are to be channels of healing and hope, instruments of justice and reconciliation, agents of change and challenge. May it be so.

SUGGESTION FOR MEDITATION: The church is invited and empowered to be a sign of this kingdom already at hand. What might change in your congregation if life was redefined by kingdom values?

[‡]Director of Public Policy and Community Outreach; Religious Leaders for a More Just and Compassionate Drug Policy; member, Hobson United Methodist Church, Nashville, Tennessee.

The psalmist sings of a God who chooses to dwell among us; a God who desires, yearns for a resting place here in our midst. It is a song that the writer of Revelation will echo as he declares, "See, the home of God is among mortals" (21:3).

The church is to be "God's contrast community," a community so marked by grace and love that its members startle the world by inviting folks into kingdom living right here and now. Base Christian Communities (BCC) often embody this kingdom living as they call people into right relationship. All over the world BCCs have been the source of radical challenge and change: churches that need no buildings or bulletins, no clergy or paid staff. They willingly trust in the God who is already bringing about a new creation. They are churches of the poor in which everyone is active as ministers, "delegates of the Word."

I wanted to learn from BCCs what it might mean to be this "church in the world." As I walked toward my first BCC meeting in Nicaragua, I realized that the house (the designated place of meeting) was already full. Disappointed but not deterred, I decided to settle outside one of the windows of the house—except that chickens were already perched on the windowsill. By the time the clucking settled down, someone hollered from the road to a man on the other side of the house. Then kids came squealing past me, chasing a pig that ran between me and the windowsill full of chickens. I could feel my frustration welling up: *I have spent two years preparing for this moment! I have read and studied, and here I am with my tape recorder, camera, and notebook!* Just then the man next to me leaned over and said, "It is good, is it not, to give God thanks in the midst of the people."

I had forgotten what I had come to see—not worship that depends upon silence in the sanctuary but this being church in the middle of the world's chaos, this eruption of praise for the God who dwells in our midst.

SUGGESTION FOR MEDITATION: **What might it mean for me to believe that God is at home in the world around me?**

Shout for joy! God has chosen to dwell among us; the poor are feasting and priests are clothed with salvation!

Hogan, age seventy-four, was pastor of a downtown congregation until he joined others carrying a casket through the streets to protest the assassination of archbishop Oscar Romero and U.S. support for right-wing death squads in El Salvador. When the congregation suggested it was time for him to retire, Hogan declared that prophetic witness was a permanent job and promptly had cards printed up, identifying himself as a "consultant on resurrection." He became a partner in the first team of witnesses for peace in Nicaragua, folks who put themselves in the middle of U.S.-financed conflict, believing their presence will decrease the violence.

In worship one Sunday in Managua, Hogan echoed what he thought the pastor was saying, "A la lucha! Amen!" It's a Spanish phrase meaning "to the struggle!" In Nicaragua, that phrase invited people to become active in the struggle for justice, liberation, and peace. Over and over, Hogan offered up what he thought he was hearing and shouted, "A la lucha! Amen!" But the pastor actually was saying, "Alleluia! Amen."

Several people tried to explain this to Hogan but couldn't get him to understand. Finally, after the service had ended, a friend leaned over, thinking Hogan would probably be embarrassed by his mistake and told him, "The pastor was saying alleluia *not* a la lucha!"

Hogan turned, stared at the friend for a moment, and declared, "Same thing! 'Alleluia,' to praise God is always to work for justice! And 'a la lucha,' to struggle for justice, always means praising God!"

PRAYER: God of justice and joy, teach us to dance in the light of your kingdom, shouting praise as we work for justice and peace. Amen.

Jesus declares, "My kingdom is not from this world. If my kingdom were from this world, my followers would be fighting to keep me from being handed over." How do we learn to live in the light of God's kingdom? How do we learn to pray "thy kingdom come" when God's kingdom so clearly disrupts, disturbs, challenges, and confronts the world in which we live?

We are invited to live in the light of God's kingdom here and now, trusting in the One who calls us and goes before us, the One who loves us into abundant life and teaches us while on the journey to pray:

Thy kingdom come, O God, thy kingdom of love and light, justice, generosity, gentleness, and joy;
kingdom of revolution, reconciliation, and redemption;
kingdom of manna, mercy, and miracles;
kingdom where chains are broken and prison doors opened,
where justice rolls down like a mighty river, where not only are tears dried, but we find laughter for our souls;
kingdom where no one waits for crumbs under the table but all are invited to sit down side by side at the banquet;
kingdom where love triumphs over division, where the power of drugs and alcohol, grief and despair is a power that has been, is now being broken by God's good grace;
Thy kingdom come! Kingdom where all belong, where folks labeled nobodies discover we are somebody wonderful, precious, and beloved, awesomely and wondrously made;
kingdom where those who are bowed down and bent over are rising up to be all God created us to be, kingdom already breaking into this world;
Thy kingdom come! Thy will be done, on earth as it is in heaven. Forever and ever. Amen.

Jesus declares that he has come to witness to the truth—to expose the contradictions, uncover the lies, dismantle the illusions, and lay bare the idols. And Pilate asks, "What is truth?"

Members of Central Methodist Church in Johannesburg, South Africa, began creating Peace, Hope, and Justice candles in the 1980s. These candles, encircled in barbed wire, were modeled (with permission) after the symbol for Amnesty International. The candles became powerful reminders of the struggle to resist evil and seek justice in a country where many churches endorsed or at least quietly consented to the brutal practices of the apartheid government.

Each week during worship, the congregation offered up the names of people who had been arrested, tortured, or executed by the apartheid government. The members then lit the candle, reading from John 1: "The light shines in the darkness, and the darkness did not overcome it" (v. 5). Even after being banned from the radio because of the candlelighting portion of their services, the congregation continued to call out names, to light the candle, and to trust in the truth of God's promise to call forth life from places of death, to undo the yokes of oppression and apartheid.

Peter Storey, pastor of Central Methodist Church at the time and later bishop, often celebrates this witness, reminding folks that the apartheid government is gone, but congregations still gather, lighting the candles and testifying to the truth of God's power and love already at work among us.

SUGGESTION FOR MEDITATION: The candles are now made available to people in this country, inviting us to live out this daring hope and outrageous courage. What might it mean for us to trust in God's promises and presence as the truth of the world in which we live?

The Book of Revelation has been used in hellfire preaching, spit out on street corners by folks carrying signs that say the end is near. It is cited in detailed predictions about last days and sudden raptures. But the Book of Revelation is not a puzzle to be solved or a riddle to be deciphered. It is a song created in the heart of God's own dreaming, a song of hope and joy, justice and love. It's a prophetic poem for now—not simply a vision of what is to come but an uncovering of what is already taking place. Its verses issue a passionate plea for Christians to bet everything on the love of God, which is even now at work among us.

Saying yes to Jesus means saying no to all other powers. There is no neutral ground. To be silent is to side with those already in power. The world expects the church to go along, encouraging congregations to become what Walter Wink refers to as "kept chaplains of an unjust order." The reign of Christ is not the reign of any Caesar; the way of love is not the way of the world. That's why saying "Jesus is Lord!" was an offense punishable by death—it was a declaration that no other power could define who and how we are. The kingdom of God exposes our compromises with a world that is often defined by consumer culture and marketplace mentality; individualism and the illusion of self-sufficiency; violence, keeping score, and getting even.

We are called to live and love like Jesus, nurturing communities that are signs of God's upside-down reign; partners with God in transforming the world so the first are last and the last really are first. The hungry are filled, and the poor find justice. Wounds are healed, and sins are forgiven.

PRAYER: Holy, wonderful, and awesome God, confront our complicity and complacency in a world where so many of your children are on the edges of death. Disturb our apathy, challenge our cooperation with the way things are, and empower us to be the church of Christ Jesus. Amen.

THE REIGN OF CHRIST

We are loved, set free, and empowered to be a kingdom community, startling the world with our wide-open loving and astonishing trust in the One who has come, is present, and will surely come again.

I knew Christmas Eve with this small inner-city congregation would be a contrast to the services I was used to—we were, after all, holding worship at the state prison instead of the church. By the time I arrived, the worship leaders had already been told we would not be allowed inside, so folks were huddled in the parking lot. It was snowing; sleet had begun to mix with the flakes, stinging our cheeks. As my two boys moved in closer, trying to hide from the wind by ducking under my coat, I considered leaving. This was not my idea of Christmas. I liked the pageantry of a sanctuary lit up in candlelight; splashed with the brilliant red of poinsettias; echoing with the wild joy of children, choirs, and trumpets.

Instead, here we were, freezing in a parking lot. I imagined sick kids, earaches, sore throats, and wondered who would even notice that we were here.

Just then the man next to me shoved a Bible into my hands, saying, "Here. Read this." So while he leaned down away from the wind, trying to light the Christ candle, I read the words from Isaiah: "The people who walked in darkness have seen a great light." Somehow he got the candle lit, and we started singing, reaching to light our smaller candles. Suddenly my younger child tugged on my coat: "Look!" And I turned to see, in cell after cell on all five floors of the prison, matches and lighters held up to the windows, splintering the darkness.

SUGGESTION FOR MEDITATION: **What might it mean for churches to be God's "contrast community," signs of God's kingdom coming even now among us?**

God's Gift of Memory and Hope

November 24–30, 2003 • *Diane Luton Blum*[‡]

MONDAY, NOVEMBER 24 • **Read Jeremiah 33:14-16**

The city of Jerusalem lies in siege, the countryside will soon be desolate, the national leaders are in confusion, and this prophet speaks from imprisonment. Jeremiah has just acted on God's word of hope, investing his money in family land. His actions express his trust that a day will come when life in Jerusalem will be restored. "Wait," says the Lord. "I will bestow blessings on Israel and Judah: A just ruler will bring safety and peace in the land again."

The prophetic words and deeds, faithfully preserved in the biblical record, offer us the gift of sacred memory. Though the people of Judah would be transformed by ruin and exile, their faith would not be extinguished; they would return and live again in Jerusalem. God's promise would become a dream realized in the life of Jesus, a sovereign who embodies for us the gifts of justice, peace, eternal security.

Where are we in exile today? What do we fear? I process these words to you just weeks after the disastrous events of September 11, 2001, and the U.S. is engaged in international conflict. Wherever you stand on this day, receive the gift of memory. God's loving history of relationship with us still speaks to us today, saying, "I have not forgotten you. I see you, I love you." Receive the gift of hope: God's promise in Christ is Emmanuel, God with us. We are not alone. Restoration is not only possible, but it is God's promise to us today.

SUGGESTION FOR PRAYER: God calls us to wait. In your time of prayer, practice active, attentive waiting for the Lord. Listen for God's promise for you in the events of this day.

[‡]A pastor of Edgehill United Methodist Church, Nashville, Tennessee; spouse to Jeff; mother to Jack and Will.

Much of our life is spent living "between," between conception and birth, between childhood and maturity, between birth and death. The days of Advent focus our attention on the memory of Christ's first coming to us through birth in Bethlehem and God's promise that Christ will come again to complete God's work of justice, peace, *shalom*. The chapters of our lives reflect this creative tension between the already and the not yet.

Paul had fervently shared the gospel in Thessalonica, and he writes to the Christians there as he waits to return. Between visits, his passionate words reveal his love and prayer for their life in Christ. Even in this in-between time, the bonds of fellowship are nurtured by these lasting words of joyous memory and hope for their life to come.

A dear friend from childhood and I have lived in different cities for more than thirty years. Our correspondence has been the key to a lively and growing bond of love for each other. She recently sent me a card in which two little girls are seated before paintings in an art museum. *Of all the great works, our friendship is still my favorite*, reads the caption inside.

Where is God calling you to reunite with someone through a word, a prayer, or a letter? The remembrance of a friend, even one far away, often sustains us. Examine the opportunity God gives you today to reach out to another with the gifts of memory and hope. May God's love work between, as well as within, our lives.

SUGGESTION FOR PRAYER: Reflect on a friendship that has blessed you in the past. Thank God for this memory. Offer prayer for this loved one, and express your prayer with a note or a call. Journal about your gratitude if this loved one has joined God beyond death.

The people of Judah had been conquered and removed from their homeland by the Babylonians. Cyrus, the great Persian emperor, led his armies into Babylon and set forth a peaceful policy that permitted the exiled Jews to return to their homeland. The dream of restoration and homecoming to Jerusalem was being fulfilled. The joy of this news, the songs and laughter, would meet with the harsh reality of rebuilding in the midst of ruins. Not every exile would join leaders like Nehemiah and Ezra in this new chapter of the biblical saga, but for those who traveled home, the seeds of memory and hope would bring a rich harvest.

Where have you prayed for the tide to turn? Where have you longed for streams of living water to fill the dry riverbeds of your life or ministry?

In 1995 several ministers in our city dreamed together of creating support programs for women who wanted to turn from prostitution and find restoration for their lives. Prayers, hard work, and love brought several programs into existence; and women have made decisions to seek new life. They have discovered support from one another and from the community that had previously given up on them. At first only a few, but now many shine with vitality in the daily process of recovery.

My husband and I have hosted a Christmas dinner several years for the graduates of these programs. As a multitude gathered last year to celebrate this miracle in their lives, we paused to remember when most had been jailed or homeless, or half-dead. We remembered dear ones who had relapsed, remembered women who had died. Then we parted after voicing our hopes that the new year would swell their ranks and that God's love would hold them safely for the days ahead.

SUGGESTION FOR PRAYER: **Give thanks to God for the seeds of hope that have grown to fullness in your life.**

THURSDAY, NOVEMBER 27 • Read Joel 2:21–27;
1 Timothy 2:1–7

THANKSGIVING DAY IN U.S.

The gifts of many holiday celebrations are the rituals that over time shape our life in community. Ritual provides a place for memory to be stored, retrieved, and shared with new generations. Personal and communal stories sweeten and strengthen our sense of God's holy presence with us on such days. The memories of our forebears become our memories. Freeing us from the narrow bondage of the present, a day of ritual remembrance and in-gathering can connect us to a past larger than our own and, miraculously, to a future larger than our own personal hope.

Paul calls Timothy and us to a life marked by prayer and thanksgiving for the saving grace of God in Jesus Christ. In the ancient eucharistic prayer of great thanksgiving, Christians claim the memory and the hope that "Christ has died, Christ is risen, Christ will come again." Our thanksgiving is larger than one prayer or one day. We give thanks in past, present, and future tenses.

On this day, so often marked by looking back, hear the prophet Joel as he looks at disaster and recognizes the waste of violence. In the midst of this reckoning, Joel proclaims the certain hope that God will restore the whole creation. Feasting will follow a season of deprivation and sorrow. I take comfort in passing a young forest that was, during my childhood, an empty field. Look for signs of God's promise to provide for all creation, for you and for me, in our present and future as in our past.

PRAYER: We thank you, living God, for the blessing of our memories found in holy scriptures. We ask you to bless this day in our lives by your abiding love. Bless us with faith and hope in your future for all your creation. Amen.

Each year as I reflect with young people in our congregation about their decisions to profess the Christian faith, to be baptized or confirmed, I urge each one to reflect on her or his vocation. I begin by saying that I am *not* talking about their livelihood—the necessity of earning or securing enough material means to be clothed, fed and sheltered. Everybody needs these provisions of livelihood. I say, "What I want you to consider is what God is uniquely calling *you* to be and to do in each part of your life."

What we hear from God, at any age or stage in our lives, depends upon our willingness to keep listening for God's voice and then to keep letting God's purpose shape our whole lives, including our livelihoods.

Putting God's plan first will shift our attention from the fears and worries that go with simply seeking food, clothing, and shelter. This focus serves as the Christian's key to a joyful life, a life that makes a difference, a life that brings a taste of God's reign to our earthly, material world.

During the Advent season in the U.S., we often experience cultural pressure to pursue the acquisition of excessive material goods in preparation for the Christmas holiday. From rich food to luxurious gifts, we often find ourselves overeating and overextending our financial means. When we put our hopes for God's reign first in our lives, God's presence in Christ can lead us through and beyond exhausting temptations.

PRAYER: God, let me put your purpose for my life first, today and always. By the light of Christ. Amen.

My sister has a vivid and painful memory from the school year when both of us were in Mrs. McKinnon's combined second- and third-grade classroom. As one of the third-grade students, I took pride in helping our teacher with the second-grade students in the room.

In an incident that I had totally forgotten, my sister recalls that I had needlessly embarrassed her before the whole class, not just the teacher. When my sister recently recounted this experience, I immediately recognized the truth of her memory. My failure to consider the feelings of others did not end with my childhood. I thank God for forgiving me the sins and offenses of my youth.

God's divine memory of us is perfect, while our memory is selective. We often choose to humble others, when God wills our humility and responsiveness to others. Our hope rests upon God's memory and mercy.

During this season of Advent search the scriptures and search your heart for memories of God's faithfulness. Recall lived experiences of God's faithful, constant love. This love can transform our youthful arrogance as well as our long-held reservoirs of pride and self-satisfaction.

During these days of Advent, we are invited to open up our vivid and powerful memories of all that God has done for us from generation to generation. We are called to tell these stories and to share them at our tables until the living Christ becomes the source of our memory and our hope.

PRAYER: Remember us, O God, in your unfailing love, so that we may seek your forgiveness and receive your guidance. Amen.

FIRST SUNDAY OF ADVENT

We practice waiting for Christ's return in the season of Advent. This practical and spiritual discipline of waiting counters the many temptations to overindulge ourselves with feasting, drinking, and profligate spending.

A few years ago, I decided to give up something for Advent, so that I could watch and wait for Christ in deeper solidarity with those whose lives are given over to poverty and suffering sacrifice. I gave up rich foods and desserts until the feast day of Christmas—hoping that my heart might be more open to the presence of Christ. It was a challenging sacrifice, one for which I endured regular inquiries, but which gave me unexpected opportunities to wait actively for Christ.

When suffering, hardship, or disaster comes, are we prepared to stand firm and place our hope in the God who has come in Jesus Christ? A South African colleague recently described the experiences of her forebears who lived during the beginning of apartheid. Families were forcibly removed in trucks from their communities and sent into exile to the so-called homelands. She described the singing that arose on those trucks as parents comforted their children. Loving parents offered songs of hope for a generation of children traveling into the destructive exile of apartheid.

Gifts of memory and hope sustain us in dark times, granting God's beloved daughters and sons the strength to stand in the face of cruel injustice. Through whatever life may bring, may God grant us the courage to seek justice and peace for all.

SUGGESTION FOR MEDITATION: **Sing and pray one of the verses from a favorite Christmas carol that you know by heart. Envision this memory moving from your mind to your heart, and then to your hands and life. Wait and watch for Christ's guidance through this Advent.**

Preparing the Way

December 1–7, 2003 • *George R. Graham*[‡]

MONDAY, DECEMBER 1 • **Read Malachi 3:1**

As the final book in the Old Testament, Malachi has long been seen as a bridge between the two testaments. In the single verse of today's reading, Malachi raises core themes of the story of our faith: the promise of a messenger, the call to prepare God's way, the hope of God's appearance in our world, and the affirmation of divine faithfulness to the covenant. These themes echo not only through this week's passages but through the entire history of salvation, setting a tone of great expectancy and joy.

Christians frequently dismiss the Old Testament as a book of judgment while holding up the New Testament as a book of grace. They also speak about a God of anger in the Old Testament and a God of love in the New Testament. Yet this one verse shows that these distinctions are neither helpful nor true. In fact, both testaments contain judgment and grace, just as God shows both anger and love from Genesis to Revelation.

The book of Malachi was probably written in the fifth century BCE, after the completion of the Second Temple. The name Malachi means literally "my messenger," and the prophet speaks to a day when people's hearts still needed to be converted. Though we live more than two millennia later, this scripture speaks to us, binding us to people of faith through the ages who sought to have their hearts transformed. In this season especially, we long for the appearance of God's messenger. We seek to prepare the messenger's way, hoping to catch a glimpse of God in whom we delight.

PRAYER: God of the ages, we give you thanks for your faithfulness to the covenant. We await your arrival with eager longing. Make us messengers who help prepare your way. Amen.

[‡]Associate for Major Gifts, Office of General Ministries, The United Church of Christ; member, Pilgrim Congregational United Church of Christ, Cleveland, Ohio.

I grew up in a steel-making town, but I have only been in a steel plant once and that was on a tour. I remember it as a hot, loud, and dangerous place. This passage from Malachi speaks of God as a refiner's fire and a purifier of metal—not particularly comforting, easy, or familiar images of God. Reconciling this passage with our concept of God may be difficult.

Reading this passage, I can feel the heat and hear the noise of the steel mill. But above all this I hear a baritone voice singing, "But who may abide the day of his coming?" from an aria in Handel's *Messiah* based on this passage from Malachi. I remember the time a number of years ago when I was a member of a small church choir, and the choir director asked me to sing this piece for an Advent service. I gulped in hesitation because I had little formal voice training, but the choir director sent me home with a simplified arrangement of the piece and a rehearsal tape. He told me to record myself regularly and then play the tape back to see where I still needed work.

I followed his instructions and recorded myself. I then listened to my wrong notes, unfocused tone, and awkward phrasing. While painful, the recordings let me know what I needed to work on. From one recording to the next, I could hear myself improve. I will never be ready for a professional singing career, but I did manage to get through the solo.

My experience in preparing this piece gave me another image of the way God works in my life as purifier and refiner. Whatever image we employ to comprehend the nature of purification, it should help us understand the importance of this dynamic in the life of faith. As we seek to prepare the way for God to enter the world, purification is a critical first step. As Malachi tells us, these efforts are not just for purity's sake but so that we may give ourselves in righteousness to God.

PRAYER: Awesome God, who can stand when you appear? Yet you work to purify and refine. Help us make right offerings that are pleasing to you. Amen.

Zechariah's words follow a very pregnant pause of at least nine months—the time it took for his wife, Elizabeth, to conceive, give birth, and name a child. One might think that the first words out of Zechariah's mouth would have been an expression of anger or an explanation for his enforced silence: that God struck him silent after he doubted an angel's message.

Instead Zechariah offers a song of praise, which is not simply thanksgiving over the birth of his son but rather an exultation that proclaims the broad sweep of the history of God's people. It encompasses God's covenant, deliverance of the people, and promise of salvation. Zechariah sees the big picture and how his family's story fits into it. By mentioning God's oath to Abraham, Zechariah surely understands that he and Elizabeth are inheritors of God's promise to Abraham and Sarah. However, his understanding of the promise is not that his descendants will be as numerous as the stars (as God promised to Abraham and Sarah in Genesis 15:5) but that God's people will be able to serve the Holy One without fear, in holiness and righteousness. The months of enforced silence allow Zechariah to prepare a message about God's faithfulness that is perhaps as important as the one delivered by his son, John.

We live in a time of great fears, yet we are inheritors of the promise that someday all people of faith might be able to serve God without fear. As we seek to prepare God's way in this season of Advent, may we set aside pregnant pauses—times of intentional speechlessness—when we can reflect on the entire story of God's salvation and our inheritance of the good news. May these times of silence magnify our praise for God and strengthen our efforts to ensure that all people can serve God without fear.

PRAYER: God of the promise, blessed are you, for you have looked favorably on your people. Make us silent until we are bursting with praise. Make us still until we are moved to action. Amen.

After Zechariah recounts the broad themes of the story of God's salvation, he directs his attention to the role that his son, John, will play in it. He speaks directly to his child who is eight days old, telling John how he will join the rank of the prophets. John will prepare God's way by giving knowledge of salvation to the people by the forgiveness of sins.

Zechariah's hopes for his child are huge. No eight-day-old child, not even one who will be called "prophet of the Most High," can understand the meaning of these words. But somehow they must have taken root. Perhaps John heard these words again and again until he began to understand what they meant and that God was speaking to him. I wonder if God's call did not make itself known to John gradually, in the same way that Zechariah describes the light of salvation breaking slowly like the dawn upon the people.

Words and images bombard children in our society. Over time, and with repetition, these words and images take root—and some are harmful. What if, from the time children were no more than eight days old, we told them and showed them in every way we could that we believed they would do great things for God and humanity? How might this change our world? How can we find inviting (rather than stifling) ways to tell children or adults who have not heard that message and encourage them to listen for God's call in their lives?

Just as Zechariah spoke directly to John, we are called to speak to young people around us about matters of faith. Preparing future generations to listen for God's word is a crucial step in preparing the way for God in the world.

PRAYER: God of tender mercy, give us knowledge of salvation and the resolve to speak directly to young people about your love and concern. Guide our feet in ways of peace. Amen.

FRIDAY, DECEMBER 5 • Read Luke 3:1-3

Bible scholars have driven themselves half crazy trying to use these verses from Luke in order to pinpoint the exact year that "the word of God came to John son of Zechariah." They try to find an intersection among the years of office of the emperor, governor, various regional rulers, and high priests.

While trying to calculate the year that the word of God came to John is an interesting endeavor, solving this conundrum is not the point of this passage. Rather, the passage enables Luke to locate the word of God concretely within a particular context. The fact that the Gospel writer lists a number of rulers at a variety of levels as well as religious leaders accentuates the fact that the word of God does not come to people in power; instead it comes to an individual living on (or perhaps beyond!) the margins. The Gospel writer locates the word of God concretely in the person of John.

We have heard nothing about John since before Jesus' birth. We know less about his early years than we do about Jesus' childhood. Yet we do know that he did not become a ruler, a high priest, or any kind of official. In fact, he had gone off to the desert, which is where the word of God comes to him.

Earlier this week, we saw how Zechariah was silenced and then eloquently spoke God's word. His son, John, went to the emptiness of the wilderness and was filled with God's word. If God spoke through one who was silenced and dwelt in one who lived in emptiness, then perhaps as we seek to prepare the way of God we should follow their lead. Perhaps we should fall silent and journey to the wildernesses of our day—those desolate places where people with power do not reside and choose not to go. God will meet us there.

PRAYER: God of desolate places, to what wilderness are you calling me to journey this Advent? When do you want me to be silent? Empty me; then fill me with your word. Amen.

John the Baptist echoes the prophet Isaiah's vision of valleys being filled, mountains made low, the crooked made straight, and the rough ways made smooth. For me this vision conjures up images of earth-moving equipment used to construct super-highways. In our age we have harnessed unprecedented power and have technological wonders for use at our fingertips. As never before, we have the ability literally to move mountains (whether or not we have faith). Yet I do not think that God's salvation will be revealed as we use bulldozers to push mountain peaks into valley floors.

Isaiah and John the Baptist speak about a different reality. They do not speak about the physical geography; rather, they refer to the landscape of the human heart. To prepare God's way, the haughty need to come down from their heights, and the lowly need to be lifted up, so that all people may meet on level ground. Crooked places where people become caught in addiction or abuse need to be straightened, and the rough places of oppression where people stumble must be made smooth.

We may want to find heavy machinery to do the hard work of leveling, straightening, and smoothing the contours of the soul, but I think the methods for changing the human spirit and working for justice have not changed much since ancient days. Relatively few technological advances have come to the fore. Soul shaping is painstaking work, like building roads without power equipment. Yet God calls us to this task, supplies us with the tools, and gives us one another so that we may work side by side. In the end, all flesh will see the salvation of God revealed. Thanks be to God!

PRAYER: Holy God, guide us as we do the slow, hard work of preparing your way in the world. Assure us when we feel like we are losing ground. As we make our way, give us glimpses of your salvation. Amen.

SECOND SUNDAY OF ADVENT

When I served as a church intern while in seminary, I began to visit a woman named Ruth who lived in several rooms in the back of a big house that her parents had bought when she was still a girl. She had lived in the house for about seventy years and was what I called a survivor: She outlived her parents, her brothers, and her husband. She had had polio as a child, which made it somewhat difficult for her to get around, but she did not let it slow her down much. In the face of her losses and adversity, her gratitude about her life amazed me. During the course of every visit I would hear Ruth say, "I am just so thankful." Sometimes she had a particular reason for saying thanks; other times that general statement summed up her posture toward life.

My friend Ruth seems to have had something in common with Paul, who wrote to the Philippians that he thanked God every time he remembered them. Paul was no stranger to adversity—he wrote to the Philippians about his imprisonment and his defense. In the face of his adversity, however, Paul saw God's grace at work. Perhaps Paul's spirit of gratitude let him see God's empowering presence even in the midst of difficult experiences.

Besides describing gratitude in this passage, Paul offers a perfect definition of compassion as holding another in one's heart. If gratitude is not the source for compassion, then it must at least be closely linked. We must recognize the gift that others can be to us before we can hold them in our heart. Through compassion we share in God's grace, and our love overflows with knowledge until Christ produces a harvest of righteousness, which completes the good work of preparing God's way.

PRAYER: Loving God, make gratitude my posture toward life and compassion my response toward others. Amen.

God in Our Midst

December 8–14, 2003 • James E. Taulman[‡]

MONDAY, DECEMBER 8 • Read Zephaniah 3:14-16

Without fear!

God in our midst! What an astounding thought! Emmanuel—God with us! The immediate context of this passage is a promise that even though Judah's people will be taken into captivity, God will forgive them. God is with them.

We can live without fear. Trusting in the Lord does not mean that we will escape all tragedies, but we acknowledge that God is with us in the midst of the tragedies. Facing tragedy with God's strength can make the situation bearable. God is in our midst. Without that divine presence, we cannot survive; with that holy presence, we can face the darkest days and know that God can take total defeat—even death—and turn it into good. As we approach Christmas, may we know the wonderful news that the babe born in Bethlehem is God with us—now and always.

Several years ago, just before Christmas, my brother-in-law died. Shortly before his death, my daughter, Beth, traveled from Chicago to Minnesota to see him. As she prepared to leave, Caleb, her four-year-old, became sad about his mother's leaving. At one point, Beth found him about to dissolve into tears. When she asked him if he were sad because she was going, Caleb nodded and said, "Couldn't you just send your uncle a card?"

How wonderful that when it came time for God's fullest revelation, God did not send a card—or even a book—but came and dwelt in our midst in the form of Jesus. How are we to live because God is in our midst? Without fear!

PRAYER: Thank you, God, for getting personally involved in my life. Help me to act out my gratitude. Amen.

[‡]Assistant to the executive director-president, Baptist History and Heritage Society, Brentwood, Tennessee.

Victoriously with renewed love

God in our midst! What an astounding thought! But that is a promise of scripture as well as the testimony of God's saints through the ages.

As we prepare for Christmas, we may find ourselves so busy helping others prepare that we do not take the time to prepare ourselves. We frequently become immune to the wonder and awe of the season. Perhaps we need to tap into God's promise of renewal in overwhelming love—God is in our midst!

Verse 19 reminds us that God will change the shame of the lame and outcast into praise. God is still in the business of changing shame into praise. If there is shame in your life over some past experience, offer it to God and be open to the marvelous possibility of seeing it turned into praise. What greater preparation for Christmas could you make?

But how does this reversal of fortune come about? Who is involved in this change? These closing verses seem to include everyone: Judah, Jerusalem, oppressors, oppressed—all the peoples of the earth. The restoration is not simply that of things lost but a restoration of relationships among people, among enemies! In this season of love and within the prophet's sense of God's renewal through overwhelming love, how do we feel when justice comes about—not in sentences meted out but through changed relationships? How willing are we both to receive and give God's love? God's overwhelming love can restore our fortunes.

We can live victoriously, not because God keeps us from experiencing problems but because God brings victory over the problems. God offers all people a future. God is in our midst! We no longer have to live in defeat! God is in our midst! So how should we live? Victoriously in God's renewing love!

PRAYER: Lord, help me experience changed relationships by living victoriously in your renewing love. Amen.

God will bring us home

Home for the holidays! Songs proclaiming that the singer will be home for Christmas—even if only in the singer's dreams—have been crooned in the department stores for weeks now.

Home! The word has a nice sound for those who remember wonderful, joyful experiences at home—especially those associated with Christmas.

However, some people shudder when they think of home. They shudder as the word brings to mind unpleasant events. For these people, home for the holidays evokes images of fear and coldness rather than of warmth and love.

Advent speaks a word to those who long to go home and those who have no desire to do so. Scripture assures us that because God is near to us, we can go home.

The prophet Zephaniah sought to encourage the people of Judah. He warns them that because they have ignored God's warnings they will be taken into exile. However, even in exile God will be with them, and they will know God's wonderful mercy. God will bring them home!

How does this scripture apply to us? We recall the boundless grace of God's mercy for us as well as for the people of Judah. For those whose memories of home bring happiness and for those whose memories of home bring pain, the promise of Advent is that God's presence will bring us to a home that exceeds our greatest expectations.

As so often happens in scripture, truth takes many forms. God not only brings us home, but God is our home! How might we act because God is in our midst? We can live in the assurance that God will bring us home!

PRAYER: Lord, I have been gone too long from you. I want to come home. Amen.

Shouting and singing for joy!

Judah, on the verge of being wiped out as a nation and her citizens being carried to Babylon as captives, hears the urging of Isaiah to "shout aloud and sing for joy." What part of reality does Isaiah not understand? A person doesn't sing for joy in the midst of defeat. But verse 2 gives the reason for singing: "God is my salvation…the LORD GOD is my strength and my might."

I'm not sure I have reached the point that I can declare, "I will trust, and will not be afraid." I want to arrive at that place; but in the face of disaster, my faith often wavers. The ability to trust and not fear resides in a personal relationship with the God of the universe. The stronger the relationship, the greater our sense of security in the face of disaster.

As my relationship with God has grown over the years, I have come to understand this statement's power: "There is no fear in love, but perfect love casts out fear" (1 John 4:18). The more we come to know, love, and trust the God who is in our midst, the greater our understanding of God's care for us in all situations, which allows us to trust and not be afraid.

Advent means turning our thoughts—and lives—to Jesus, who is in our midst. Knowing his presence can calm us even when a powerful enemy threatens.

Advent means we can celebrate our relationship with Jesus. All of us face serious issues in our lives: illness, death, loss, hurt, and pain. But "great in [our] midst is the Holy One of Israel."

So how should we live since God is in our midst? By shouting and singing for joy!

Prayer: Dear God, help me to celebrate your presence with joy! Amen.

Gently and without worry

A documentary television program dealt with bullies in school. The explanation given for bullies' existence is that we all like people who dominate us, and vicariously we get our thrills by seeing them act.

What a contrast with Paul's statement about how believers are to live in the world. Because "the Lord is near," we let our "gentleness be known to everyone." The Lord's "nearness" serves to remind us that Jesus models this gentleness.

This advice is 180 degrees from the counsel we receive from society—including those in the church. "Good guys finish last" has been used to reinforce our bullying instincts. Our emphasis on hard-hitting competitive sports leaves little place for gentleness. Business seldom finds room for a gentle approach.

Paul's mention of the Lord's nearness refers to Christ's coming again. As those before Christ's birth lived in the hope of his first coming, we on this side of his birth live in hope of his coming again. Regardless of where we are in history, the Lord is near—so we need to live like it. The Lord's nearness requires that we live gently—and without worry!

Is there a correlation between the two—gentle living and not worrying? One can only wonder: If we lived more gently would we have less to worry about? In our post-9/11 age, gentleness and kindness are not highly sought-after commodities. Yet the verse is still in the Bible. It still flies in the face of conventional wisdom.

So, then, how should we live because of the Lord's nearness? With gentleness and without worry!

PRAYER: Lord, at times I do not want to be gentle. Forgive me, and help me realize that you have dealt gently with me when I didn't deserve it. Amen.

Bear fruits worthy of repentance

Where are the Christmas gifts in this passage? We say we give gifts because God gave the greatest gift to us and because the wise ones brought gifts. But this scripture says nothing about gift giving in preparation for the Messiah's coming. What it does demand of our discipleship is that we bear fruits that indicate we have repented.

Instead of asking if friends have all their shopping done, perhaps a more appropriate question would be this: Have you borne all the fruits worthy of repentance you need to bear to get ready for Christ's coming this year?

I am struck by the fact that when people ask John how to get ready for the Messiah's coming, he does not tell them to do a single thing that could be considered "religious"! Everything he tells them to do involves their everyday lives: share food and clothing, work honestly, and live with a sense of satisfaction with what you have.

Which seems the better response in celebration of Jesus' birth: giving gifts to people who have so much already or sharing our abundance, working with integrity, and expressing gratitude for what we have?

Because Jesus' coming is near, John tells us that we need to prepare ethically: no religious duties, no Bibles read, no worship attended, no religious language used. Why would John urge this kind of preparation? For John the answer is simple: Jesus is more concerned with our daily lives and how we live than with our religious lives. We can fake religion; it is hard to fake a whole life. After we have prepared for acts of social justice, our Bible reading, worship, and prayer will take on new meaning.

So how are we to live because the Lord is near? By bearing fruits worthy of the Lord we claim to follow!

PRAYER: Lord, help me show you my love by the way I live during these busy days of preparation for your coming. Amen.

Humbly and expectantly

Advent is a time for us to prepare for Jesus' coming. Advent is Christmas-not-yet. My grandson came home from preschool singing:

Advent is a time to wait,

Not quite time to celebrate.

It is not quite time to celebrate, but it will be soon. Before Christmas Day arrives, we have some preparation to do. Jesus is coming! He who is God in a human suit of clothes. He who put a face on the God of the universe. We can't prepare for his coming in a casual way. What is left? Since Christ's coming is so close, what more can we do? We can live humbly and expectantly.

Humble living, like gentleness, goes against conventional wisdom. John feels unworthy; we feel unworthy. But Jesus did not come to "worthy" people. Instead, he came to people who needed help in finding a way to God. Those who admitted their need and sought Jesus' help could discover God's presence in their midst. The same is true today. All we can say when we have done our best is that "we are worthless slaves; we have done only what we ought to have done!" (Luke 17:10).

We often picture the shepherds kneeling at the manger in adoration of the Christ child. Have you knelt in a barn lately? It can be a humbling experience!

No, it's not yet time to celebrate, but we can wait expectantly. Hope is one of the hallmarks of Advent.

So how should we live because the Lord is near? Humbly and expectantly!

PRAYER: Lord, I wait. Sometimes I'm not too humble, and sometimes it seems like you are so far away and will never come. But come, Lord Jesus. I believe. Help my unbelief. Amen.

Beginnings

December 15–21, 2003 • *Roberta C. Bondi*[‡]

MONDAY, DECEMBER 15 • Read Luke 1:39-45

At the beginning of this lection, it is far from Christmas. Mary's cousin Elizabeth has been pregnant for six months. Gabriel has only now brought Mary the message announcing her own pregnancy. Mary assented to it, yes, but she has clearly not yet thought out the meaning of the strange thing that is taking place in her own body. Rather than shut herself up in her room to ponder it all in private, Mary went "with haste" to her older cousin's house when the angel left.

What the scripture passage does not tell us is why exactly Mary goes, but the reader can easily make some guesses. At best Mary's feelings would be ambivalent. Considering Elizabeth's long barrenness, Mary would have wanted to congratulate her cousin. She might have wondered at God's selecting her; been afraid for her child who would be "the son of God" and afraid for herself and the coming scandal around her pregnancy. Perhaps she is excited, yet she also probably worries that it will be the end of her chances to marry.

Elizabeth, however, has no such ambivalence when Mary appears on her doorstep. "Blessed are you among women," she cries, "and blessed is the fruit of your womb!" Only with this greeting and in conversation with her cousin can Mary clarify her thoughts so that she might respond, "My soul magnifies the Lord!"

PRAYER: Beloved God, as we await your birth, we thank you for the community around us that helps us recognize the meaning of your presence in us. Amen.

[‡]Author; member of Emmaus, an ecumenical house church; teacher, Candler School of Theology, Decatur, Georgia.

From whence will come the Messiah? Christians through the centuries have read these verses as a prophecy about Jesus' birth, and with good reason. Whatever the prophet Micah originally had in mind for Israel's rescue, the elements of what seems to be an ongoing Christian life experience are all here as they are represented in the life of Jesus: interiorly or exteriorly the people of God are oppressed, unsettled, scattered, in exile. By the brutal and dehumanizing forces that seem to control the world, our city is under siege, and God appears to have abandoned us to it.

Into this pain Micah speaks an Advent promise: God's help is coming and from the most unexpected place—from little Bethlehem, which belongs to one of the most insignificant of the clans of Judah. But there is more to Bethlehem than its size: from it also came Jesus' anointed ancestor David, who brought the chaos of the tribes into a single nation.

For us in a similarly painful world, the promise of the new Messiah is that through this child, in spite of appearances, the entire world will ultimately be renewed as God originally intended it.

SUGGESTION FOR MEDITATION: What signs do you see—in your home, in your community, in your church—of the presence of God's renewing power, even in the darkness of our world?

PRAYER: Lover of the world, groaning, we wait for you. Quickly come to us and renew the face of the earth. Amen.

Hardly any of us would be surprised to hear that the early church understood this passage as a statement that the body of Jesus Christ, offered for the sake of the world, would fulfill and replace the ancient law of temple sacrifice. What is more surprising to most modern Christians is the fourth- and fifth-century church's equally strong conviction that this body, which God makes God's own in Jesus, is also our collective human body, our single human identity, so to speak, for transformation within God.

This body is also the church—the body of Christ—to which all Christians, past, present, and future, belong and in which we share a common life. If this is true, when Jesus says, "See,…I have come to do your will," he is speaking to God not just for himself but on behalf of all of us who are his body.

As Christmas approaches let us meditate with the author of Hebrews on how God's incarnation in us implies that when Jesus says to God, "See,…I have come to do your will," he speaks for us as well.

PRAYER: Loving God, help us to understand what it means to say that the same Jesus Christ who came to us as a baby lives in us now as his body. This Christmas, help us to remember who we are as the presence of your love in your world. Amen.

Sometimes in the season of Christmas, when we long to celebrate the birth of that baby who is God among us, we find it hard not to resent the voices who whisper to us, "How can you rejoice in the presence of all the pain in the world? Why won't you accept that Christmas is no more than a nostalgic, sentimental dream?"

At that point we have to remind ourselves that Christmas is not about sentiment or nostalgia; and it is certainly not about the denial of suffering in the world. Rather, it is precisely because the world is so dreadfully wounded, because suffering is so real and pervasive, and because we so thoroughly participate in causing as well as enduring that suffering that we need the promises of Christmas. Through the promises of Christmas, we receive the needed restoration and salvation for which the psalmist yearns.

These promises assure us that God has not abandoned God's creation; in the person of that baby God enters into it fully to redeem it and heal it and save it. "O God of hosts; let your face shine, that we may be saved" is not a cry from the good old days. It is a cry we hear daily, but God's assurance in the baby of Bethlehem allows us to get out of bed in the morning, acknowledge the reality of suffering, and still bless God and bless the day.

PRAYER: Loving God, help us never to celebrate your birth in such a way that we blot out the sight of suffering. Fill us, rather, with the courage of your compassion till all things are transformed in you. Amen.

This passage that begins the Letter to the Hebrews reminds us that the baby whose birth we celebrate in this season is more than a very good human being. In this baby is incarnate the God who created the heavens and founded the earth.

None of this universe, which is so precious and familiar to us, is permanent. The writer of Hebrews reminds us that all of it is changing constantly, and not necessarily for the better. Indeed, ultimately everything we can imagine will be worn out like a piece of clothing that is discarded.

This would be bad news if this were the whole content of these verses. Blessedly, it is not. What this passage promises is that however impermanent everything familiar is, the God whose tender, gentle, and particular love for us is present and visible in Jesus from his birth to his resurrection is *not* impermanent. Though we do not know the shape our future will take, we do know that God will never abandon us, for God's faithfulness will always be "the same, and [God's] years will never end."

SUGGESTION FOR MEDITATION: **What changes in your life seemed, at the time, too much to bear? Reflect on the ways God has brought you through them to new life.**

PRAYER: **Loving God, we ask you to hold us in the knowledge of your love for us, so that we may love your world in return as you intend. Amen.**

How much we need Isaiah's words this Christmas season! In our deepest hearts we know that we are, indeed, "the people who have walked in darkness," and we walk there still. On the verge of God's birth among us, we find our hearts broken. Bowed down by our wounds and the knowledge of wounds we have inflicted upon others, we are blind to where we have been and where we are to go to be true to God's love.

Our oppressors—our fear of loss, our acquisitiveness, our need for acceptance, our callousness, our perfectionism—live in our hearts in such a way that we can hardly imagine how to love our neighbors as we are called to love. But soon, quite beyond our imaginations, our own God will come among us as a great light shining into a land of deep darkness.

This baby, so little, so vulnerable, so absurd, and yet so bright is a pledge to us that as God once created everything from nothing, God will ultimately, in ways we cannot now even imagine, heal every wound and relieve us of the burden of our sorrows.

SUGGESTION FOR MEDITATION: This Advent season what pain in your life needs God's healing? Speak it aloud to yourself and to God. Reflect on ways God can use you to love others as you await your own healing.

PRAYER: Lover of our souls and bodies, shine on our hearts this night, filling us with a knowledge that all things in our broken world will finally be taken up and healed in you. Amen.

★A lection from Christmas Eve day not otherwise addressed.

FOURTH SUNDAY OF ADVENT

The Advent season continues, and today's Gospel lesson confronts us with the greatest paradox Christianity has to offer: In the very baby whose birth we celebrate, in the tiny infant born obscurely under terrible conditions to an ordinary young woman in ancient Palestine we find ourselves face to face with the great God through whom creation came to be and all life continues to come.

As Christians have confessed for centuries in the Easter liturgies of our churches, this God whom we meet in Jesus is our Light, and this "light shines in the darkness, and the darkness did not overcome it." And what is the character of this divine light in whose being we can see all things as they really are? The fourth-century writer Ephrem the Syrian, addressing the baby Jesus in a Christmas hymn, sums it up for us: "How bold you are, Babe, who bestows himself upon all. At everyone who meets you, you smile....It is as if your love hungers for human beings. You distinguish not your parents from strangers....From where did it come to you so to hunger for human beings?"**

The mighty light of God of which John speaks and which illumines all things that ever were is the eager light we see in the face of a baby who indiscriminatingly holds out little arms to anyone, friend or stranger, who would pick him up. This is the light of love.

PRAYER: God of love, thank you that the light of your love has come among us and that nothing can extinguish that flame. Amen.

---

*A lection from Christmas Day not otherwise addressed.

**Ephrem the Syrian: Hymns, translated by Kathleen McVey (New York: Paulist Press, 1989). "Hymns on the Nativity," Hymn 13; 139.

The Gift

December 22–28, 2003 • *Arvin R. Luchs* ‡

MONDAY, DECEMBER 22 • **Read Samuel 2:18-20, 26**

Hawaii's Ironman Triathlon World Championship is considered to be one of the most grueling athletic challenges, involving a full marathon run, over a hundred miles of competitive bicycling, and a 2.6 mile ocean swim. In the 1999 event, Dick and Rick Hoyt entered and competed together because Rick has cerebral palsy. So his father, Dick, pulled his son in a small dinghy, balanced him on a special seat on their cycle, and pushed him on a three-wheeled chair. Late in the day they finally finished. They won no medals, just everyone's heart. In a post-race interview a reporter asked Dick why he undertook such a challenge. He replied simply that he had promised it to his son.

Sometimes the gifts that yield the most blessing both to giver and receiver are promises sincerely offered and faithfully kept. That is true of Hannah. She and her husband, Elkanah, have prayed and hoped for a child. Year after year they have been bitterly disappointed. In her prayers, Hannah promises that if a child were to be theirs, she would dedicate him to the Lord. Samuel's birth fills the couple with joy, but Hannah remains faithful to her promise and offers her cherished son to God as an apprentice to Eli the priest. Each year, as the parents visit their son, Eli singles her out for a special blessing that finds fulfillment in other children to fill their household. Hannah's faithfulness to her promise is counted to her as blessing.

Advent reminds us of the faithfulness of God who has promised to deliver the people. In the gift of a tiny child, God gave the beloved Son; the blessings of that gift are ours forever.

PRAYER: Ever-giving God, fill us with confidence and hope to wait patiently for the fulfillment of your promises in our hearts and lives. Amen.

---

‡Senior pastor, First United Methodist Church, Portland, Oregon; former Associate General Secretary, United Methodist Communications.

Among my childhood memories is a twilight summer evening on an ocean beach with my father. I remember asking my dad how big the sky was. "Bigger then you can imagine," he replied.

I persisted, "Is it bigger than the United States?"

"Yes," he responded, "bigger than that."

"Bigger than the ocean?"

"Even bigger than that," he answered. I remember persisting until his patience grew thin, and I knew it was time to stop. But I still pause every now and then to wonder about the immensity of the universe.

At such moments I identify with the psalmist. I suspect that this ancient poet was staggered by thoughts of the grandeur and glory of God. Ordinary language couldn't express it, wasn't big enough to encompass it. For the psalmist, God's power and righteousness is beyond all comprehension. Praise to God's majesty rises from the hosts of celestial beings that populate the heavenly courts; crescendos in sun, moon, stars, and planets from the sky; and echoes from the earth and all living beings. Everything, anywhere, in all creation praises God who is bigger than anything the psalmist can imagine and whose glory transcends every created thing.

The message of Christmas is that this same God came to earth as a baby in a manger in Bethlehem. That moment redirected the course of earthly history. It has more than celestial impact. It is an event of more than cosmological significance. It is bigger than anything anyone can imagine. And in that creation-shaking moment, God's incalculable love was given to finite people like you and me. And so, with sages of old, we join with all creation in singing praise to God who is bigger than everything but given to us all.

PRAYER: Almighty God, who is beyond all human comprehension, open our hearts and our eyes to glimpse the wonder of your immense love in the coming of your Son. Amen.

CHRISTMAS EVE

In 1942 the darkness of war blanketed the world. In March, the Japanese occupied the Dutch East Indies and with a policy of "Asia for the Asians" interred all non-Asians. Conditions in the internment camps were grim. Cockroaches, rats, bedbugs, and lice infested everything. Food was scarce, and more than half of the internees did not survive.

A Presbyterian missionary, Margaret Dryburgh, and Norah Chambers, a graduate of London's Royal Academy of Music numbered among the prisoners. They were determined to offer their gift of music to the camp, but they had no musical scores and no instruments. The two women painstakingly recreated four-voice arrangements of works by Schubert, Dvorak, and Chopin from their memory. Prisoners' voices substituted for instruments. Just after Christmas sixty years ago the "vocal orchestra" presented its first concert.

In the midst of that dark night of the soul, amid hatred and violence, the prisoners sang. They sang because it lifted sagging spirits and brought hope to weary souls. They sang to bring a ray of beauty to brighten their bleak world. They sang to proclaim their confidence in the presence of a Spirit that the darkness could not stop. They sang to praise God.

On the eve of Jesus' birth, songs of praise to the glory of God startled the shepherds in the hills of Judea. These songs praised a God who had come into the world's darkness, bringing the light of love in the birth of a baby in Bethlehem. Christ comes again into our dark night bringing hope and peace. May our voices join the chorus of praise on this night.

PRAYER: Ever-present God, come to us again today. May your love and glory be ever praised. Amen.

CHRISTMAS DAY

On my office wall hangs a framed block print of a first-century man. His shoulders are squared, arms rippling with muscles and his jaw set firmly, the image of power and strength. By himself he appears to be an unstoppable warrior—fearful to any adversary. Yet cradled tenderly in the cupped hands of the fierce strongman is a tiny, fragile bird—a nestling finding safety and support.

Isaiah agonized over the plight of Israel in the bonds of captivity and exile. This Isaiah, commonly known as Deutero- or Second Isaiah, proclaims the end of that darkness and the first light of a new day. He extols the harbinger of peace and praises God who has by the sheer strength of holy power brought the nation out of slavery to freedom. All creation—even the ruins of Jerusalem—lifts its voice in song. Yet Isaiah declares that this mighty God has tenderly comforted and supported God's people through the struggle and suffering.

Today we celebrate the coming of God in the innocence of a baby—but a baby whose power and glory is heralded by angelic messengers, worshiped by simple shepherds, and honored by the wise. Today we welcome both the inbreaking of God's power that will turn aside evil, bringing justice to all creation and the infusion of God's presence offering love, comfort, and hope.

We too might break forth in singing. We too shall see the salvation of our God through a tiny baby who redeems us all.

PRAYER: God of power, God of tender mercy, come once more to our world and bring us your peace. Amen.

In my family, there was mandatory duty reserved for the day after Christmas. Until it was done, I was forbidden to play with the new toy truck tantalizingly parked under the tree or dash next door to exchange tales of Santa's abundance with my friends.

December 26 was "thank-you letter day." I could plead all I wanted, but until an expression of gratitude matched each gift, I could do nothing else. "Don't just say 'thanks,'" mom would warn; "tell them what you are going to do with their gift." She was saying that Christmas was not complete until the gifts were acknowledged and the giver understood what difference their generosity would make in my life.

The Colossian Christians were struggling to understand and appreciate God's gift of Jesus Christ. Apparently, some understood their faith as a mystical experience and Jesus as a sort of divine apparition. Paul says no! Christ is not a philosophical model of an ideal human but the living, breathing presence of God. Through Jesus' life, death, and resurrection, God broke into human life bringing the power to change and reshape the lives of all who would believe.

The gift of Jesus means that our lives have changed and are being remolded. Because we have been loved, we can love. Because we have been forgiven, we can forgive. This gift brings wisdom, harmony, peace, and joy. This gift is not one to be pondered internally, then put on a shelf as a curiosity. This gift is to be lived each day in faithfulness and thanksgiving.

PRAYER: Generous God, we give you thanks for the great gift of Jesus. May our lives be made new and our world reborn through him. Amen.

A few years ago my seat assignment on an airplane was next to a well-known television performer. From the public's eye he had suddenly catapulted to success because of a part in a beloved comedy series. As we talked, he told me of the years he had spent in school and regional theater. He lamented the countless auditions and callbacks. He said, "It took me fifteen years to be an overnight success."

Many of us read the Bible stories of the men and women who have encountered God and seem to have been transformed instantly into vessels of divine power. It is easy to overlook references to their growth and preparation. Moses retreated to Midian before his call to lead Israel from Egypt. Samuel, we are told, apprenticed with the priest Eli and grew "both in stature and in favor with the LORD and with the people" (1 Sam. 2:26). Many years passed between Isaiah's call and his prophetic ministry.

Luke tells us that John the Baptist "grew and became strong in spirit" (Luke 1:80) before his ministry. Luke also tells us that Jesus' divinity, promised before his conception and evident to growing numbers of people throughout his infancy, must have been evident to the teachers in the Temple who quiz him and are amazed. Luke carefully notes that the young man still needed to grow intellectually, socially, and spiritually before he was ready to fulfill his ministry and destiny.

Over the centuries, men and women like you and me have heard and responded to God's call. God's grace beckons each of us to share in the work of the Spirit and the building of God's reign. How are you prepared to respond?

PRAYER: Touch our hearts and our minds, gracious God, that we may sense your call and be ready. Amen.

I heard recently of a university sociology class that decided to test the proverb: "The clothes make the man." They dressed a student in various garb—ragged clothes, worker's coveralls, jeans and a sweatshirt, a chauffeur's uniform, and a tailored business suit—and observed his behavior. He unconsciously acted and interacted very differently when wearing the different outfits. The class members concluded that his clothing affected his self-image.

The Colossian church was torn by disputes and disagreements. Paul, hearing of their bickering, reminds them of Christ's love and sacrifice. He urges them to understand that through Christ they have become a new community held together by bonds of God's love. He suggests that they embrace the nature of Christ like a huge cloak that engulfs them in the qualities of the life in the Spirit: compassion, kindness, humility, meekness, patience, and forgiveness. Their spiritual clothes will shape their self-image. In the clothes of Christ they will live into a harmony and a unity that brings peace.

Christmas reminds us that God came to a broken and needy world. In the Son, all humankind, even you and I, can see and know a better way to live. The clothing of the Spirit—the way of the Christ—can be our way. Who we are, what we do, how we live, will change. Then our hearts, our relationships, indeed, our world, can know God's peace.

PRAYER: God of love, grant us the wisdom and courage to embrace the way of the Christ that we might be clothed in your love and peace. Amen.

The Promise

December 29–31, 2003 • *Helen R. Neinast*[‡]

MONDAY, DECEMBER 29 • **Read Isaiah 60:1-6**

The rich and glorious images of light call out from the darkness that covers the earth and its peoples. God's light and the salvation it brings are described with great joy by Isaiah. "[T]he glory of the LORD has risen upon you" the scripture says, "and nations shall come to your light."

The promise is clear. The promise is great. Light will replace deep darkness. Vision will replace blindness. Radiant hearts will rejoice—hearts that had been weighed down by darkness and exile. This passage is about coming home—coming home to God, coming home to salvation, coming home to joy.

Isaiah wrote these words to the people of Israel during a very dark time, the time of their exile in Babylon. These words from God carried the promise and hope to Israel in its time of desperate need.

Where in your life do you need to hear God's words of light and promise? What dark places in the world need the witness of God's light? How are you called to be a bearer of light and promise to others?

PRAYER: Lift my eyes, O God, to your light. Let me arise from my prayers to carry your light into the world. Amen.

[‡]United Methodist campus minister at Emory University, Atlanta, Georgia; ordained elder in the New Mexico Conference of The United Methodist Church.

This psalm is a prayer for God's blessing on Israel's king, probably King Solomon. It asks God to give the king justice and righteousness in his rule of the kingdom, and that request becomes a prayer for God's just and righteous reign in the whole world.

Over and over again, this prayer for Solomon lifts up the needs of the weak, the poor, the needy, those who have no helper. In no uncertain terms, it becomes clear that God's reign—and therefore Solomon's—is focused on the peace that comes only with justice. When God's rule is done, the psalm says, peace will abound "until the moon is no more!" It is only when justice reigns that the world is as God intends it to be.

That justice is lovely, the psalm says. It is like the rain that falls on the grass, or the showers that water the earth. Yet as the poor and needy are defended, so the must oppressors have justice served. The oppressors will be crushed; peace—God's peace—demands it. In God's reign, oppressed and oppressor alike will be reconciled to God.

As you pray this psalm, remember leaders in the United States and around the world. Pray that God may give them a thirst for justice so that they may govern with righteousness.

PRAYER: God of peace, help me to seek justice in my life with my family. Help me to seek justice in my life at work. Help me to seek justice in my life as a citizen of your world. Amen.

Two groups—sheep or goats, eternal life or everlasting punishment. And the measure of God's judgment here is not confession of faith in Christ; the measure is whether one has acted with love and care for the needy.

In this passage, Matthew states it quite starkly: When people respond to the needs of others or fail to respond to those needs, they are in truth responding or failing to respond to Christ himself. This fact surprises both groups! Those who responded to other people's needs with loving-kindness are surprised when God reveals that this is the deeper meaning of human compassion. Those who failed to respond to other people's needs are also surprised; they had no idea that they had failed Christ each time they failed the needy.

This scripture issues both encouragement and warning: encouragement to us to be faithful in our deeds of mercy, love, and kindness toward the needy; warning us by showing just how critical compassion is in God's measurement of faithfulness. Be encouraged—and reminded—of what God values in the way we live our lives every day.

PRAYER: Let me follow Christ's example today, God. Keep me mindful of the needy this day, that I may see Christ and respond with compassion. Amen.

The Revised Common Lectionary[‡] for 2003
Year B – Advent / Christmas Year C
(Disciplines Edition)

January 1–5
Jeremiah 31:7-14
Psalm 147:12-20
Ephesians 1:3-14
John 1:1-18

> #### NEW YEAR'S DAY
> Ecclesiastes 3:1-13
> Psalm 8
> Revelation 21:1-6*a*
> Matthew 25:31-46

> #### January 6
> #### EPIPHANY
> *(These readings may be used for Sunday, January 5.)*
> Isaiah 60:1-6
> Psalm 72:1-7, 10-14
> Ephesians 3:1-12
> Matthew 2:1-12

January 6–12
BAPTISM OF THE LORD
Genesis 1:1-5
Psalm 29
Acts 19:1-7
Mark 1:4-11

January 13–19
1 Samuel 3:1-20
Psalm 139:1-6, 13-18
1 Corinthians 6:12-20
John 1:43-51

January 20–26
Jonah 3:1-5, 10
Psalm 62:5-12
1 Corinthians 7:29-31
Mark 1:14-20

January 27–February 2
Deuteronomy 18:15-20
Psalm 111
1 Corinthians 8:1-13
Mark 1:21-28

February 3–9
Isaiah 40:21-31
Psalm 147:1-11, 20*c*
1 Corinthians 9:16-23
Mark 1:29 39

February 10–16
2 Kings 5:1-14
Psalm 30
1 Corinthians 9:24-27
Mark 1:40-45

February 17–23
Isaiah 43:18-25
Psalm 41
2 Corinthians 1:18-22
Mark 2:1-12

February 24–March 2

TRANSFIGURATION

2 Kings 2:1-12

Psalm 50:1-6

2 Corinthians 4:3-6

Mark 9:2-9

March 3–9

FIRST SUNDAY IN LENT

Genesis 9:8-17

Psalm 25:1-10

1 Peter 3:18-22

Mark 1:9-15

> **March 5**
>
> ASH WEDNESDAY
>
> Joel 2:1-2, 12-17 (*or* Isaiah 58:1-12)
>
> Psalm 51:1-17
>
> 2 Corinthians 5:20*b*–6:10
>
> Matthew 6:1-6, 16-21

March 10–16

SECOND SUNDAY IN LENT

Genesis 17:1-7, 15-16

Psalm 22:23-31

Romans 4:13-25

Mark 8:31-38 (*or* Mark 9:2-9)

March 17–23

THIRD SUNDAY IN LENT

Exodus 20:1-17

Psalm 19

1 Corinthians 1:18-25

John 2:13-22

March 24–30

FOURTH SUNDAY IN LENT

Numbers 21:4-9

Psalm 107:1-3, 17-22

Ephesians 2:1-10

John 3:14-21

March 31–April 6

FIFTH SUNDAY IN LENT

Jeremiah 31:31-34

Psalm 51:1-12

  (*or* Psalm 119:9-16)

Hebrews 5:5-10

John 12:20-33

April 7–13

PASSION/PALM SUNDAY

> *Liturgy of the Palms*
>
> Mark 11:1-11
>
>   (*or* John 12:12-16)
>
> Psalm 118:1-2, 19-29

> *Liturgy of the Passion*
>
> Isaiah 50:4-9*a*
>
> Psalm 31:9-16
>
> Philippians 2:5-11
>
> Mark 14:1–15:47
>
>   (*or* Mark 15:1-47)